NAKED FOOD

the way food was meant to be

Jane Grover

with photography by Steve Brown

I dedicate this book to
my wonderful parents
Geoffrey and Annabell Kelleher
two of the most encouraging and generous people I've known.
They have always been willing to help me in the pursuit of my passions,
rather than limit and contain me with the expectations of the mainstream.
I have seen them both live exemplary lives, displaying to me what it is
to work hard, to dare to follow your dreams and to be kind and generous to
others along the way. Over time the seeds of this kind of living were sown in
me, and this book is the fruit of those seeds and a piece of my dreams.

Geoffrey William Kelleher - 3rd June 1934 – 21st Sept 1989

my husband
Paul
how thankful I am that you came into my life, just as my dear father passed out
of this life. You have believed in me every day. You are my best friend.

our darling children
Thomas Geoffrey, Molly Annabell and Jacob Paul
it is such a joy and privilege to be your mother. How proud we are of you all.
No matter what we do in this life, you will always be what we count as our
greatest achievement.

"He has made everything beautiful in its time"

Ecclesiastes 3:11

contents

introduction...

If you love eating but don't really enjoy cooking, if you lack confidence in the kitchen and are bored with your current repertoire of recipes, or if you want to start cooking and eating in a more healthy way, to live a long health filled life, then keep reading. Your answers are here in *Naked Food - the way food was meant to be*.

Naked means *'without clothes', 'without the usual covering', 'not hidden, open'*. Food means *'any substance that people or animals eat or drink, or that plants absorb, to maintain life and growth'*. Naked food is food that is not hidden, not covered, not compromised by additives, flavourings and preservatives - it is food undressed. It is food in its natural state, designed to add to your body and help you to maintain life and growth. Naked food is letting the produce speak for itself, so you can enjoy the incredible flavours, colours and textures that naturally occur in food. To me it is the way food was meant to be.

A key to enjoying naked food is to understand that food is produced according to seasons and it is best to learn to cook and eat produce in season. When you eat in season there is an abundance, the produce tastes better and is available at a more affordable price. Modern day food production and transportation has in many ways led to a disregard of the seasons, deeming that we can eat what we want, when we want - in essence, we can have everything we want all year round. Often this means importing food or treating food to preserve its shelf life - way beyond what is natural. In doing so the quality, taste, colour and texture of our food is compromised and often the nutrition and the price of our food is adversely affected. Basically tomatoes are red ripe, taste incredible and are reasonably priced in their summer season, so that is when you should enjoy them in abundance.

It is my hope that this cookbook will help you discover what it is to enjoy naked food, cooking from scratch, in season, simple, healthy recipes that taste great and are good for you. The recipes are not complicated, anyone can cook them. Each chapter of the book contains recipes designed to provide you with a variety of options, whether you are looking for a nourishing breakfast, a raw salad, a summer bbq menu, fast food for a midweek dinner, slow food as a winter warmer or something sweet to celebrate with, it is all here.

Let me encourage you to read through the complete recipe before beginning, allowing you to take advantage of all the information provided. With each recipe I have provided notes on ingredients, especially ingredients that you may not be familiar with, explaining their origins and nutritional benefits. I have also tried where possible to provide a gluten-free (GF) or vegetarian (V) alternative, by suggesting how you can substitute ingredients, so you too can enjoy cooking and eating each dish.

Although I have not specified in each recipe, but rather left room for you to make your own choices, I do whenever possible opt to cook and eat using certified organic and biodynamic produce. This includes using certified organic eggs, chicken, pork, beef and biodynamic lamb, as well as sustainably harvested Australian seafood. It is also my preference to source produce as local as possible and of course Australian owned and produced. I prefer to cook with an Australian extra virgin olive oil and use Australian organic extra virgin olive oil for raw food recipes, where you can appreciate the full flavour. I favour butter over margarine and full cream dairy products over low fat or lite. When using sugar I prefer to use rapadura sugar, produced from the sugar cane juice of organically grown sugar cane. When storing food I prefer glass containers over plastic and baking paper over plastic wrap.

My desire to support and consume certified organic produce, is motivated by my understanding that farming without the use of chemicals is better for everyone. It promotes a healthier life for the farmer, the plants, the livestock, the future of our land and environment and us the consumer. Throughout the book I have also shared *'my story'* with you, as well as *'meet the people'* and *'feature recipes'*, introducing you to many amazing people, who work incredibly hard to passionately produce the food you buy, cook and eat daily. My true aim with this cookbook is to equip and empower you to be unafraid to cook and eat well, meaning you can live a healthier life - you, your family and the next generations. Of equal importance I'd like to acknowledge and appreciate those who work so hard to produce our food, which enables us in Australia to access and enjoy abundant fresh produce. It is the year of the farmer in Australia in 2012. Wouldn't it be wonderful to get behind our local farming communities, choosing to buy Australian produce, and in doing so show them we are grateful for what they do.

x jane

my story...the early years and learning to cook

I love to tell a story, and the life you've lived makes your story. I love to ask people to tell me their story, and in doing so you continue to learn from and about others. This is my story.

I grew up in a happy family on Sydney's north shore, with loving, generous and encouraging parents, an older brother Arthur, older sister Catherine and younger brother David. I had a wonderful childhood and was fortunate to attend a private girl's school. At school I discovered there were two things I was really good at, talking and playing sport. I gave all my time to both; the talking often saw me sent out of class or on detention! My report card consistently read that *"Jane should pay more attention in class"*, however in the sports report it read *"Always enthusiastic and keen to participate"*.

When I thought about what I would like to do for a career, my first choice was to be a PE teacher. I loved sport and played some kind of sport six days a week. However, it appeared that my average academic results may not see me get the marks required to study PE teaching at university. The only other thing I was really interested in was cooking! In my final year of high school, my Dad, who always believed and lived 'where there is a will, there is a way' helped me find a week's work experience in a commercial kitchen, and we began looking into applying for an apprenticeship as a chef for me. That week in the kitchen, I cut myself badly enough that it required many stitches to two of my fingers. Despite that setback I just loved the kitchen experience and decided that this was where I wanted to be.

My favourite teacher at school, was my modern history teacher, despite my lack of interest in the subject, she was very encouraging and patient with me. She wrote in my yearbook a famous quote from the poem 'The Road Not Taken' by Robert Frost (1874-1963). These words below have definitely rung true for me as I have journeyed through life.
'Two roads diverged in a wood, and I, I took the one less travelled by, and that has made all the difference.'

After completing my schooling, I began my four year apprenticeship as a chef, while attending Ryde Catering College, doing the Commercial Cookery course. My classmate and friend at college was the now-famous celebrity chef, Matt Moran. Matt opened my eyes to the opportunities of working in an a la carte restaurant, and helped instigate my move out of catering into a small French restaurant in Sydney's CBD, called *Our Pleasure*. Here, under the talented chef and owner Ron Hughes, I learnt how to cook everything from scratch, making all our own pastry, bread, pasta, sauces, desserts, ice cream and chocolates. It was a magnificent foundation for my cooking future. Over the following years I furthered my experience, working at other restaurants such as *Bilsons* at Circular Quay with Chef Peter Kuruvita, *Faulty Bowers* at Shelley Beach, Manly, with Chef Kenneth Leung and then finally at *EJ's* in Macquarie Street, Sydney, again with Chef Ron Hughes and Janet Hughes.

After eight years in restaurants and now married to Paul, I retired from the restaurant world to be a full time mum to our three children, first Tom, then Molly and then Jake! My passion for food and all things cooking was somewhat suppressed for a time, as I mastered mashing vegetables, making Vegemite sandwiches and icing cupcakes, while loving and raising our three kids!

top left to right: Jane aged 3, aged 8, aged 18
centre: Geoff and Annabell Kelleher (Jane's parents)
bottom left to right: Jane aged 12, Jane with siblings

basics

basic; *forming an essential foundation; fundamental,*
consisting of the minimum needed or offered.

Like most wonderful creations, it often comes down to the basics forming the foundation of the work. Cooking too has its basics, which often are the taste makers in each dish. Here are my basics, which appear in my recipes throughout this book. These are your foundations, which you can cook from scratch yourself. Have them stored in the pantry, fridge or freezer to access as you need them. Alternatively, good quality versions of these basics are available ready-made, from fine food stores, organic food suppliers or at local growers markets.

guacamole

Everyone loves this avocado-based dip which originated in Mexico.
Traditionally it is made by simply mashing ripe avocado with a little salt, though
some recipes include tomato, onion, lime juice, chilli and other seasonings.
This is my version - and I find it easier to do the mashing with a fork on a dinner plate.

makes about 2 cups
what you need

2 avocados

½ small red onion, finely chopped

1 large tomato, deseeded,
finely chopped

juice of 1 lemon

pinch of sea salt

freshly ground black pepper,
to taste

V GF
what you do

1. Cut the avocados in half, remove the seed, and scoop out the flesh.
Combine the avocado flesh and lemon juice on a dinner plate or in a
bowl, and mash with a fork until smooth.

2. Mix in the onion and tomato, and season to taste.

Note: Guacamole is best made close to serving time. If you need to make
ahead, cover the surface with a piece of baking paper cut to size. Keep in
the fridge for up to a couple of hours.

tomato salsa

Salsa is a dance, but it is also a sauce! It usually refers to the spicy,
often tomato-based hot sauces typical of Mexican cuisine, particularly those used as dips.
This recipe is for a raw, fresh tomato salsa with fragrant coriander and a hint of chilli.

makes about 2 cups
what you need

6 ripe tomatoes

½ red onion, finely diced

½ bunch coriander
(roots, stalks and leaves),
finely chopped

juice of 1 lime

½ tsp rapadura sugar

pinch of sea salt

1 small red chilli, deseeded
and finely chopped (optional)

V GF
what you do

1. Cut the tomatoes into quarters, and remove the cores and seeds.
Cut the flesh into a large dice.

2. Combine the tomato with the remaining ingredients.

Note: For information on rapadura sugar see page 18. Tomato salsa
is best served at room temperature within one hour of making.

basil pesto

Pesto is a sauce which originated in the Liguria region of northern Italy.
It is traditionally made using a mortar and pestle, but this is my quick and easy version
in the food processor. Pesto has so much versatility, whether it is tossed through hot pasta,
added to savoury breakfast dishes or used as a spread on sandwiches and wraps.

makes about 1 cup
what you need

¼ cup (40g) pine nuts

1 small garlic clove,
roughly chopped

1 cup basil leaves (firmly packed)

²/₃ cup (50g) freshly
grated parmesan

½ cup (125ml) extra virgin
olive oil

V GF
what you do

1. Place the pine nuts and garlic into a food processor and
process until they form a creamy consistency.

2. Add the basil leaves and process until well chopped, then with
the motor running, add the oil in a thin stream until combined.
Finally add the parmesan and process until combined.

Storage: Transfer to a glass container. If not using immediately, cover the
surface with a thin film of oil. Cover tightly and store in the fridge for up
to one week.

tomato sauce

This is a basic tomato sauce which can be made with a surplus of tomatoes in season.
Out of season you can use half fresh and half canned tomatoes.
It takes no time to make and you will find it useful for so many recipes.
Great as a pasta sauce, or as a sauce base on pizzas.

makes 4 cups
what you need

2 tbsp extra virgin olive oil

1 onion, finely chopped

2 garlic cloves, halved

1kg tomatoes, diced

seasonal fresh herbs of your
choice (see note)

pinch of sea salt

V GF
what you do

1. Combine the oil, onion and garlic in a large saucepan, and cook
for 2 minutes over medium heat, stirring often.

2. Add the tomatoes, and cook for a further 5 minutes. Cover and bring
to the boil, then reduce the heat and simmer, covered, for 30 minutes.

3. Transfer to a large bowl and add herbs. Use a hand blender or upright
blender to puree until smooth. Season to taste.

Note: Use your favourite fresh herbs in season, such as a good handful
of basil or parsley, or slightly less oregano or thyme.

Storage: Tomato sauce will keep in an airtight container for up to 5 days
in the fridge. It can also be frozen for up to 2 months.

pizza dough

Making your own pizza dough is an enjoyable process, and if you have children get them involved - they'll love it. It is something you can easily do amidst doing other things. Using part wholemeal flour goes way against Italian tradition, but does loads to increase your nutrition.

makes four 30cm bases
what you need

2¼ cups (360g) wholemeal plain flour

2 cups (300g) unbleached white strong bakers flour (see note)

1 tsp rapadura sugar

7g sachet dried yeast (or 2 tsp)

½ cup (125ml) extra virgin olive oil

pinch of sea salt

V

what you do

1. Combine all the ingredients in a large bowl with 350ml warm water, and use your hands to mix to a soft dough. (This can be done in a mixer, if you have one with a large bowl and dough hook attachment.) The dough should be moist but not sticky. Knead on a lightly floured surface for about 5 minutes, until the dough is smooth and elastic.

2. Transfer to a large, lightly oiled bowl. Cover with a clean tea towel, and leave in a warm place for at least 30 minutes (or up to one hour), until doubled in size.

3. Knock the dough down and knead briefly again. Divide the dough into four pieces and roll out to rounds to fit your pizza trays. Allow to prove on the trays for another 5 minutes in a warm place, before topping and cooking (see page 189 for toppings).

Note: Look at the supermarket for flour labeled 'pizza and bread flour'. It is higher in gluten and gives a good structure to your dough. For information on rapadura sugar see below.

Storage: Pizza dough can be made up to 4 hours in advance, and kept in the fridge until needed. It will rise again slightly, so knock the dough down again, and roll out as instructed.

rapadura sugar *is a whole sugar that undergoes minimal processing. This allows it to retain a higher nutrient content than white sugar, which when refined to create crystals loses much of its nutrients. Rapadura sugar is simply the product left behind after evaporating the water from sugar cane juice and has a unique, caramel flavour. Substitute the same quantity of rapadura sugar for regular sugar in any recipe. It is available from health food shops, and is usually an organic product.*

hummus

Hummus is a spread popular in the Middle East. It is simply made from mashed cooked chickpeas, blended with tahini (sesame seed paste), lemon juice, salt and garlic. Served with bread, it forms a complete protein given the combination of grain and pulse, making it useful in vegetarian and vegan diets. My version, with the addition of onion, cumin and coriander, is great on sandwiches, wraps and burgers. It is also a delicious and healthy dip to have as a snack, or to serve at a party, with lavosh crackers or raw vegetable sticks.

makes about 2½ cups
what you need

1 tbsp olive oil

1 onion, finely chopped

2 garlic cloves, crushed

1½ tsp ground cumin

400g can chickpeas,
rinsed and drained

½ cup (125ml) tahini

½ cup (125ml) lemon juice

¼ cup extra virgin olive oil
(plus extra to serve)

½ bunch fresh coriander
(roots, stems and leaves),
washed and roughly chopped

1 tsp ground paprika
(plus extra to serve)

V GF
what you do

1. Heat the olive oil in a frying pan. Add the onion and garlic and cook over medium heat for about 3 minutes, stirring often, until soft and transparent. Add the cumin and cook a further one minute.

2. Transfer to a food processor and allow to cool for 5 minutes.

3. Add the chick peas, tahini, lemon juice, extra virgin olive oil, coriander (reserve a few leaves for the top) and paprika. Process until smooth.

4. To serve as a dip, spoon onto a serving plate or shallow bowl. Drizzle with a little extra virgin olive oil, and sprinkle with paprika and reserved coriander leaves.

Storage: Hummus will keep in an airtight container in the fridge for up to one week.

lentil dahl

Dhal (which can also be spelt dal, daal, or dahl) is a thick, soupy stew of pulses, such as lentils, beans and/or dried peas. It is a good source of protein, particularly when combined with bread or rice to make a complete protein. It can be served as a side dish with curry or as a base for soups, pies or patties.

makes about 2 cups
what you need

1 tbsp olive oil

1 onion, finely diced

2 garlic cloves, crushed

1 tsp ground cumin

¾ cup (150g) red lentils

1 cup (250ml) vegetable stock
(see basics page 21)

V GF
what you do

1. Heat the oil in a small saucepan and add the onion, garlic and cumin. Cook for 2-3 minutes or just until soft but not coloured.

2. Add the lentils, stock and one cup (250ml) water. Bring to the boil, then reduce the heat to low and simmer uncovered for 15 minutes, stirring occasionally. Serve warm as is, or cool to use in other recipes.

Storage: Dhal will keep in an airtight container in the fridge for up to one week.

meet the people...

I was first introduced to Lettuce Deliver Organics by my neighbour Kerry, who had been having Lettuce Deliver organic produce home-delivered to her for many years. Over four years ago I placed my first online order, and received my first weekly delivery of organic produce to the door of my home. I have been enjoying it ever since.

Emma Stuart caught the passion for organics working at Mary's Organics back in 1996. Cheryl and Bob Stuart, Emma's parents, then encouraged their daughter to look into starting her own organic home-delivery service. At the same time the owners of Lettuce Deliver were looking to sell their small shop and handful of home deliveries in Sydney's eastern suburbs. Emma and Cheryl decided to take on the challenge in 1999. It didn't take long for the home delivery service to expand, to such an extent that Bob decided to join the business full time. Then in 2000 an opportunity arose for the Stuart family to purchase Mary's Organics, expanding the business even further.

The next step was to relocate to Homebush and focus on Sydney-wide home delivery of fresh organic produce. Ben Slade came to the business in 2001, and he and Emma married in 2005. Emma's sisters Peta and Kathleen have also worked in the business. Today, Lettuce Deliver is bigger than ever, with an unmatched reputation in the market place - a family-owned business, run with real passion.

Says Emma, *"Today, the extended Lettuce Deliver family includes close to 20 staff members, many of whom have been with the Stuart family for years, all with a genuine passion for organic produce. We have dozens of Australian farmers and suppliers, many of whom we have been co-operatively trading with for over a decade, not to mention the many happy, healthy families we deliver to each week across Sydney."*

Lettuce Deliver continues to sponsor JaneCOOKS Cooking Classes and generously provided much of the organic produce used for the recipe testing and food photography in this book.

lettuce deliver organics

Emma Slade and Cheryl Stuart

Unit 8/177 Arthur St,
Homebush,
NSW Australia 2140

t: 61 2 9763 7337

www.lettucedeliver.com.au

my story...jane cooks is born

After a season of raising small children, soon all three were at either preschool or school and I returned part time to the paid work force. Initially I worked with my husband Paul, in an administrative and accounts role, at our engineering company. This was the most sensible decision for us at the time, especially financially, as the company grew. In 2009 the role became a full time position, so I resigned, knowing it was time for me to move on - but with not much idea of what I was moving on to!

The same year I read a book about inner health, and how what you eat affects the health of your body. It was a life-changing read for me and my family, and we began to focus more on the quality of the food we were consuming and getting to know where it had come from. This lead to me further educating myself in this area, and we began to see the benefits of eating both organically grown produce and eating in season. This same year an opportunity arose for me to do some cooking demonstrations, teaching others to cook. I just loved the experience and so with all these factors combined, I began to think about running a cooking school.

In April 2009, my ever-believing, entrepreneurial husband Paul encouraged me to go for it and start the cooking school. In May 2009 we set up a company called Jane COOKS. The idea was to run a series of cooking classes that would empower people to learn how to cook and eat well for themselves and their families. Simple, healthy recipes cooked from scratch, using local, seasonal and where possible, organic and biodynamic produce. It was a way for me to combine my training as a chef, my new found passion for healthy eating and my experience as a parent, to help others.

It has been quite a journey, with lots of hard work. Delightfully, old connections have been revived and new ones made, with some very talented and lovely people. People who are passionate and have integrity in what they do, who helped get me through the first twelve months of establishing a new business. Graphic designer Nicky Kukulka designed the Jane COOKS logo, Paul and I spent many late nights building the website and I spent many hours designing the cooking class concept and planning the variety of classes, menus and recipes.

In October 2009 we took another step, redesigning and overseeing the renovation of our home kitchen, making it more suitable for the classes. Lettuce Deliver Organics, who were recommended to me by my neighbour Kerry, generously agreed to sponsor my classes with organic produce, and friend Wendy Kendrew kindly agreed to take on the role of kitchen assistant.

Finally, in February 2010, Jane COOKS Cooking Classes were launched, as well as my ridiculous idea to post a recipe each week on the Jane COOKS website, and start writing a blog *Live, Laugh, Love...
Real Stories of Food and Travel*, later re-named
'Naked Food the way food was meant to be'.

breakfasts

breakfast; *the first meal of the day.*

orange, ginger and
parsley juice

banana smoothie

seasonal fruits with
toasted nuts and seeds

bircher muesli with
pears and raisins

sourdough french toast
with seasonal fruit

spelt and blueberry
pancakes

bruschetta with
tomato and basil

eggs benedict

savoury muffins

scrambled eggs with
garden spinach

poached eggs with roast
tomato, mushroom and
basil pesto

tomato, avocado and
hummus on toast

mushroom, tomato
and sage frittata

feature dish:
scrambled eggs with
feta and parsley
(Beachwood Café, Yamba)

Breakfast is my favourite meal of the day.
A nourishing breakfast or brunch, depending on
what time you rise, is an excellent start for your
body, to sustain you for the day ahead.

I have found entertaining family and friends for
breakfast or brunch, is such a simple and enjoyable
option too. You get to catch up together, without
experiencing the unnecessary expense and stress of
trying to put on a flash dinner party, after a long day!

Depending on how much time you have and the
occasion, you can cook just one or combine many
of these dishes, to create your own little breakfast
buffet. I hope these simple and nutritious recipes will
help you to enjoy a delicious breakfast for family and
friends…then you can have the rest of the day off!

orange, ginger and parsley juice

This is a great kick start to the day and your body will love you for it.
In our house freshly squeezed juice has become a daily habit.

serves 4

what you need

12 oranges

2cm piece ginger, peeled and finely grated

¼ cup flat-leaf parsley, finely chopped

V GF

what you do

1. Halve the oranges and extract the juice (preferably with a small motorised citrus juicer). Take 2 tablespoons of the pulp, removing any seeds, and place into a blender with the juice, ginger and parsley.

2. Blend until evenly combined. Serve immediately.

oranges are renowned for their high quantity of vitamin C, and they are also high in dietary fibre. Sweet, juicy and very good for you, they are known to help lower high blood pressure as well as cholesterol, and have strong anti-inflammatory properties. Vitamin C, which is also vital for the proper function of a healthy immune system, is good for preventing colds and may be helpful in preventing recurrent ear infections. Research has shown that consuming vitamin supplements does not provide the same protective benefits as drinking a glass of fresh orange juice.

banana smoothie

This is a quick and easy high protein and high fibre breakfast, or could be an afternoon pick-me-up. It's a great way to use up ripe bananas and is an excellent quick breakfast option for those mornings when you are on the run.

serves 4

what you need

2 large or 3 small bananas, peeled and chopped

½ cup (125ml) natural yoghurt (european or greek style)

3 cups (750ml) almond milk (see note)

¼ cup (25g) wheatgerm

1 tsp freshly grated nutmeg

1 tsp chia seed

2 tbsp honey

1 cup ice cubes

extra nutmeg, to serve

V GF

what you do

1. Place all the ingredients into a blender and blend until smooth and frothy. If your blender doesn't have an ice crushing capacity, replace the ice with ½ cup (125ml) cold water (you don't want to destroy your blender!).

2. Serve with a little freshly grated nutmeg on top.

Note: Using almond milk and the chia seed will give you the best source of protein. You could substitute rice milk, soy milk or full cream cow's milk if you like.

chia seed is known as nature's complete super food. Chia is an ancient seed that has more omega-3 and dietary fibre than any other food in nature and is high in protein. It promotes heart health, digestive health and aids regularity. It supports joint function and mobility, and is gluten-free. You can sprinkle it on raw foods, smoothies, add to salads, soups, bread and muffin recipes. Soaking chia seed overnight will double its antioxidant value.

bruschetta with tomato and basil

Seasonal eating at its best, this is a fabulous way to enjoy your glut of tomatoes! Tomato and basil were created for one another, and when you combine them with a lovely Australian organic extra virgin olive oil it is a 'naked food' sensation.

serves 6

what you need

6 thick slices of crusty bread (see note)

1kg tomatoes

1 garlic clove, halved

handful basil leaves, torn

1 tbsp extra virgin olive oil

pinch of sea salt

freshly ground black pepper, to serve

V

what you do

1. Preheat the oven to 150°C (130°C fan forced). Arrange the bread slices onto an oven tray, and bake for 15 minutes each side, until crisp.

2. Meanwhile, bring a large saucepan of water to the boil. Use a small sharp knife to remove the core of each tomato and then score a small cross into the base on the other side. Prepare a large bowl of iced water.

3. Place the tomatoes in the boiling water for 1-2 minutes, until you see the skins begin to come away. Lift out with a slotted spoon, drain, then place into the iced water. This stops the cooking process, so they don't become mushy. Lift each tomato out, drain well, then the skins will peel away easily by hand.

4. Cut each tomato into quarters lengthways, and remove the seeds. Cut each quarter into long strips (1.5cm wide) and then cut each strip on an angle to make a large diamond-shaped dice.

5. Remove the bread from the oven and rub each slice with the cut garlic clove while still warm. In a bowl combine the tomato, basil and oil, season with salt. Spoon onto the bread, and serve immediately, sprinkled with pepper.

Note: I use either an olive sourdough bread or a ciabatta, but you could use any hearty sourdough or Italian style bread.

GF option: Use gluten-free bread.

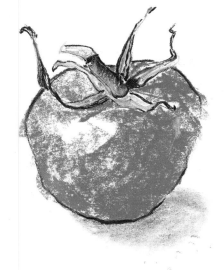

tomatoes are botanically a fruit, but in the culinary sense are a vegetable. They are rich in vitamin A and C, and also have good amounts of calcium, potassium, sodium and phosphorus. A real benefit is that they are a rich source of the antioxidant lycopene, which is said to help prevent prostate cancer. Bright red fruit indicates that it is high in lycopene as well as beta-carotene (which converts to vitamin A in the body). Consuming olive oil or avocado with tomato aids in the absorption of these nutrients - and luckily they taste great together!

eggs benedict

This one has become a family favourite. You can be traditional
with the smoked leg ham, or try my vegetarian option.
Rather than serving the eggs on a traditional English muffin,
try some organic wholemeal sourdough or wholemeal Turkish bread.

serves 4
what you need

4 small tomatoes

1 tbsp olive oil

1 tbsp white vinegar
(see note)

1 tsp extra virgin olive oil

8 eggs

4 pieces wholemeal turkish
bread, split and toasted

2 cups (500ml) hollandaise sauce
(see basics page 25)

freshly ground black pepper,
to serve

traditional:
8 thin slices free range
smoked leg ham

vegetarian:
1 avocado, thinly sliced

1 tbsp lemon juice

½ cup (15g) baby spinach leaves

V
what you do

1. Preheat the oven to 180°C (160°C fan forced) and lightly grease a large oven tray. Cut the tomatoes in half and place them onto the tray. Drizzle with the oil, and roast for 15 minutes. Set aside, and preheat the grill.

2. To poach eggs bring a small saucepan of water to the boil and stir in the vinegar. Reduce the heat so the water is simmering. Carefully crack 2 eggs into the saucepan. Cook gently for 1-2 minutes, or until the whites have just set.

3. Lift the eggs from the water one at a time with a slotted spoon, allowing the excess water to drain away. Transfer to a plate. Repeat step 2 to cook the remaining eggs two at a time.

4. Cut the avocado in half and remove the seed. Cut each piece in half again, and remove the skin. Slice the avocado flesh, and sprinkle with lemon juice.

5. Meanwhile, arrange the toast onto two large oven trays. Place either a slice of leg ham, or spinach and avocado, onto the toast. Top each piece with a poached egg. Spoon hollandaise over each egg, and place under the hot grill for one minute, until just slightly browned. Serve immediately, with the tomatoes and season with pepper as desired.

Note: Unless your eggs are extremely fresh (as in you have your own hens), adding a little white vinegar to the poaching water will help to keep your eggs together. For this recipe, use an avocado which is 'medium ripe'. It should have a little 'give' when gently prodded, but not be too soft to slice.

GF option: Use gluten-free bread.

leg ham *is a cut of meat from the thigh of the hind leg of an animal, usually pig, which is either fully cooked or cured. Cured ham is uncooked preserved pork. It is cured (a preservation process) usually in large quantities of salt and sugar. Then hot smoked (hung over a hot, smokey fire but out of direct heat) to preserve it more. Sodium nitrite is usually used for the curing of meat, because it prevents bacterial growth, this is also what causes the product to have a dark red, pinkish colour. There is nitrate free ham available for those who have concerns about consuming sodium nitrate.*

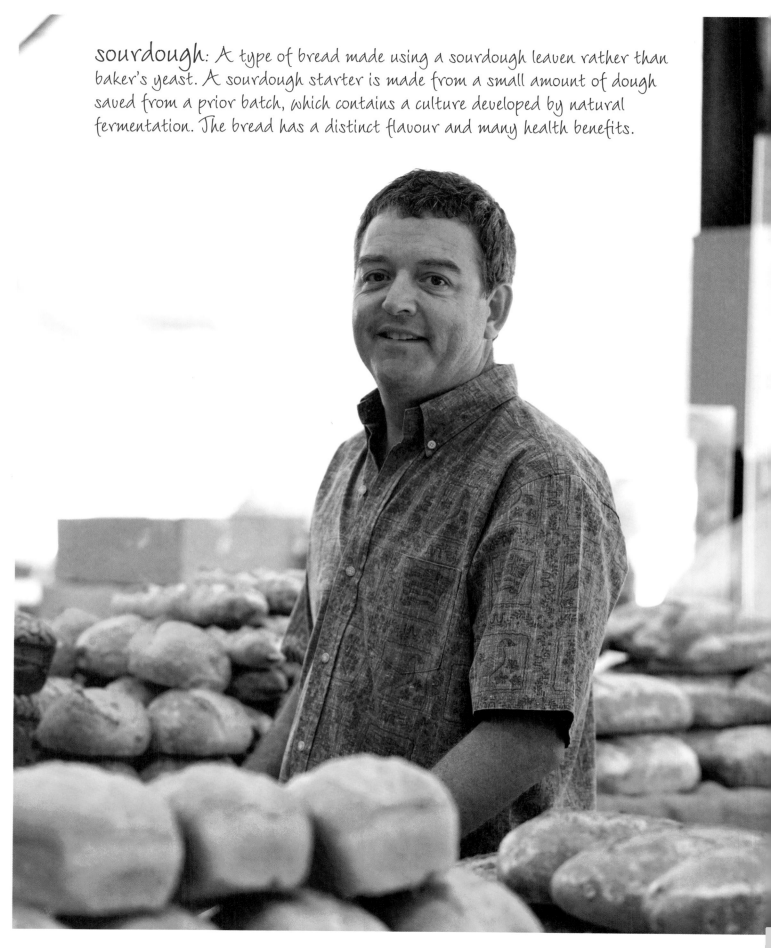

sourdough: A type of bread made using a sourdough leaven rather than baker's yeast. A sourdough starter is made from a small amount of dough saved from a prior batch, which contains a culture developed by natural fermentation. The bread has a distinct flavour and many health benefits.

meet the people...

I first met Mark Anthony at his La Tartine Organic Bakery stall at Eveleigh Farmers' Market in 2010. What struck me, apart from the sensational sourdough bread, was his incredible passion for organics.

La Tartine initially began in France, in the Alpine area between Switzerland and Italy. In the late 1990's, after nine years of baking in France, Nick and his lovely wife Lotti brought the La Tartine sourdough concept, as well as specialised bakery equipment, to begin baking in Australia. Mark then joined his brother Nick in the business and they began producing authentic organic sourdough for the Sydney market.

Nick and Mark Anthony are sourdough purists, with an uncompromising commitment to pure sourdough and certified organics. Their organic flour comes directly from a family-run mill in Gunnedah, NSW. Both Nick and Mark believe that many consumers are not aware of the difference between 'organic' and 'certified organic'. Mark says *"Certified organic includes controls to keep flour from contamination right up to the point of consumption. For example, trucks that deliver certified organic flour must be certified as being suitable for the task. These considerations are enforced by regular inspections."* Mark regularly makes the point to his customers that *"any bread containing bakers yeast cannot be certified organic, as bakers yeast is not an organic product."*

I recently visited the La Tartine bakery at Somersby, on the NSW Central Coast. It was a wonderful experience, to meet the passionate team and see the breads being shaped, proved and then baked in the large ovens. The aroma as baker Jan removed the freshly baked bread from the ovens, and the taste of bread, still warm, is hard to beat.

Their range of certified organic sourdough breads are unmatched in the market place. The flagship fruit loaf with whole almonds, figs and apricots, the unbleached white breads (including a delicious olive sourdough), the wholemeal grain, as well as the rye and caraway loaf, are some of our favourites.

La Tartine breads are available direct from the bakery ovens every Friday, or from several outlets in Sydney, including Lettuce Deliver Organics or at the La Tartine stall at Eveleigh Farmers' Market every Saturday.

la tartine organic bakery

Nick and Mark Anthony

Unit 2/11 Wiseman's Ferry Rd, Somersby NSW 2250

t: 61 2 4340 0299

savoury muffins

These are a delicious and nutritious snack, suitable for breakfast, brunch, served for lunch with a leafy green salad or popped into the school lunchbox. When I am cooking these for breakfast I usually measure and prepare the ingredients the night before, then throw them together and into the oven first thing in the morning.

makes 16

what you need

1½ cups (240g) wholemeal plain flour

1½ cups (225g) unbleached plain white flour

2 tsp baking powder

1 tsp paprika

1 cup (100g) grated mozzarella

1 red onion, finely diced

1 red capsicum, finely diced

2 green shallots, finely sliced

1 zucchini, grated

1 cup fresh corn kernels (from 2 cobs)

handful of fresh herbs, chopped (see note)

120g feta, diced

3 eggs

1 cup (250ml) full cream milk

½ cup (125ml) tomato sauce (see basics page 15) or 1 tbsp tomato paste

125g butter, melted and cooled

V

what you do

1. Preheat the oven to 200°C (180°C fan forced) and lightly grease 16 medium muffin tins, or line with paper cases.

2. Sift the flours, baking powder and paprika into a large mixing bowl, and return the husks. Add the mozzarella, onion, capsicum, shallots, zucchini, corn, herbs and feta.

3. In a separate bowl, lightly beat the eggs and milk with a fork, then add the tomato sauce or paste and the butter. Add the wet ingredients to the dry ingredients and fold together until evenly combined (don't overbeat, or the muffins will be tough). Spoon evenly into the prepared muffin tray.

4. Bake for 35-40 minutes, until risen and golden brown. Serve warm or at room temperature.

Note: Use any one, or a mixture of the following herbs: chives, parsley, basil, oregano.

Storage: The cooked muffins can be kept, tightly wrapped in foil, for up to 3 days in the fridge or in the freezer for up to one month. Reheat in a moderate oven to serve.

GF option: Substitute the wholemeal and plain flour with 3 cups of rice flour. Use gluten-free baking powder.

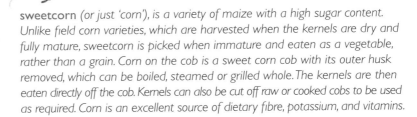

sweetcorn *(or just 'corn'), is a variety of maize with a high sugar content. Unlike field corn varieties, which are harvested when the kernels are dry and fully mature, sweetcorn is picked when immature and eaten as a vegetable, rather than a grain. Corn on the cob is a sweet corn cob with its outer husk removed, which can be boiled, steamed or grilled whole. The kernels are then eaten directly off the cob. Kernels can also be cut off raw or cooked cobs to be used as required. Corn is an excellent source of dietary fibre, potassium, and vitamins.*

scrambled eggs with garden spinach

This is my favourite breakfast of all. Some say the real test with eggs, is whether you can soft poach them successfully, but for me it all comes down to how you scramble them! The freshest eggs, real milk and some freshly picked garden spinach should return you a fluffy, moist masterpiece of yellow with flecks of rich green. Can you tell I'm passionate about my scrambled eggs?

serves 4

what you need

6 eggs

¼ cup (60ml) milk

1 cup finely shredded spinach or silverbeet (see below)

1 tsp extra virgin olive oil

1 tsp butter

pinch of sea salt

toasted sourdough bread and freshly ground black pepper, to serve

V

what you do

1. Crack the eggs into a large glass mixing bowl. Add the milk and lightly beat with a fork or whisk. Stir in the spinach.

2. Heat a saucepan over high heat, add the oil and butter and then immediately pour in the eggs, so oil doesn't smoke and the butter doesn't burn.

3. Reduce the heat to low and cook for 3 to 5 minutes, stirring regularly. The eggs should be moist and yellow (not browned at all), so as soon as they appear to be almost (but not quite) done, turn off the heat, add a pinch of sea salt and stir for half a minute more.

4. Serve immediately, on toasted sourdough bread and season with pepper as desired.

GF option: Serve on gluten-free toast.

spinach and silverbeet *are quite different - silverbeet is actually a type of chard (in fact it is sometimes called Swiss chard) and is more closely related to beetroot. Spinach is often called English spinach, to differentiate it from silverbeet. There are lots of types of spinach, but most have fairly small (10-30cm), soft leaves, and are often used raw in salads. You can also buy baby spinach leaves. Silverbeet has much larger (30-60cm) leaves, which are thicker than spinach and very crinkly. It also has a white, or sometimes red or yellow stem. Both are good sources of iron, and are rich in vitamins, minerals, protein and omega-3 fatty acids.*

poached eggs with roasted tomatoes, mushrooms and basil pesto

Many people love to order poached eggs when they eat out for breakfast, often because they are not confident cooking them at home. Unless your eggs are extremely fresh (as in you have your own hens), adding a little white vinegar to the poaching water will help to keep your eggs together. This breakfast combo is one of my husband's favourites.

serves 2
what you need

3 roma tomatoes

4 medium field mushrooms

1 tbsp extra virgin olive oil

1 tbsp white vinegar

4 eggs

¼ cup (60ml) basil pesto
(see basics page 15)

toasted bread and freshly ground black pepper, to serve

V
what you do

1. Preheat the oven to 180°C (160°C fan forced) and lightly grease a large oven tray. Cut the tomatoes in half and place them onto the tray. Place the whole mushrooms at the other end of tray. Drizzle the vegetables with one tablespoon of the oil, and roast for 15 minutes.

2. Bring a small saucepan of water to the boil and stir in the vinegar. Reduce the heat so the water is simmering. Carefully crack 2 of the eggs into the saucepan. Cook gently for 1-2 minutes, or until the whites have just set.

3. Lift the eggs from the water one at a time with a slotted spoon, allowing the excess water to drain away. Transfer to a plate and repeat step 2 to cook the remaining 2 eggs.

4. Serve the eggs on toast, with the mushrooms and tomatoes on the side, drizzled with the basil pesto. Season with pepper as desired.

GF option: Use gluten-free bread.

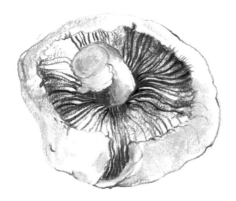

mushroom *is the 'fruit' of a fungus, as it carries the spores, which is its 'seed'. It grows above ground in soil, or on its food source. Mushrooms are very low in kilojoules, and a good source of B vitamins, and minerals such as selenium, copper and potassium. They come in many shapes and sizes, and can be eaten raw or lightly cooked.*

tomato, avocado and hummus on toast

There are always tomatoes and avocados in my fruit bowl and hummus in the fridge, making this my number one easy breakfast. It is quick to prepare and full of nutrients, tastes great and fills you up - what more could you want?

serves 2

what you need

4 slices rye and caraway sourdough bread (or bread of your choice)

I large avocado

I tbsp lemon juice

4 small tomatoes

½ cup hummus (see basics page 20)

I tbsp extra virgin olive oil

freshly ground black pepper, to serve

V

what you do

1. Lightly toast the bread if you like, or leave fresh. Cut the avocado in half and remove the seed. Cut each piece in half again, and remove the skin. Slice the avocado flesh, and sprinkle with lemon juice.

2. Cut tomatoes into thick slices. Spread the hummus thickly onto the bread. Arrange the avocado, then the tomato slices on top. Serve immediately, drizzled with the extra virgin olive oil and season with pepper as desired.

Note: For this recipe, use an avocado which is 'medium ripe'. It should have a little 'give' when gently prodded, but not be too soft to slice.

GF option: Use gluten-free bread.

avocados *are a fruit rather than a vegetable, and though we usually use them in savoury dishes, in some cultures they are used in sweet dishes. The flesh is smooth and creamy with a subtle flavour. The creaminess can be attributed partly to the fat content - avocados are one of a very small number of fruits which contain fat. It is a monosaturated fat (a 'good fat'), similar to the kind found in olive oil. They are a good source of essential fatty acids, and also contain vitamins B, E and K, as well as potassium and fibre. The flesh can turn brown quite quickly when exposed to air. Brush cut surface with lemon juice (or combine with mashed avocado) to prevent this.*

mushroom, tomato and sage frittata

This can be served warm, or served later at room temperature - great for a picnic. Frittatas are very versatile, so don't feel like you are restricted to this ingredient combination. Use different vegetables, such as roasted sweet potato, pumpkin or boiled potatoes, and flavour with different types of herbs. You could also use cheddar or feta instead of parmesan.

serves 6

what you need

¼ cup (60ml) extra virgin olive oil

200g mushrooms, roughly chopped

2 green shallots, finely chopped

8 sage leaves, roughly chopped

6 eggs

10 grape tomatoes, halved

¼ cup (20g) finely grated parmesan

V GF

what you do

1. Preheat the oven to 200°C (180°C fan forced). Using a 24cm (top measurement) ovenproof frying pan, heat the oil on a medium heat.

2. Cook the mushrooms for 5 minutes over medium heat until soft, then add the shallots and sage and cook for one minute, until soft.

3. Lightly beat the eggs with some freshly ground black pepper. Reduce the heat to medium-low, and pour the eggs over the mushrooms. Cook for about 5 minutes, until the underside is golden brown (use a palette or non-serrated knife to carefully lift away from the side of the pan a little, to check the colour).

4. Arrange the tomatoes over the top of the frittata, and sprinkle with parmesan. Place into the oven for 5 minutes, to cook through, then place under the grill for 2 minutes to brown the top. Loosen the frittata by running the knife around the edge. Cut into wedges to serve.

Note: If your pan isn't 'scratch-proof', slide the frittata onto a board before cutting.

Storage: Frittata will keep tightly covered in the fridge for up to 3 days.

sage usually known as common sage or garden sage, is a soft leaf herb, with greyish green leaves and blue to purplish flowers. It is available in both fresh and dried form. Sage provides nutritional benefits, as it is a rich source of vitamin A, and contains calcium, iron, potassium and a small amount of sodium. It is best added to dishes towards the end of the cooking time to experience its full flavour. Fresh sage leaves are often fried until crisp in a little oil and used as a garnish. Sage will stay fresh in the fridge for several days, wrapped in some damp paper towel and stored in an airtight container.

feature recipe...

Beachwood Café is tucked away on a peaceful side street, right in the heart of the seaside town of Yamba, on the NSW far north coast. You can enjoy the casual outdoor setting, with the fragrances from their fresh herb garden. Beachwood Café enjoys a close connection with local farmers, fishermen and their produce. Deliveries vary each day from fresh seafood straight off the trawler, Iluka sardines, free-range eggs, to locally-grown herbs and vegetables. The food is connected to a face and a story and customers see for themselves how fresh and beautiful the local produce is and how good it tastes.

The menus change to reflect the seasons. They are fresh and creative, with a delicious Mediterranean twist to many of the dishes. Breakfasts, full flavoured mains and fresh from the oven sweet treats, such as baklava, as well as famous home-made jam, delicious coffee, homemade mint tea and freshly squeezed organic juices and smoothies.

Café owner, the lovely Sevtap Yuce, has recently released her first cookbook *Turkish Flavours - Recipes from a Seaside Café* published by Hardie Grant. She has kindly shared this beautiful breakfast recipe. Beachwood Café is licensed, and is open Tuesday to Sunday. Breakfast is served from 7am – 11am, and lunch from 11am – 3pm.

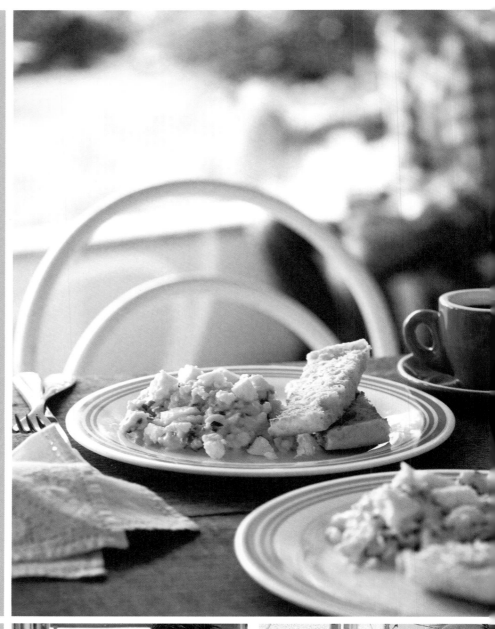

beachwood café

22 High Street, Yamba NSW

t 61 2 6646 9781

www.beachwoodcafe.com.au

scrambled eggs with feta and parsley

This delicious breakfast recipe comes from our recent visit to Beachwood Café, a cosy little café in the seaside town of Yamba, on the north coast of NSW. Owner Sevtap Yuce has recently launched her own delightful book called *Turkish Flavours - Recipes from a Seaside Café* published by Hardie Grant. She has kindly agreed to share this recipe for you to enjoy.

serves 2
what you need

4 eggs

100ml pouring cream

pinch of sea salt

3 tbsp chopped flat-leaf parsley

20g butter

50g bulgarian feta

toasted turkish bread, to serve

V
what you do

1. Gently whisk the eggs with the cream, salt and parsley.

2. Melt the butter in a non-stick frying pan over low heat. Pour in the egg mixture and gently fold and stir for about 5 minutes, until just set.

3. Spoon onto serving plates and crumble the feta over. Serve immediately, with the toasted turkish bread.

Note: Bulgarian feta is a rich and creamy sheep's milk cheese. This feta is much stronger in flavour, more salty and more creamy than other feta cheeses. It is a product of Bulgaria.

GF option: Use gluten-free bread.

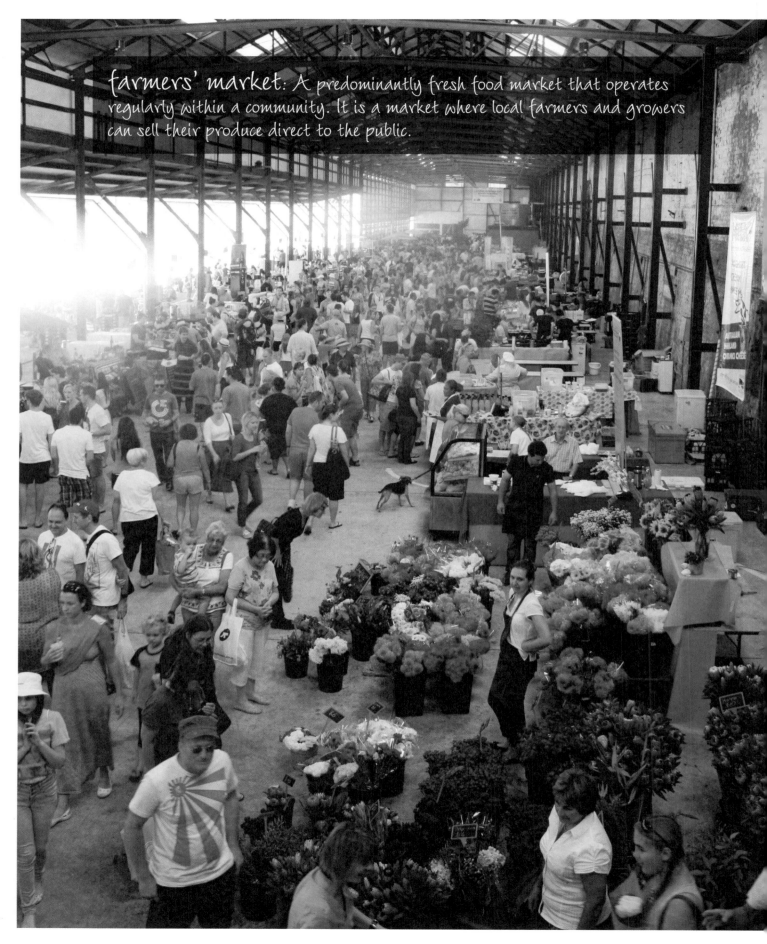

farmers' market: A predominantly fresh food market that operates regularly within a community. It is a market where local farmers and growers can sell their produce direct to the public.

meet the people...

I first visited Eveleigh Farmers' Market in October 2010, after reading about it in *SBS The foodies' guide to Sydney (Hardie Grant)*, and in Kylie Kwong's wonderful book *It Tastes Better (Penguin)*. What an amazing experience it is to walk through the markets on a Saturday morning, meeting the producers, hearing their passion, tasting and buying their fresh produce.

Eveleigh Farmers' Market first commenced trading on Saturday 28th February 2009, with great support from the local community and food lovers across Sydney. It is an award-winning authentic farmers' market, where NSW-based farmers and artisan food producers bring their fresh and seasonal produce, which they grow, rear and make themselves, direct to the community.

The market is home to over 70 regular stallholders, who sell a wide range of farm-fresh products, straight from the source. I start my market experience with breakfast from Kylie Kwong at *Billy Kwong's Homestyle Chinese Cooking* stall, or with a crooked madame from Alex Herbert's *Bird, Cow, Fish* stall.

Highlights of a trip to the markets for me are picking up some real dairy products, including *Pepe Saya* hand churned butter and *Highland Organic Cheeses*, from lovely Ester on the *Country Valley* stall. I always have a chat with Mark and grab some of his delicious bread at the *La Tartine Organic Sourdough Bakery* stall. I love to see Lesley and her team at their *Kurrawong Organics* stall, with their freshly picked organic vegetables and herbs. It is also a joy to see Kim and Chris Margin, selling their freshly picked, chemical free mushrooms from the *Margins Mushrooms* stall.

Eveleigh Farmers' Market has become a fortnightly outing for my husband Paul and I, then on the first Saturday of each month I take a car load of aspiring foodies on a JaneCOOKS tour to the market. Without fail they all come away inspired and satisfied, and of course pulling a red trolley filled with fresh produce behind them.

Eveleigh Farmers' Market is held every Saturday from 8am to 1pm. It is undercover so weather is not an issue.

Jane COOKS Market Tours

Eveleigh Farmers' Market
1st Saturday of the month

www.janecooks.com.au

eveleigh farmers' market

243 Wilson Street,
Darlington NSW 2008
(near Redfern Station)

t: 61 2 9209 4735

www.eveleighmarket.com.au

my story...oh, is that where food comes from

The cooking school had a wonderful first year, with lots of friends and new faces coming to learn and be inspired to cook and eat in a whole and healthy way. With my revived passion for all things food and my new interest in where my food was coming from, we began to turn our family holidays into foodie road trips.

Since beginning the cooking school and website, we have enjoyed many such trips, which I have then shared on my blog. We have explored regional areas such as the southern highlands and the blue mountains of NSW, the southern coastline of NSW, particularly the shoalhaven region and north-eastern NSW, particularly the northern rivers region. We also did a quick visit to the Margaret River region of WA and I am keen to explore that further, as well as other states of Australia. It has been a fascinating opportunity to meet wonderful people who are passionate about their produce, visiting farmers' markets, farms, wineries, olive groves and bakeries, as well as restaurants and cafes along the way. We have picked our own produce on a berry farm, toured a biodynamic winery and tasted the freshly crushed grape juice, picked and packed broccoli at an organic farm and witnessed the art of freshly made sourdough, how it is formed, proved and baked. Many of these farmers and producers are featured in the 'meet the people' sections of this book, or in the 'where to shop and eat' guide at the end of the book.

My discovery of, and passion for, the local farmers' markets as we travelled, made me seek out and visit a handful closer to home. Traditionally farmers grow a select variety of produce on their own farm. Some grow potatoes, others grow oranges or olives, while some rear lambs for meat, or goats to make cheese. The idea of a community-based food market is where one day a week the farmers bring their own produce into town to the market place and the community buy from one another. This means the produce available is straight from the farm, at reasonable prices and everyone goes home happy with fresh produce, as well as reward for their own labour.

The first modern farmers' market began in Australia in Victoria in 1999 and the Australian Farmers' Market Association was convened in 2003 by a group of volunteers, to create a networking entity to support the development and growth of best practice, and sustainable farmers' markets across Australia. The creation of these markets has been a positive contribution to our existing food systems. Eight years ago farmers markets were a rare breed, with only 28 in NSW and 70 across Australia. Conservative figures indicate that the numbers have now swelled to 43 in NSW and 152 nationally, with new markets springing up weekly. Farmers' markets are trading in capital cities, regional centres, and country towns from Carnarvon, WA, to Byron Bay, NSW, and beyond.

In February 2011, I began Jane COOKS market tours, taking people on a three-hour weekend tour to Eveleigh Farmers' Market, to discover where their food comes from and more importantly appreciate the people who work so hard to produce it. It is a rewarding experience to see people connect with those who grow the food. Customers realise that there is a face and devoted passion behind producing the food that ends up on their plate.

salads and sides

salad; *a cold dish of raw vegetables, a cold dish of various mixtures of raw or cooked vegetables, usually seasoned with oil, vinegar, or other dressing.*

Salads are such a great opportunity to incorporate raw, wholefoods into your diet. Each season brings some great produce to work with, fruit and vegetables rich in antioxidants, as well as natures super foods in the form of seeds and grains. Eat them in abundance, and where possible eat them raw.

side; *additional or less important: a side dish, sometimes referred to as a side order or simply a side, a food item that accompanies the entrée or main course at a meal.*

These sides can serve as a vegetable accompaniment to the main event, however with a recipe such as the asparagus it can also be served as a starter or light lunch.

tomato, basil and feta salad

This is a simple seasonal summer salad which is quick and easy, and tastes great.
My favourite dishes involve using fresh produce in season, which require you to do
very little and rather let the food do the talking!

serves 6
what you need

**1kg tomatoes (homegrown
or organic for best flavour)**

60g feta

¼ cup fresh basil leaves

1 tbsp extra virgin olive oil

**1 tbsp caramelised balsamic,
or balsamic vinegar**

V GF
what you do

1. Cut the tomatoes anyway you like, depending on size and variety, such as thick slices, quarters or halves. Arrange onto a serving plate.

2. Break up the feta and sprinkle evenly over tomatoes. Scatter the basil leaves over. Drizzle with the oil and balsamic, and serve immediately.

feta is a brined curd cheese traditionally made in Greece. It is commonly produced in blocks, and has a crumbly and slightly grainy texture. It is cured in a brine solution (based on water or whey) for several months. When removed from the brine, it dries out rapidly, which is why it is often stored in liquid. It was initially made with goat or sheep milk, though nowadays it is made commercially from pasteurised cow's milk. It can be used in sandwiches and salads, or cooked in pastries and other dishes. It is a good source of protein, riboflavin (vitamin B2), cobalamin (vitamin B12), calcium and phosphorus, though is high in cholesterol, sodium, and saturated fat, so should be eaten in moderation, combined with salads and vegetables.

tabouli

My husband used to enjoy eating Lebanese food just about daily, from Cleveland Street eateries, as he studied at the University of New South Wales many years ago. Apparently this now makes him an expert on tabouli, and this is my best attempt to gain his approval!

serves 6-8

what you need

1/3 cup (55g) burghul

1/2 cup lemon juice

1 bunch flat-leaf parsley

1 cup mint leaves

1 bunch green shallots

2 tomatoes, deseeded

1/2 cup (125ml) extra virgin olive oil

pinch of sea salt

V

what you do

1. Place the burghul into a bowl and add the lemon juice. Leave to soak while you prepare the other ingredients.

2. Roughly chop the herbs, and finely slice the green shallots. Cut the tomatoes into quarters and scoop out the seeds, then finely dice the flesh.

3. Add the herbs, shallots, tomato, olive oil and sea salt to the burghul mixture and mix well. Leave to stand for 30 minutes for the flavours to develop before serving. Serve as a side salad, or in wraps with meat and hummus.

Note: For information on burghul see below.

GF option: Substitute cooked quinoa for the burghul. For information on quinoa see page 183.

burghul (also known as bulgur, bulghur or bulgar) is made from wheat, most commonly durum wheat. It is used widely in Middle Eastern cuisine in dishes such as tabouli, pilafs and kibbeh. It is considered a whole grain product as it retains more nutrients than refined, processed wheat, which has been stripped of many beneficial components. It is also low in fat and high in fibre, and has a delicious nutty flavour.

crunchy brown rice salad

A lovely high fibre salad that everybody loves. A friend who dared to cook for 'the chef', made this salad for me and I asked her for the recipe. This is my similar version of that recipe, as I have adjusted the dressing ever so slightly. As for the origin of the original recipe we are unsure.

serves 6

what you need

2 cups (400g) brown rice

6 green shallots, finely chopped

1 red capsicum, deseeded, finely diced

1/3 cup (55g) currants

60g roasted unsalted cashews, finely chopped

2 tbsp sunflower seeds, toasted

1/2 cup flat-leaf parsley, finely chopped

soy sauce dressing:

1/4 cup (60ml) olive oil

2 tbsp sesame oil

2 tbsp soy sauce

2 tbsp lemon juice

1 tbsp caramelised balsamic vinegar

1 garlic clove, crushed, grated or finely chopped

freshly ground black pepper, to taste

V GF

what you do

1. Place the rice into a sieve and rinse under cold running water; drain. Place 4 cups of water in a large saucepan and bring it to the boil.

2. Add the rice, stir briefly, return to the boil and cook for 10 minutes. Reduce the heat to low, cover and cook for a further 15 minutes. Remove from the heat and stand with the lid on for 5 minutes, then spread out onto a flat tray to cool.

3. For the dressing, put all the ingredients into a glass jar. Seal tightly and shake well to combine. Set aside.

4. Combine the cooled rice and the remaining ingredients in a large bowl. Drizzle with the dressing, and mix well. Leave to stand for at least 30 minutes for the rice to absorb all the flavours (place in the fridge if leaving for more than 30 minutes).

brown rice is rice which has had the husk removed, but retains the germ and bran layer (unlike white rice which has had all these removed). For this reason it is more nutritious than white rice, as it retains the thiamine (vitamin B1) and niacin (vitamin B3), as well as iron and fibre from the unprocessed grain. Both forms of rice have the same amount of kilojoules, carbohydrates and protein, but brown rice is the much healthier option. Brown rice has a nuttier flavour and slightly more chewy texture than white rice and takes around twice the time to cook.

mediterranean salad

The Mediterranean diet traditionally includes fruits, vegetables, pasta, rice and olive oil, lots of seafood, moderate poultry and dairy, and less often meat. Each meal has at its base fruit, vegetables, wholegrains, beans, nuts, legumes, seeds, herbs and spices and olive oil. This salad is my version of the traditional Greek salad and is a favourite at our place.

serves 6

what you need

120g mixed salad leaves

2 lebanese cucumbers, diced

3 celery stalks, thickly sliced

1 red onion, finely sliced

1 punnet grape tomatoes, halved

1 red capsicum, diced

1 green capsicum, diced

½ cup (60g) pitted kalamata olives

100g feta, roughly diced

½ cup fresh basil leaves

basil dressing:

½ cup fresh basil leaves

¼ cup (60ml) extra virgin olive oil

2 tbsp lemon juice

1 tbsp balsamic vinegar

½ tsp sweet paprika

1 tsp honey

V GF

what you do

1. Combine all the salad ingredients in a large bowl, and toss to mix evenly.

2. For the dressing, either smash the basil leaves with a mortar and pestle to a paste, or finely chop. Place all the ingredients into a small glass jar, seal tightly and shake to mix thoroughly.

3. Drizzle the dressing over the top of the salad, toss lightly and serve.

olives are the fruit from the olive tree. The olive tree is native to the Mediterranean region, as well as western Asia and northern Africa. Olive trees are a vital agricultural industry in the Mediterranean as they are the source of olive oil production. This is also a growing industry in Australia. Olives are a naturally bitter fruit, which makes freshly picked olives not very palatable. Therefore the fruit are usually fermented or cured in sea salt or a brine (salty water) solution, then often marinated to make the fruit even more tasty. Olives can be green or black, and their different names (such as black kalamata or green manzanillo) represent the different variety of olive trees they come from. All olives contain plenty of great vitamins and minerals.

feature recipe...

The Peasants Feast Organic Restaurant is a cosy restaurant in Newtown, NSW, which makes delicious food using all certified organic ingredients.

When you dine at The Peasants Feast Organic Restaurant you eat for life, eat for health and eat organic. There is a wide variety of dishes on the menu at very affordable prices and they can cater to every dietary requirement

From his many years in medical research, owner Dr. Robert Warlow has concluded that *"What you put in your mouth determines whether you stay healthy or become ill and how long you live. You can't change your genes but you can change your eating habits to avoid diseases. You truly are what you eat!"*

His goal is to provide healthy food which prevent diseases rather than causing them. Serving food without artificial additives, antibiotics, hormone supplements, pesticides or other synthetically derived chemicals.

The Peasants Feast Organic Restaurant is one of our favourite places to eat. Chef James Limnios has provided two of his health-filled recipes, which we often enjoy when we visit the restaurant.

The restaurant is BYO and is open for dinner from 6pm Tuesday to Saturday.

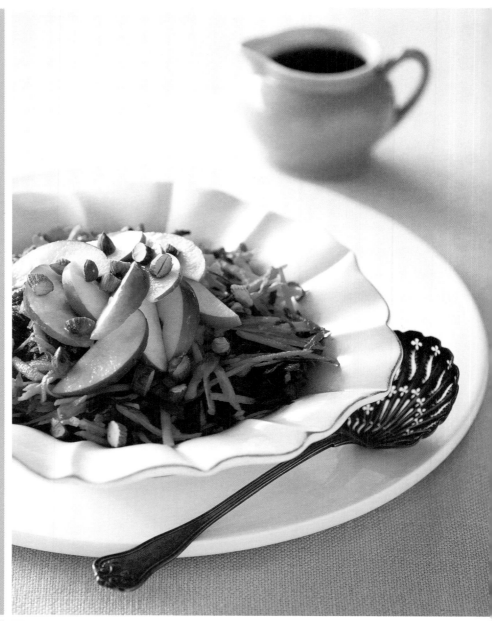

the peasants feast organic restaurant

121A King Street, Newtown
NSW 2042

t: 61 2 9516 5998

www.peasantsfeast.com.au

organic raw salad with ginger and chilli dressing

This recipe comes from Chef James Limnios, of
The Peasants Feast Organic Restaurant in Newtown, NSW.

serves 2

what you need

2 medium carrots, grated

2 medium beetroot, grated

1 apple (fuji or other variety),
quartered, cored and sliced

16 raw almonds, roughly chopped

dressing:

50g ginger, peeled and sliced

1 chilli, sliced

2 garlic cloves, bruised

finely grated zest of ½ small
orange

½ star anise

1 black peppercorn

1 clove

50ml extra virgin olive oil

50ml sunflower oil

35ml tamari

75ml white wine vinegar

V GF

what you do

1. For the dressing, combine the ginger, chilli, garlic, orange zest, star anise, peppercorn, clove, olive oil and sunflower oil in a saucepan. Bring up to a simmer, cook gently for 2 minutes then turn off the heat and leave to infuse until cooled to room temperature.

2. Strain the mixture, reserving the oil, and place the solids into a small blender or food processor. Blend to crush the solids, adding a little of the oil to help it move. Strain back into the oil and press with the back of a spoon to extract as much flavour as you can. Discard solids. Whisk the tamari and vinegar into the oil.

3. Toss the dressing with the carrot and beetroot. Serve topped with sliced apple and chopped almonds.

Note: Star anise is the seed pod of an evergreen tree grown in China and Japan. It is about one inch high with eight segments and a dark brown rust colour, shaped like a star and with a licorice taste similar to regular anise, only stronger. Star anise plays a key role in the slow cooked dishes that characterise Eastern Chinese cuisine. Star anise is one of the spices in five-spice powder. You will find it in the herbs and spices section of your supermarket or fine food store.

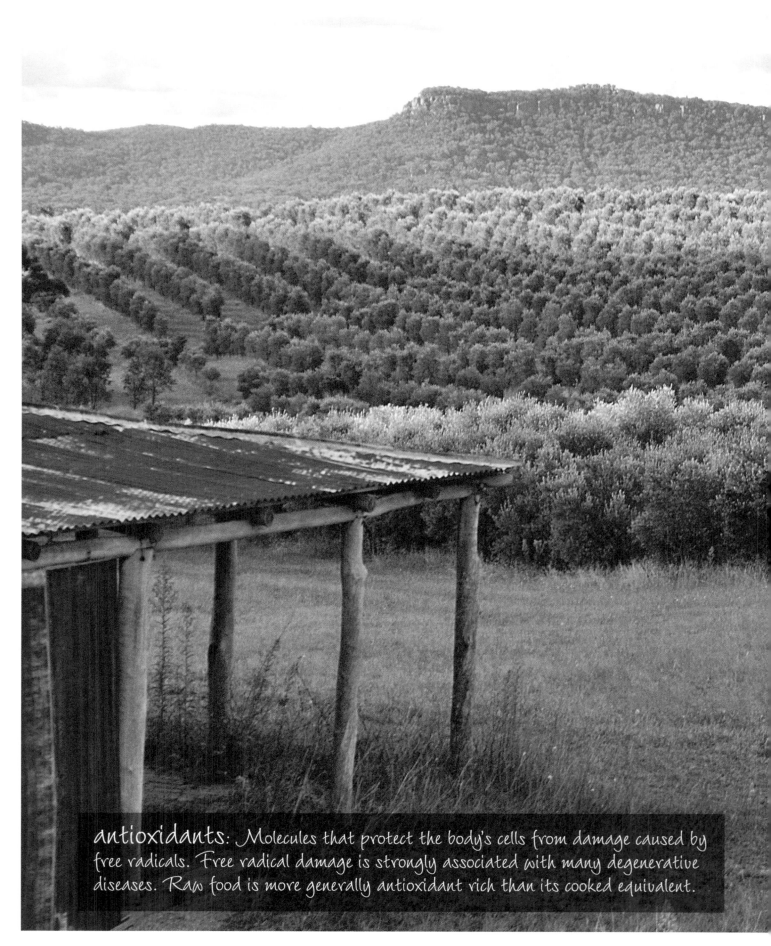

antioxidants: Molecules that protect the body's cells from damage caused by free radicals. Free radical damage is strongly associated with many degenerative diseases. Raw food is more generally antioxidant rich than its cooked equivalent.

meet the people...

I was first introduced to Rylstone Organic Extra Virgin Olive Oil when I tasted it at the *Good Food and Wine Show* in Sydney in 2009, and have since made it an essential ingredient in my diet.

Rylstone is a gorgeous country town in the Central Tablelands of NSW. It is about a 30 minute drive from Mudgee, or 3 hour drive from Sydney, and it is well worth a visit.

On 127.5 hectares of old grazing country in the Rylstone area, Jayne Bentivoglio, with the support of her husband Peter and a team of 13 people, has developed an 8000 olive tree grove and a state-of-the-art olive oil processing facility. With its high altitude, hot summers and consistent rainfall, Rylstone resembles Tuscany, and is ideal for olive growing.

At Rylstone Olive Press, right from the start in 1997, organic principles have been followed, with no herbicides or synthetic fertilisers used at any stage. The olive trees are only irrigated as a supplementary measure, as the rainfall in the area is consistent, with a dominant winter distribution, which is good for olives. The operation has an impressive commitment to high standards, and both the olive grove and the processing plant are certified organic.

The olives for the beautiful Rylstone Organic Extra Virgin Olive Oil are grown and processed on the estate. Extra virgin olive oil (known as the best olive oil) is top of the range in terms of health benefits, antioxidant levels and fruity olive flavour. Coming from Rylstone Olive Press, you can be assured it is certified organic, and an Australian made product.

Jayne Bentivoglio's mission statement reads: *'Rylstone Olive Press contributes to improving the health of family, friends and society. We are committed to protect the environment that is entrusted upon us and to impart knowledge and guidance to future generations for the sustainability of the olive industry and the environment that nurtures it.'*

Rylstone Organic Extra Virgin Olive Oil is available from organic stores and most fine food outlets.

rylstone olive press

Jayne Bentivoglio

Rylstone, NSW

t: 61 2 6379 1485

www.rylstoneolivepress.com.au

steamed asparagus with toasted pine nuts

Asparagus remains one of the few great examples of real seasonal eating. Spring time comes around and it means that fresh asparagus is on its way. This recipe is great as a side to fish, or to accompany one of the recipes from the 'on the bbq' chapter. It can also be enjoyed as an entrée or light lunch all on its own.

serves 4
what you need

¼ cup (40g) pine nuts

2 bunches asparagus, woody ends trimmed

juice of ½ lemon

1 tsp caramelised balsamic vinegar

1 tbsp extra virgin olive oil

parmesan, shaved and freshly ground black pepper, to serve

V GF
what you do

1. Heat a small frying pan over medium heat and dry fry the pine nuts for 1-2 minutes, until golden brown. Transfer to a plate to cool.

2. Cook the asparagus in a steamer for 3-5 minutes, until just tender and bright green (test with a small sharp knife). The cooking time will depend on the thickness of the spears. Remember it will continue to cook once removed from the steamer, so get it out sooner rather than later.

3. Arrange the asparagus on a platter and sprinkle with the toasted pine nuts. Drizzle with the lemon juice, caramelised balsamic and extra virgin olive oil. Top with shaved parmesan and season with pepper as desired.

Note: Caramelised balsamic vinegar is balsamic vinegar which has been boiled to reduce it in quantity, producing a thicker and sweeter syrup consistency. On some occasions sugar is added at the time of boiling to add further sweetness and help with the caramelising.

smashed potatoes with rosemary

Recently I visited Kurrawong Organics Farm on the Central Tablelands of NSW. Lesley Bland cooked me a lovely meal using fresh organic vegetables from their market gardens. This is my take on the delicious potatoes she cooked for me that evening with her freshly dug, new season potato crop.

serves 6
what you need

1kg kipfler or chat potatoes, scrubbed

¼ cup (60ml) olive oil

1 tbsp sea salt

1 tbsp rosemary leaves

V GF
what you do

1. Preheat the oven to 250°C (230°C fan forced) and line a large baking tray with non-stick baking paper.

2. Cook the potatoes in a steamer for 20 minutes until tender. Dry any moisture from potatoes. Arrange the potatoes in a single layer.

3. Using a fork or potato masher, gently crush or smash the potatoes so they break open but still retain their form. Drizzle with the olive oil, and sprinkle with sea salt and rosemary.

4. Bake on the top shelf for 30 minutes, until golden brown with a crispy outside and fluffy inside.

Note: Use the highest setting on your oven, preferably fan forced, for the best crunchy result.

green beans with almond and mint crumble

In my opinion fresh green beans are best just eaten raw, but that doesn't really qualify as 'a recipe' for a cookbook! In this dish the beans are lightly steamed, then served cold, with sweet balsamic vinegar and a crunchy nut crumble.
A perfect side dish for the warmer months of the year.

serves 6
what you need

¼ cup (40g) whole raw almonds, roasted

500g green beans

handful of mint leaves

drizzle of extra virgin olive oil

drizzle of caramelised balsamic vinegar

V GF
what you do

1. Preheat the oven to 160°C (140°C fan forced). Place the almonds onto a baking tray and roast for 20 minutes. Cool.

2. Cook the beans in a steamer for 3-5 minutes, until just tender and bright green. Meanwhile prepare a large bowl of iced water.

3. Remove from the steamer and plunge into the iced water to stop the cooking process (this ensures the beans will be crunchy and vibrantly coloured). Drain immediately and pat dry with paper towel.

4. Place the almonds into a food processor and process until coarsely chopped. Add the mint and process until finely chopped and evenly combined.

5. Place the beans onto a serving plate, and drizzle with oil and caramelised balsamic. Finish by sprinkling with the almond and mint crumble mixture.

roast vegetables

Roast vegetables are a favourite of mine. I am both fascinated by and attracted to the amazing transformation of texture and flavour that occurs to these vegetables once cooked. The vegetables naturally caramelise with the olive oil, becoming even sweeter and more tender to the tooth, and the garlic becomes a creamy sweet delight.

serves 6
what you need

3 onions

3 red onions

1 bunch baby carrots

1 bunch beetroot (small bulbs)

2 small parsnips

500g sweet potato

4 tbsp olive oil

10 small garlic cloves

pinch of sea salt

V GF
what you do

1. Preheat the oven to 220°C (200°C fan forced).
Cut the onions into 6 wedges each. Scrub the carrots and beetroot, and trim the carrot tops. Cut the beetroot into thick wedges. Quarter the parsnips lengthways, and cut the sweet potato into batons.

2. Drizzle the olive oil over two oven trays, and arrange the vegetables onto the trays. Add the garlic cloves, leaving the skin on. Sprinkle with sea salt, and toss to distribute the oil and salt evenly.

3. Bake for 45-60 minutes. (If not using a fan forced oven, swap the trays from top to bottom shelf halfway through cooking.)

4. When ready the vegetables will be a caramelised golden brown colour and be tender when pierced with a small sharp knife.

garlic and white bean mash

I began to introduce more legumes and pulses into my diet a few years back. This mash with its combination of flavours makes a nice change from rice or potatoes accompanying every dish.

serves 6

what you need

1 tbsp olive oil

1 small onion, finely chopped

3 garlic cloves, sliced

2 x 400g cans cannellini beans, rinsed and drained

1 tbsp butter

pinch of sea salt

freshly ground black pepper, to taste

V GF

what you do

1. Combine the olive oil, onion and garlic in a small saucepan. Cook over medium heat for about 3 minutes, until soft and transparent.

2. Add the beans and ½ cup (125ml) water, and bring to the boil. Reduce the heat and simmer for 10 minutes, stirring occasionally until the liquid has almost all gone.

3. Add the butter, then using a potato masher, mash to a smooth paste. Season to taste. This is great served with lamb cutlets, pan-fried chicken or grilled fish.

potato wedges

As a child one of my favourite things to eat was hot chips with lots of salt! Times have changed and most hot chips are not what they used to be. These wedges offer me a homemade alternative, and the golden crunch and fluffy potato bring back great memories. Occasionally I make a batch or two of these on a cold rainy day and we eat them between slices of buttered fresh bread, with sea salt and tomato sauce. What my dad used to call a chip butty!

serves 6

what you need

6 large desiree potatoes (see note)

400g sweet potato

2 tbsp olive oil

pinch of sea salt

what you do

1. Preheat the oven to 250°C (230°C fan forced). Peel the potatoes and sweet potato if you like, or leave the skins on and scrub them well.

2. Cut into even sized wedges or batons, and steam or boil until tender but not falling apart. Remove from the steamer and use paper towel to dry off any remaining moisture.

3. Place the wedges onto an oven tray. Drizzle with oil and sprinkle with salt, then toss to coat evenly. Cook for 30 minutes, turning over halfway through cooking, until golden and crunchy. Serve straight away.

Note: You can really use any type of potato, but desiree are lovely, and especially good with the skin left on.

my story...out in the garden, growing my own

Inspired by my visits to farmers' markets and meeting those hard working people who grow the fresh produce, I decided it was time to start growing some of my own produce at home. I have always enjoyed gardening and am forever fascinated by the miraculous transformation that occurs from seed to fruit. I had a lovely older neighbour a few years back named Kevin, who was a legend at growing his own vegetables. His compost was worth more than money can buy and occasionally he would share some with me, as well as some of his fresh produce and marigold seedlings for my garden. I learnt a lot from him and his amazing backyard garden.

When visiting the *Organic Expo and Green Show* in Sydney for the first time in 2010, I was fortunate to meet Toni Salter, aka *The Veggie Lady*, who was exhibiting there. Toni runs backyard veggie classes, as well as therapeutic gardening workshops from her own garden at her home in western Sydney, as well as online courses. At the end of our first year of running the cooking classes, Wendy and I attended one of Toni's gardening classes together on backyard veggies, and learnt so much about getting a vegetable garden started. I spent the following six months planning, building, planting and establishing our own vegetable patch. A couple of months later, we began to harvest our own produce at home. I attempted to grow many things from seed, which returned to me about a fifty percent success rate and so I became a bigger fan of growing only a few things from seed and most things from seedlings.

It was also my great pleasure to meet Rebekah Brauman from *Ready 2 Plant Organics* at the show the following year. Later I discovered that she is a regular at the *French's Forest Organic Markets* (every Sunday 8am – 1pm), selling her organic seedlings and vegetables. You can also order the seedlings online to be delivered to your door. I now regularly fill my patch with organic seedlings, which I buy from Rebekah at the markets. With some quality soil, water, organic fertiliser and winter sunshine, we enjoyed an abundant harvest of lettuce, silverbeet, kale, beetroot, coriander and garden peas in our first Autumn/Winter season last year. This was followed by our first Spring/Summer season harvest of tomatoes, eggplant, basil, capsicum, chillies, beans, cucumbers, eggplant, parsley, rocket, more lettuce and an attempt at corn, which unfortunately something else ate before we could!

Growing your own produce is not rocket science, you can begin with a couple of pots, an old wine barrel or a small patch in an existing garden. The satisfaction, flavour and freshness of growing something yourself is unmatched and I think even my old mate Kevin would be impressed by my recent efforts.

top left: Toni Salter
bottom left: Rebekah Brauman

Vege Patch

Bed 4

on the bbq

barbeque; *an outdoor meal or party at which food is grilled over a charcoal fire.*

For me having a bbq is one of the easiest and most pleasurable ways to cook. It is a real treat in the warmer months of the year, making meal times a little more casual and enabling you to enjoy the outdoor lifestyle. These recipes are a little different to your classic steak and sausages! Utilising quality seasonal produce, herbs and spices, then cooking them on the bbq, adds an extra edge of flavour to your barbequed 'naked food'. But please people do remember, just because you are cooking on the bbq, does not give you license to serve up burnt offerings…it is after all a meal, not a sacrifice!

seasonal vegetable skewers

These skewers can be done on the bbq in Summer and Spring, or pan-fried or char grilled on the stove in Autumn and Winter. Choosing seasonal vegetables, feel free to mix up your vegetable combinations. Substitute tomatoes with peeled and steamed sweet potato pieces, capsicums with peeled and quartered red onions, basil leaves with sage leaves and basil pesto with drizzles of balsamic vinegar as an alternative in the cooler seasons.

serves 6

what you need

2 medium zucchinis

1 large red capsicum

1 punnet cherry tomatoes

200g button mushrooms

24 fresh basil leaves

¼ cup (60ml) extra virgin olive oil

**½ cup (125ml) basil pesto
(see basics page 15)**

V GF

what you do

1. Cut the zucchinis into thick slices, and cut the capsicum into pieces about 3cm square.

2. Thread the vegetables and basil leaves onto 12 skewers, alternating the reds and greens, finishing with a mushroom on top. Brush with extra virgin olive oil.

3. Preheat the bbq on medium heat. Place the skewers onto the bbq, and cook for a few minutes until they have coloured a little, turning frequently to avoid burning. Reduce the heat to low and cook for a further 5-10 minutes, until the vegetables are tender (depending on how crunchy you like your vegetables!).

4. Serve the skewers on a platter, drizzled with basil pesto.

Note: If using bamboo skewers, soak them in cold water for 15 minutes, to prevent them burning while cooking.

basil *(sometimes known as sweet basil) is a culinary herb, most commonly used fresh, and of course used to make basil pesto. When used in cooked dishes it is best added at the last minute to maximise the colour, flavour and fragrance. Basil is easy to grow yourself, although it is very sensitive to the cold, so plants will always produce and thrive better in the warmer seasons of the year.*

garlic prawn and haloumi skewers

A family favourite, these skewers were always a popular menu item on new years' day. When our children were small we found it too hard to party all night to see in the new year, so instead we celebrated with a bbq with good friends on new year's day!

serves 6
what you need

1kg green prawns
(medium king or banana)

2 garlic cloves, crushed

¼ cup (60ml) extra virgin olive oil

180g haloumi

12 cherry tomatoes

freshly ground black pepper and lemon wedges, to serve

V GF
what you do

1. Peel the prawns, leaving the tails on. Using a small sharp knife or scissors, cut down the back of the prawn from top to tail and remove waste tract. Combine the prawns, garlic and olive oil in a mixing bowl. Cover and refrigerate for about 30 minutes.

2. Soak 12 bamboo skewers in cold water for 15 minutes, to prevent them burning while cooking. Cut the haloumi into pieces about 3cm x 2cm x 1cm.

3. Thread 2 prawns and a piece of haloumi alternately onto each skewer, and finish with a cherry tomato.

4. Preheat the bbq on high heat. Place the skewers onto the bbq plate, making sure to space them well apart to avoid overcrowding and stewing the prawns (cook in two batches if necessary). Cook for 2-3 minutes each side, until golden brown and cooked through.

5. Transfer to a serving platter, season with pepper as desired and serve immediately with lemon wedges.

Note: For information on haloumi cheese see below.

haloumi *is a soft or semi-hard Cypriot cheese with a salty flavour, made from either sheep or goats' milk. It has a high melting point and so can easily be fried, grilled or barbequed. It is a good source of calcium and protein. It can be soaked in milk to remove some of the saltiness prior to use.*

spicy lamb cutlets with white bean mash

Lamb cutlets are the lamb fillet sliced still on the bone, which is why they are both so tender and pricey to buy. They don't need to be marinated for tenderness, however this spicy marinade makes for great flavour on the bbq and paired with the creamy mash they are always a winner.

serves 6

what you need

12 lamb cutlets

white bean and garlic mash
(see salads and sides page 99)

harissa marinade:

2 tsp harissa paste
(see basics page 24)

¼ cup fresh mint leaves,
finely shredded

½ cup (125ml) natural yoghurt
(european or greek style)

GF

what you do

1. To make the marinade, combine the harissa paste, mint and yoghurt.

2. Coat each cutlet in the marinade. Place into a shallow dish in two layers, cover and refrigerate for 30 minutes.

3. Preheat the bbq on medium heat. Cook the cutlets for 2 minutes each side, then reduce the heat to low and cook for a further 5 minutes.

4. Transfer the cutlets to a platter, cover loosely with foil and rest for 5 minutes, while you warm the white bean mash in a saucepan. Serve cutlets with the mash.

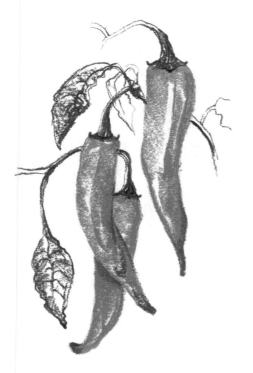

chillies *are the fruit from a plant which is in the same family as capsicums. Originating in the Americas, their use has spread into most of Asia, and have been incorporated into their local cuisines. Also known as chilli peppers, their most obvious characteristic is heat, though they do have subtle flavour differences ranging from sweet to fruity. They can be used fresh or dried. The membrane which holds the seeds contains the most heat, so removing the seeds and membrane will reduce the spiciness in most cases. Yellow and green chillies are the unripe fruit, which usually turn red when ripe. They all contain good amounts of vitamin C, which when served with beans or grains help the body with the absorption of iron.*

lentil and sweet potato patties

If you are not familiar with cooking with lentils, this is a great recipe to start with. You will enjoy the flavour and nutrition of these served as a patty with a salad or steamed vegetables, or on a bun as a family-friendly burger. If you don't want to bbq, you could cook them in a large frying pan on the stove.

makes 10
what you need

750g sweet potato, peeled and thickly sliced

2 tbsp olive oil

¾ cup (150g) red lentils

1 tbsp extra virgin olive oil

1 onion, finely diced

2 garlic cloves

1 tsp cumin

1 cup (250ml) vegetable stock (see basics page 21)

1 red chilli, deseeded and finely chopped (optional)

1 bunch coriander, stalks and leaves roughly chopped

6 green shallots, roughly sliced

2 eggs, lightly beaten

1 cup (200g) cooked brown rice

1 cup (200g) brown rice flour

pinch of sea salt

burger buns, hummus (see basics page 20), salad leaves, sliced tomato and grated carrot to serve

V GF
what you do

1. Preheat the oven to 180°C (160°C fan forced) and line an oven tray with baking paper. Brush the sweet potato with half of the olive oil, and arrange onto the tray. Roast for 20-30 minutes, until tender.

2. To prepare the lentils, place into a sieve and rinse under running water; drain. Heat the extra virgin olive oil in a small saucepan, and cook the onion, garlic and cumin over medium heat for 2-3 minutes, until soft. Add the lentils, stock and one cup (250ml) water. Bring to the boil, then reduce the heat and simmer uncovered for 15 minutes, stirring occasionally, until lentils are tender and the mixture is thick. Cool.

3. Combine the cooled lentil mixture with the chilli (if using), coriander, shallots, eggs, rice, rice flour and salt. Mix well. Take ½ cupfuls of the mixture and shape into 10 patties about 2cm thick.

4. Preheat the bbq flat plate over medium heat and drizzle with the remaining olive oil. Cook the patties for 5 minutes each side, until golden brown.

5. Serve on the burger buns with the hummus and salad leaves, tomato and grated carrot.

Storage: The patties can be frozen, cooked or uncooked.

lentils *are an edible pulse or seed, grown in a pod from a plant in the legume family. Lentils come in a range of sizes and colours, with or without skins, whole or split and therefore cooking times vary from 15 minutes up to an hour. The lentils with their husk intact remain whole during cooking (like puy lentils), while the lentils without husk tend to disintegrate into a thick puree (like red lentils). Most commonly used in soups, patties or as a side dish to accompany curries, lentils are highly nutritious, being a good source of protein, iron and dietary fibre.*

lime, coriander and coconut chicken skewers

A friend brought some chicken in a similar marinade to a bbq at our place over 10 years ago now. She shared the marinade recipe with me and I've been using it ever since!
You can also use this marinade for lamb or seafood, such as white fish, calamari and prawns. When using it for seafood it is best to marinate for no more than an hour.

serves 6
what you need

500g chicken thigh fillet

500g chicken breast fillet

lime, coriander and coconut marinade:

juice of 1 lime

2 garlic cloves, crushed

3cm piece fresh ginger, peeled and finely grated

½ bunch coriander, including stems and roots, roughly chopped (keep a handful of coriander leaves to serve)

400ml can coconut milk or cream

GF
what you do

1. To make the marinade, combine the lime juice, garlic, ginger, coriander and coconut milk in a bowl.

2. Trim the excess fat from chicken and cut into 3cm pieces. Thread onto skewers, alternating thigh and breast meat. Place the skewers into a shallow glass dish and coat with the marinade. Cover and refrigerate for at least 4 hours, or preferably overnight.

3. Preheat the bbq on high heat. Cook the skewers for one minute each side, until the chicken is golden brown all over.

4. Reduce the heat to medium and cook for a further 10 minutes, turning occasionally, to cook through. Serve on a platter, sprinkled with fresh coriander leaves.

Note: If using bamboo skewers, soak them in cold water for 15 minutes, to prevent them burning while cooking. You can use just thigh or just breast fillet if you prefer, but I find using a combination gives the best flavour, with the thigh pieces keeping the breast pieces moist and tender.

coriander *which is known as cilantro in other parts of the world, is a soft leafy green herb. It is also a spice, as it produces a globular shaped seed. All parts of the plant are edible - leaves, stalks, roots and seeds. The seeds are used as whole dried seeds or in ground form. Ground coriander seeds do lose flavour in storage, so it is best ground fresh just before using. Roasting or dry-frying seeds prior to grinding will give greater flavour and fragrance. Coriander, like many herbs and spices, is high in antioxidants.*

flathead fillets with tartare sauce

Over the years I have discovered and learnt a lot about fish from my husband,
who loves nothing more than to go for a fish and catch some! Flathead would have
to be one of the ugliest fish I have seen, but they make for succulent eating.
It is best not to overdo the flavours when cooking with fish. Keep it simple,
just bbq or grill with a squeeze of lemon and a lovely homemade tartare sauce.

serves 6

what you need

12 small or 6 large flathead fillets

1 tbsp olive oil

pinch of sea salt

freshly ground black pepper,
to taste

1 lemon, cut into 6 wedges

tartare sauce:

1 cup (250ml) mayonnaise
(see basics page 22)

3 gherkins, finely diced

1 tbsp capers, rinsed and
finely chopped

½ cup chopped flat-leaf parsley

1 tbsp lemon juice

V GF

what you do

1. To make the tartare sauce, combine the mayonnaise, gherkins, capers, parsley and lemon juice in a bowl. Refrigerate until required.

2. Brush the flathead fillets with olive oil and season to taste.

3. Preheat the bbq on high heat. Place the fillets onto the bbq plate, taking care to space them well apart to avoid overcrowding and stewing. Cook for 2 minutes on each side, or until cooked through.

4. Transfer the fillets to a plate to rest for 2-3 minutes. Serve hot with a dollop of tartare sauce and a lemon wedge.

gherkins *are a fruit which look like a miniature cucumber, and are in fact of the same species. Usually pickled in a vinegar or brine solution and stored in jars, they are also known as pickled cucumbers, dill cucumbers or dill pickles, due to the addition of the herb dill added in the pickling process.*

capers *are the edible flower bud, from the caper bush. They are picked young, then salted or pickled in a vinegar or brine solution and stored in jars. They are used as a seasoning in sauces or as a garnish. The more mature fruit of the caper bush are prepared the same way and sold as caper berries.*

salmon fillet with cucumber and herb salsa

Known as the super-easy super-food, salmon certainly is easy to cook and enjoy.
Cooked on the bbq or pan-fried, it is a delicious way to eat well.

serves 6
what you need

6 x 100g portions boneless salmon, skin on (see note)

1 tbsp extra virgin olive oil, plus extra to serve

1 lime, cut into 6 wedges

freshly ground black pepper, to taste

cucumber and herb salsa:

1 tsp honey

2 lebanese cucumbers, deseeded and finely diced

2 green shallots, finely diced

handful coriander leaves

handful mint leaves, roughly chopped if very large

1 tsp brown rice vinegar

1 tbsp lime juice

1 red chilli, deseeded and finely sliced (optional)

GF
what you do

1. For the salsa, dissolve the honey in ¼ cup (60ml) boiling water, then leave to cool. Combine with the remaining ingredients in a bowl, and mix well.

2. Preheat the bbq on high heat. Brush the salmon fillets with extra virgin olive oil, and place flesh side (presentation side) down onto the bbq plate; cook for 5 minutes. Turn over and cook for a further 5 minutes, reducing the heat to low for the last 3 minutes.

3. Transfer to a plate to rest for 5 minutes. Serve with the cucumber and herb salsa, with a drizzle of extra virgin olive oil and lime wedges on the side. Season with pepper as desired.

Note: Ask your fishmonger to pin bone the fillets for you.

salmon *is classified as an oily fish and considered to be very good for you, as it is high in protein, omega-3 fatty acids and vitamins. All Atlantic salmon caught in Australia is farmed, commonly from Tasmania. Wild caught salmon is usually imported frozen from places such as Alaska. There is concern that farmed salmon are becoming the battery hens of the sea, with talk of chemicals and antibiotics involved in the farming processes of the salmon, which may then be present in the fish we are eating. Just another case for being aware of where your food comes from, and how it is being produced.*

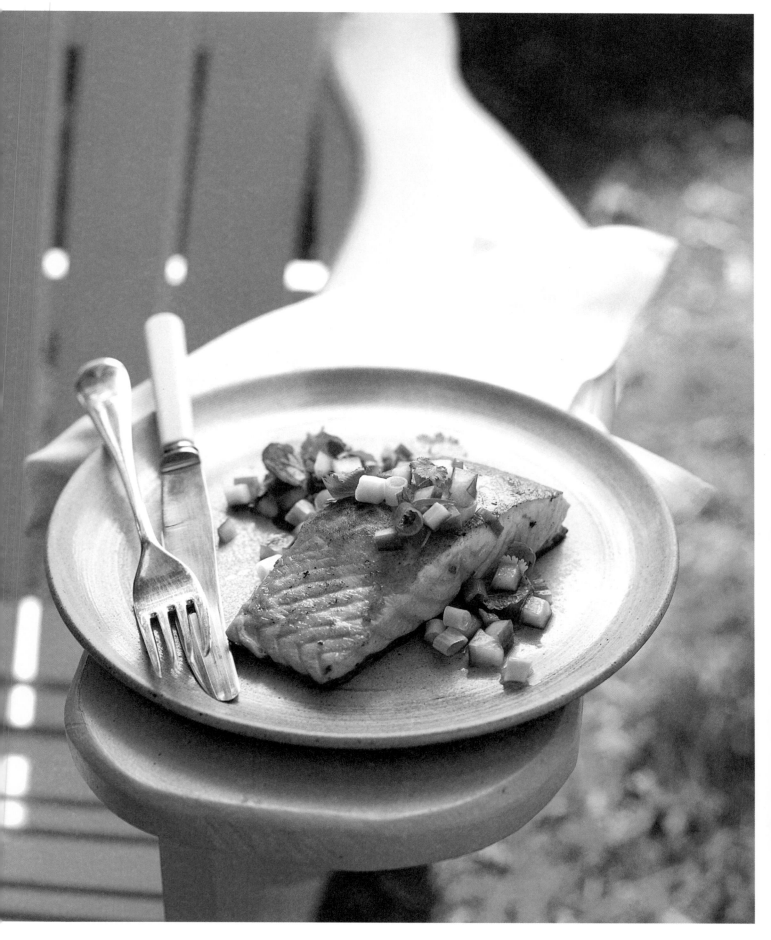

feature recipe...

Hungry Duck is a modern Asian restaurant in Berry, NSW. They use organic produce, most of which is sourced locally, and some is grown by restaurant owners David and Nicole Campbell.

Chef David Campbell has worked with many well known chefs, in various fine dining restaurants. He has taken the skills he acquired while working at Wokpool and Billy Kwong in Sydney, and at MJU with Tetsuya in London, and opened his own modern Asian restaurant in the heart of Berry on the south coast of NSW, just a 2 hour drive south of Sydney.

David, his wife Nicole and their two children relocated to Berry from Sydney in 2008 and are now living on fifteen hectares, farming Angus beef cattle and free range chickens for their eggs. Both the beef and eggs are served in the restaurant.

Hungry Duck features a landscaped kitchen garden which is a source of organic herbs and vegetables for the restaurant. We have visited Hungry Duck a few times on our south coast road trips and always really enjoy the experience. Chef David kindly shared with me the recipes for two of my favourite dishes.

Hungry Duck is fully licenced, no BYO on Friday and Saturday nights, and is open 6 days a week from 6pm. Closed Tuesdays.

hungry duck restaurant

85 Queen Street, Berry
NSW 2535

t: 61 2 4464 2323

www.hungryduck.com.au

chicken and lemongrass skewers with peanut and tamarind sauce

This recipe comes from Chef Dave Campbell from Hungry Duck Restaurant, Berry NSW.
We enjoyed this dish on our first visit to Hungry Duck a couple of years ago,
so I asked Dave to share the recipe with me, so I could share it with you.

serves 6

what you need

sauce:

1-2 red chillies (for milder sauce use 1 chilli and remove seeds)

2 garlic cloves

4 eschallots

½ lemongrass stalk, trimmed and finely chopped

2cm piece ginger or galangal, finely chopped

roots from 1 bunch coriander

½ tsp ground cumin

½ tsp shrimp paste

100ml vegetable oil

270ml can coconut milk

¼ cup (55g) caster sugar

2 tbsp fish sauce

100g unsweetened tamarind puree

125g peanuts, coarsely chopped

skewers:

1kg chicken mince

100ml yuzu juice

finely grated zest of 1 lemon

½ cup (20g) fresh breadcrumbs

6 lemongrass stalks, each cut into two to create 12 skewers

what you do

1. To make the sauce, combine the chillies, garlic, eschallots, lemongrass, galangal, coriander roots, cumin and shrimp paste in a food processor with 50ml of the oil. Blend to a smooth paste.

2. Remove the solid cream from the coconut milk, leaving the milk aside. Place the cream into a saucepan with the remaining oil, and bring to a simmer over medium heat. Cook for one minute, until the cream and oil split. Add the prepared paste, and fry for 2 minutes, until it smells toasty.

3. Stir in the sugar and cook for 2 minutes, until caramelised. Add the fish sauce and taste to check the balance of sweet and salty. Stir in the tamarind puree and the reserved coconut milk. Bring to a simmer and cook for 5 minutes. Stir in the chopped peanuts.

4. For the skewers, combine the chicken mince, yuzu juice, zest and crumbs thoroughly, then divide into twelve equal portions (about 100g each). Use wet hands to roll each portion into a sausage shape, and mould onto the lemongrass 'skewers'.

5. Preheat the bbq on medium-high heat. Brush the mince with a little oil to prevent sticking. Cook for 5 minutes, turning often, until golden brown and cooked through. Serve two skewers per person with the sauce.

Note: Yuzu is a type of citrus fruit. The zest and juice are used in Japanese cooking. 100% Yuzu juice (no msg) is available in bottles from Asian food shops, but you can substitute lemon juice and a pinch of salt, if you like.

GF option: Substitute rice crumbs for breadcrumbs. For information on rice crumbs see page 151.

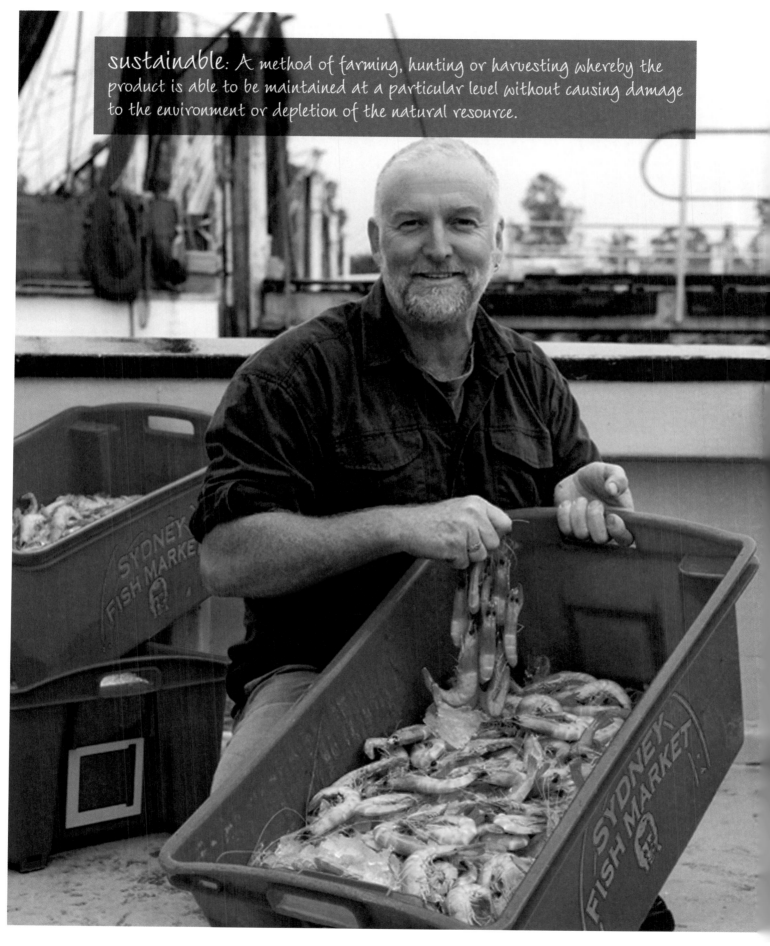

sustainable: A method of farming, hunting or harvesting whereby the product is able to be maintained at a particular level without causing damage to the environment or depletion of the natural resource.

meet the people...

Freshly caught seafood is such an enjoyable experience to cook and eat. Whenever we take a road trip along the coastline in Australia, we often seek out the local fish co-op to buy fresh seafood. Back home in Sydney we have the luxury of a large fish market, the Sydney Fish Market at Pyrmont, which is a 30 minute (early morning!) drive from our home on Sydney's Northern Beaches, to access the greatest variety of fresh seafood, at the best prices.

Sydney Fish Market is the largest market of its kind in the Southern Hemisphere. It is also the world's second largest seafood market, in terms of variety, outside of Japan.

As dawn approaches and the rest of Sydney sleeps, the hard working fishing fleets return to their moorings to unload their catch. Over one hundred species of freshly harvested seafood from all over Australia and New Zealand are sold on the state-of-the-art auction floor at the Sydney Fish Market each weekday. Sydney Fish Market sources product both nationally and internationally, and trades over 14,500 tonnes of seafood annually.

As a leader in the Australian seafood industry, Sydney Fish Market Pty Ltd actively pursues and promotes strict environmentally sustainable practices at all levels of its business. On an operational level, it promotes the availability of, and trade in, quality seafood that comes from ecologically sustainable wild fisheries and environmental best practice aquaculture.

Sydney Fish Market employs approximately 57 staff to run the weekday wholesale auction, to promote Sydney Fish Market as the centre of seafood excellence, to operate daily behind-the-scenes tours, and to run the popular Sydney Seafood School.

It is a wonderful experience for the whole family to visit the Sydney Fish Market, take an early morning 'behind the scenes' tour, purchase fresh seafood to take home and to have a seafood lunch by the water at Blackwattle Bay.

sydney fish market

Bank Street
Pyrmont
NSW 2009

t: 61 2 9004 1100

www.sydneyfishmarket.com.au

my story... 'eggciting' - raising chickens in suburbia

With the vegetable garden beginning to produce, we decided we would add to our little suburban farm and get some chickens, which would soon grow into hens and daily lay the freshest of eggs. My mother had spent her childhood growing up in the country and had told me stories of the colour and taste of farm fresh eggs.

Meeting Daniel from *New Leaf Nursery*, Ingleside, our local nursery just up the hill from our home, helped solve all our questions and requirements for obtaining and keeping chickens. We found ourselves a lovely recycled timber coop and a laying box for sale at the nursery and after building a chicken wire enclosure around it to keep our dog out, we picked up our nine week old chickens from Daniel and bought them home to our backyard.

We have seven chickens in all, five Isa Browns and two black Australorps, which we were told were the best two breeds for laying. Since that day it seems nothing is wasted at our place, with a family of five, a dog, seven chickens and two compost bins, a lot of feeding and recycling goes on and on!

The chickens settled in well and we gave them all names. After three months of caring for our chickens, patiently waiting and watching them grow, they grew to double their size. The funny thing was, the names didn't really stick, as we couldn't tell them apart once they had grown (except the black ones from the brown of course!). At about twenty weeks of age they all began to lay eggs, which was very 'eggciting' for us and they haven't stopped laying since!

Raising chickens and keeping hens in suburbia has been very enjoyable and entertaining. They are fascinating animals to watch, extreme excavators, always busy scratching around, bathing in the dust and clucking. Occasionally they escape from their enclosure, usually with the help of our dog, who digs under the wire to get their scraps. They exit to greener pastures, often leaving the dog stuck in their enclosure unable to get back out!

So now we enjoy fresh eggs at our place daily, and they are as good as my mum had told me they would be. Still warm from the coop, with a brilliant yellow yolk, eggs don't come any fresher and they do taste better.

bottom left: Daniel Yakich

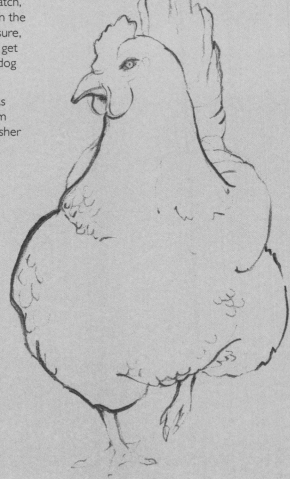

123

fast food

fast food; *cooked food sold in snack bars and restaurants as a quick meal.*

The reality is, that by the time you order it in or go out to pick up fast food or take away food, you could have cooked some real food fast yourself! These recipes have been created to allow you to cook real food in real time. Food that is healthy, nutritious and delicious, creating meals in no more than sixty minutes. The idea is once you have organised and shopped for your ingredients, you can be home at 6pm and have dinner on the table by 7pm!

prawn and mango with grilled haloumi salad

My husband Paul grew up eating fresh caught and cooked school prawns.
Although they are laborious to peel, he has now convinced me that they
are the sweetest and tastiest prawns you can eat.
This salad was inspired by a kilo of 'as fresh as you'll find' school prawns,
that we were fortunate enough to purchase from a local fisherman just cooking
his morning's catch on the shores of Lake Macquarie last summer!

serves 6

what you need

200g haloumi cheese, sliced thinly

120g mixed salad greens

½ cup fresh coriander leaves

2 lebanese cucumbers,
cut into 3cm dice

2 mangoes, peeled and flesh
thinly sliced

1 avocado, peeled and cut
into 3cm dice

1 small red chilli, deseeded and
finely sliced (optional)

juice of 1 lime

1 tbsp extra virgin olive oil

1kg cooked school prawns,
peeled and chilled

juice of ½ lemon, to serve

GF

what you do

1. Cook the slices of haloumi cheese in a dry frying pan, over medium heat, for one minute on each side until golden brown. Set aside to cool.

2. Combine all the ingredients, except the prawns, in a large bowl and toss to dress.

3. Arrange the salad on a platter. Sprinkle the prawns over, then the haloumi slices. Finish by squeezing the lemon juice over the prawns and haloumi.

Note: This salad is best eaten immediately, as the lemon, lime and prawn juices will cause the salad leaves to wilt and soften.

V option: Substitute toasted whole almonds for the prawns.

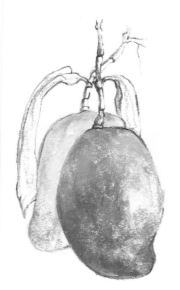

mangoes come from a tropical fruiting tree, which produce a fleshy stone fruit, oval in shape, yellowy orange in colour and sweet to taste. Mangoes which are native to India, are now grown all round the world and make up approximately half of all tropical fruits produced worldwide. Rich in antioxidants, vitamins and nutrients, they are best eaten raw as a fruit or included in a salad. Very ripe mangoes are perfect for making a sauce or chutney.

sweet pumpkin and ginger soup

A sweet, fragrant soup, vibrant in colour and taste.
Plain old pumpkin never tasted this good!

serves 6

what you need

1 tbsp olive oil

1 onion, diced

2cm piece ginger, finely chopped

6 saffron threads

1 tsp freshly ground nutmeg
(plus extra to serve)

1.5kg pumpkin, peeled, seeded
and diced (1kg flesh)

300g sweet potato,
peeled and diced

6 cups (1.5 litres) vegetable stock
(see basics page 21)

sea salt, to taste

½ cup (125ml) natural yoghurt
(european or greek style) and
handful coriander leaves,
to serve

V GF

what you do

1. Heat the oil in a large pot over medium heat. Add the onion, ginger, saffron, nutmeg, pumpkin and sweet potato, and sauté without colouring for 2-3 minutes.

2. Add the stock and bring to the boil. Cook, covered, for 15 minutes. Remove the lid, reduce the heat slightly and simmer uncovered for a further 15 minutes, or until the vegetables are tender.

3. Use a hand blender to blend the soup in the pot to a chunky consistency (or smooth if you prefer). Alternatively, cool slightly and puree in batches in a food processor. Season with sea salt. Serve with a dollop of natural yoghurt, a sprinkle of freshly ground nutmeg and fresh coriander leaves.

pumpkin is a humble backyard vegetable that is rich in vital antioxidants, vitamin A, vitamin C and vitamin E. It is low in kilojoules, containing no saturated fats or cholesterol, and is a good source of dietary fibre.
The flesh is a golden-yellow to orange colour, with a sweet flavour and creamy texture. Pumpkin seeds are also a great source of protein, minerals, vitamins and omega-3 fatty acids. Pumpkin can be cooked in a variety of ways, either baked, added to soups, curries and stews or steamed, allowing maximum retention of nutrients.

asian style coconut and chicken noodle soup

This fragrant and spicy soup is simple to prepare and quick to cook.
It will warm you inside and out.

serves 6

what you need

2 x 400ml cans coconut milk

¼ cup green curry paste
(see basics page 24)

500g chicken thigh fillets,
finely sliced

270g packet dried noodles
(any asian variety)

1 tbsp fish sauce

juice of 1 lime

3cm piece ginger, finely sliced

1 red chilli, deseeded
and finely sliced

3 green shallots, finely sliced

225g can bamboo shoots, drained

½ bunch coriander
(roots, stalks and leaves),
washed and finely chopped

handful each of coriander leaves
and vietnamese mint leaves, to
serve

what you do

1. Combine the coconut milk, curry paste and 100ml water in a large saucepan. Bring to the boil, then reduce the heat and simmer, uncovered, for 5 minutes. Add the chicken, simmer for a further 5 minutes.

2. Meanwhile, cook noodles in a separate pan of boiling water for 5-10 minutes, depending on variety and thickness. Once noodles are cooked, drain and refresh under cold running water to prevent them from over-cooking.

3. Add all remaining ingredients (except the herb leaves) to the soup, and simmer for a further 5 minutes. Add the noodles, cook for a further 2 minutes to heat through. Serve topped with fresh herb leaves.

V option: Substitute diced and steamed vegetables (such as pumpkin or sweet potato) for the chicken.

GF option: Use rice noodles rather than wheat.

coconut milk *is widely used in Southeast Asia and other tropical countries. It is often the staple fat source in these cuisines, where the rest of the diet is mainly fish, a little meat, and fresh fruit and vegetables. From a nutritional perspective, it's an excellent choice. It's high in saturated fatty acids and medium-chain triglycerides (MCT), which are both easily burned as fuel by the body. Canned coconut milk is readily available at the supermarket. Once opened it must be refrigerated and used within a few days or it will sour.*

chicken san choy bau

Fresh, light and fragrant, this is a leaner and
less oily version of the traditional Asian dish.

serves 6

what you need

2 tbsp sesame oil

1 onion, finely diced

500g chicken mince

2 garlic cloves, crushed

3cm piece ginger, peeled and
finely grated

2 tbsp tamari or soy sauce

230g can water chestnuts,
drained, finely diced

1 red capsicum, finely diced

5 green shallots, finely chopped

330ml bottle ginger beer

6 medium iceberg lettuce leaves,
chilled

1 green shallot, finely shredded,
to serve

what you do

1. Heat a large frying pan or wok over high heat. Add the sesame oil,
onion and chicken mince, and stir-fry for 5-7 minutes, until the onion is
soft and chicken mince changes colour. Break up any lumps of mince
with a wooden spoon as it cooks.

2. Add the garlic, ginger, tamari and water chestnuts; mix well. Stir in the
capsicum, shallots and ginger beer. Cook for a further 5-10 minutes,
stirring occasionally, until the liquid reduces and thickens.

3. Cool slightly, and serve spooned into the iceberg lettuce leaves,
topped with finely shredded shallot.

Note: For information on tamari see below.

GF option: Use wheat-free tamari or wheat-free soy sauce.

water chestnuts *are not actually a nut at all, but an aquatic vegetable that
grows in marshes. The name 'water chestnut' comes from the fact that it
resembles a chestnut in shape and colouring. Indigenous to Southeast Asia, it
has been cultivated in China since ancient times. Unless you live in an area
where they are farmed locally, it will be difficult to obtain them fresh, however
canned water chestnuts are readily available in supermarkets. They add a
delicious crunch to dishes and are a good source of potassium and fibre.
They are low in sodium, and fat is virtually non-existent.*

tamari *is a Japanese-style soy sauce, available from most supermarkets. It
is lower in wheat content than regular soy sauce, and is also available in a
wheat-free version.*

lamb, pine nut and mint burgers

Who doesn't love a burger?
This is a very tasty combination that can be easily pan-fried or done on the bbq.
Searing first then finishing in the oven ensures a juicy result.
Serve these on toasted Turkish bread instead of rolls, if you like.

serves 6

what you need

½ cup (80g) pine nuts

600g lamb mince

1 red onion, finely diced

2 eggs, lightly beaten

½ cup (20g) rice crumbs
or wholemeal breadcrumbs

1 cup mint leaves, roughly
chopped

½ cup flat-leaf parsley leaves,
roughly chopped

1 tsp ground cumin

1 tsp sweet paprika

pinch of sea salt

freshly ground black pepper,
to taste

1 tbsp olive oil

toasted wholemeal burger rolls,
salad leaves, sliced beetroot,
avocado, and tomato chutney
(see basics page 29), to serve

what you do

1. Preheat the oven to 160°C (140°C fan forced) and line a baking tray with non-stick baking paper.

2. Heat a small frying pan over low heat. Add the pine nuts and dry-fry for 1-2 minutes, until golden brown. Place the pine nuts into a large bowl with the mince, onion, eggs, crumbs, mint, parsley and spices. Season to taste. Mix well until thoroughly combined.

3. Divide mixture evenly into 6 portions. Using wet hands, roll mixture into balls, and then flatten to form large, round patties about 2-3cm thick.

4. Heat the oil in a large frying pan over high heat. Cook the burgers in 2 batches, for 2-3 minutes each side until browned. Transfer all the burgers to the prepared tray and finish cooking in the oven for about 10 minutes (time in oven depends on thickness of burger, and how well done you like your meat).

5. Serve on the rolls with the salad leaves, beetroot, avocado and tomato chutney.

Note: For information on rice crumbs see page 151.

GF option: Use rice crumbs in patties and gluten-free bread rolls.

pine nuts *are the edible seeds from trees. About 20 species of pine produce seeds large enough to be worth harvesting; in other pines the seeds are also edible, but are too small to be of great value as a human food. The time it takes for a pine tree to grow and the difficulty in harvesting leads to a limited supply and reflects the usual high price. Pine nuts contain thiamine (vitamin B1) and protein.*

chicken and sweet corn soup with white beans

Everybody can make this easy to prepare, nutritious soup, in any season.
This is a simple meal to share with family and friends. It is something I like to cook and drop
in for a friend who has been unwell or has just had a new baby and needs a bit of tender
loving care. High in both fibre and protein, it is a sustaining meal in a bowl!

serves 6
what you need

500g chicken thigh fillets

4 corn cobs

**2 cups (500ml) chicken stock
(see basics page 21)**

1 large onion, diced

2 garlic cloves, crushed

**400g can cannellini beans,
rinsed and drained**

2 celery stalks, finely sliced

pinch of sea salt

**freshly ground black pepper,
to taste**

2 green shallots, finely sliced

GF
what you do

1. Place the chicken into a large pot and add one litre of water.
Cover and bring to the boil. Remove the lid, reduce the heat and simmer
for 15 minutes. Transfer the chicken to a plate, and cover to avoid drying out.
Reserve the cooking liquid in pot.

2. Meanwhile, using a small sharp knife, cut the kernels from the corn cobs.
Place half of them into a food processor and puree to a creamy paste.
Reserve the remaining whole corn kernels.

3. Add the chicken stock, onion and garlic to the reserved cooking liquid
remaining in pot. Return to a simmer and cook for 15 minutes, to reduce
slightly and intensify the flavour.

4. Add the creamed corn, reserved whole corn kernels, cannellini beans,
and celery. Simmer a further 10 minutes.

5. Finely chop the chicken meat and add to the soup. Cook for a final 5 minutes
to heat the chicken through. Season to taste, and serve sprinkled with green
shallots.

Note: You can use one cup (200g) dried cannellini beans, soaked overnight then
boiled for 30 minutes, in place of the canned beans, if you like.

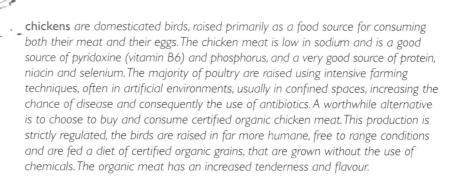

chickens *are domesticated birds, raised primarily as a food source for consuming
both their meat and their eggs. The chicken meat is low in sodium and is a good
source of pyridoxine (vitamin B6) and phosphorus, and a very good source of protein,
niacin and selenium. The majority of poultry are raised using intensive farming
techniques, often in artificial environments, usually in confined spaces, increasing the
chance of disease and consequently the use of antibiotics. A worthwhile alternative
is to choose to buy and consume certified organic chicken meat. This production is
strictly regulated, the birds are raised in far more humane, free to range conditions
and are fed a diet of certified organic grains, that are grown without the use of
chemicals. The organic meat has an increased tenderness and flavour.*

prawn caesar salad

This is a fresh alternative to traditional caesar salad,
high in protein and raw goodness.
It's great for a summer meal or as a Christmas day treat.

serves 6

what you need

6 thin bacon rashers,
rind removed

4 slices wholemeal sourdough
bread, torn into 2-3cm pieces

2 cos lettuce, washed, dried
and roughly chopped

2 lebanese cucumbers,
roughly chopped

250g cherry tomatoes, halved

1 cup (250ml) caesar salad
dressing (see basics page 28)

1kg cooked king prawns,
peeled and deveined

shaved parmesan, to serve

what you do

1. Preheat the oven to 180°C (160°C fan forced). Cut the bacon into 3cm pieces, and spread onto an oven tray. Arrange the bread pieces onto another oven tray. Cook the bacon and bread pieces for about 15-20 minutes, until golden brown. Transfer the bacon to a plate lined with paper towel, to drain and cool. Cool the bread croutons.

2. In a large bowl, combine the lettuce, cucumber, tomatoes and caesar salad dressing, tossing to coat evenly.

3. Arrange the dressed salad onto a platter. Top with the bacon, croutons and prawns, then scatter shaved parmesan over the top.

V option: Substitute grilled haloumi slices and toasted pinenuts for the bacon and prawns.

GF option: Use gluten-free bread.

prawns *and shellfish are worth including in your diet because like fish, they are rich in omega-3 fatty acids, which are thought to promote a healthy heart. They are also a rich source of protein. Although it's true that prawns and shellfish contain some cholesterol, they are also very low in saturated fats - unless of course you are eating them battered, crumbed or fried!*

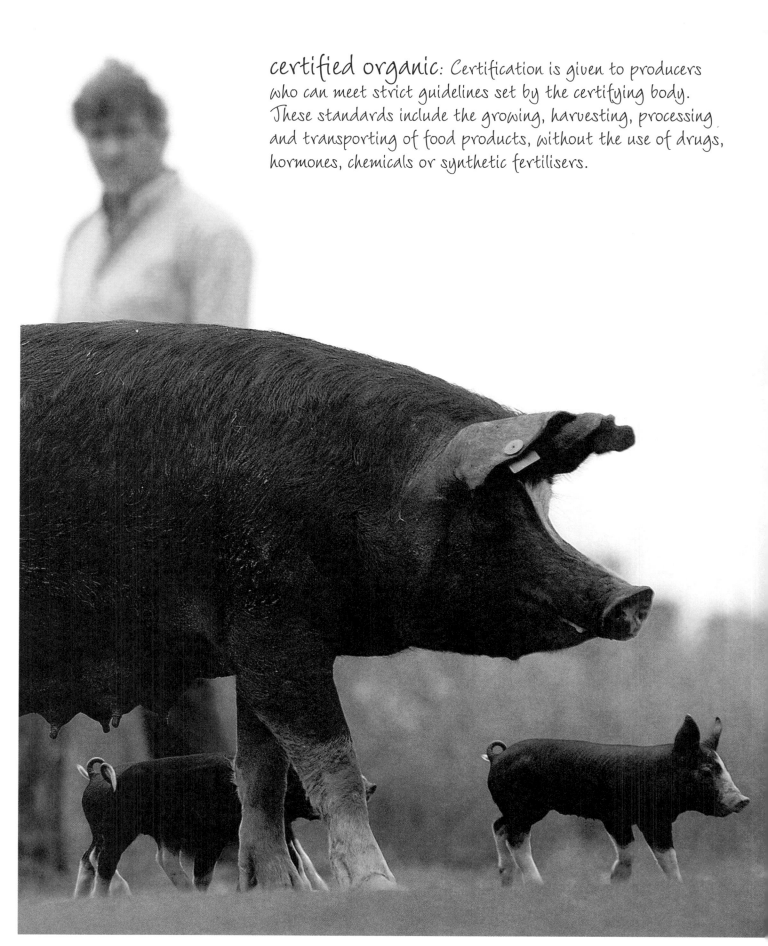

certified organic: Certification is given to producers who can meet strict guidelines set by the certifying body. These standards include the growing, harvesting, processing and transporting of food products, without the use of drugs, hormones, chemicals or synthetic fertilisers.

meet the people...

I first met pig farmer Jack Nielson at an organic farmers' market in 2009, selling his Pasture Perfect Pork direct from his pig farm. He has wonderfully succulent pork, nitrate-free bacon and ham, and at the time had some delicious handmade pork sausages.

Pasture Perfect Pork is the largest certified organic pork producer in Australia, and the only certified pork producer growing Berkshire pigs (which are also sometimes known by the Japanese name of Kurobuta). The pigs live on 200 hectares of lush green pastures in the New England region of northern NSW.

The pigs are 100% free-range, 100% Australian pasture-raised, 100% certified organic and 100% chemical free. No chemicals are used on the animals or the land, and no antibiotics are used on any animal sold as organic. The animals are fed a balanced mix of organic grains that contain no genetically modified ingredients.

The pigs are free to run, graze, play, dig and show all of the characteristics true to their nature. They are always outdoors, with shelter available. All of the infrastructure that they have built for the pigs is mobile, so that they can better manage the land and the animals.

Jack's mission statement: 'We aim to provide excellent quality meat at the same time as improving the quality of life for animals. With a holistic approach to the management of our herd and land, we intend to improve the soils and pasture, thus improving the quality of feed available to the animals, and of the food available to you.'

Pasture Perfect Pork products contain no chemical nitrates or preservative E220. For cured meat products to gain organic certification they have to be processed without the use of nitrates or other chemical preservatives. The team have spent 6 years researching to find a curing method that meets the certified organic standards, but still has the same appeal in taste and colour that the consumer is accustomed to. Pasture Perfect Pork products are available direct from the farm via online ordering, or selected organic food stores.

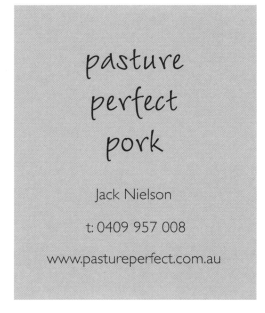

pasture perfect pork

Jack Nielson

t: 0409 957 008

www.pastureperfect.com.au

spaghetti with meatballs

I have given you two great choices of tasty meatballs. Choose either a lovely combination of sweet pork, fresh basil and the heat of the chilli, or the Mediterranean flavours of succulent lamb, fresh basil and feta - both served with a high fibre wholemeal pasta.
Give the wholemeal pasta a go, you'll enjoy the difference.

serves 6

what you need

500g pork (or lamb) mince

1 onion, finely diced

1 garlic clove, crushed

1 red chilli, deseeded and finely chopped (if making pork meatballs)

100g feta (if making lamb meatballs)

½ cup basil leaves, finely chopped

2 eggs, lightly beaten

pinch of sea salt

2 tbsp olive oil

500g wholemeal spaghetti

3 cups (750ml) tomato sauce (see basics page 15)

freshly ground black pepper and parmesan, grated, to serve

what you do

1. To make the meatballs, combine the mince, onion, garlic, chilli or feta (depending on which meatballs you are making), basil, eggs and salt in a large bowl. Use your hands to mix thoroughly. Shape heaped teaspoons of mixture into small round meatballs (you should get about 30).

2. Heat half the olive oil in a large frying pan over high heat. Fry the meatballs in 2 batches for 5 minutes each, shaking the pan occasionally to turn them, until golden brown and cooked through. Transfer to a tray or plate and set aside.

3. Meanwhile, cook the pasta in a large saucepan of boiling water for 8-10 minutes or until 'al dente'(see note). Heat the tomato sauce in a saucepan or frying pan, over medium heat. Add the meatballs to the sauce. Drain the pasta.

4. Serve the hot pasta topped with the sauce and meatballs. Season with pepper as desired and sprinkle with parmesan to taste.

Note: For information on 'al dente' see page 150. If you don't have any homemade tomato sauce on hand, you can use a good quality purchased tomato pasta sauce.

V option: Substitute spinach leaves and crumbled feta for the meatballs.
GF option: Use gluten-free pasta

pork is sweet and succulent meat, very high in thiamine (vitamin B1). Pork with its fat trimmed is leaner than the meat of most domesticated animals, but is still high in cholesterol and saturated fat. Choose to cook with certified organic pork that has been raised in free to range, humane conditions, enjoying organic feed and pastures. These pigs get their vitamins and minerals from the plants and soil they eat as nature intended. The risk of disease to a well cared for outdoor herd is minimal, avoiding the problems created by raising animals in unnatural conditions. Drugs only become a necessity in a confined, artificial environment.

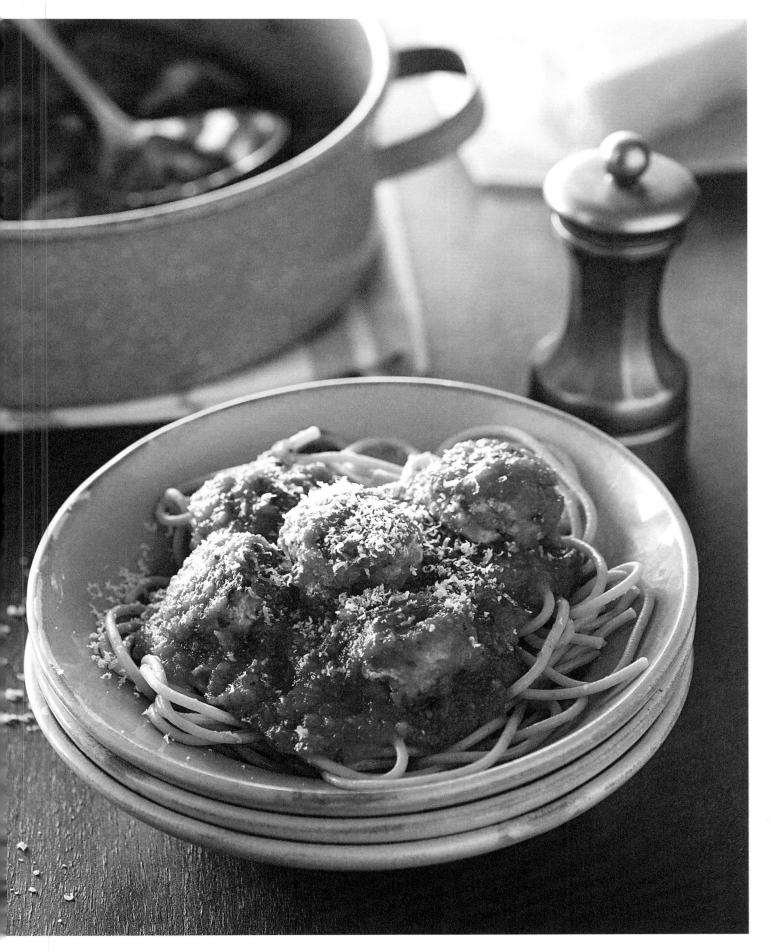

herbed crumbed pork cutlet with caramelised apple

Pork and apple just go together so nicely and the herbed crumbs add great flavour and texture to the dish. This crumbing mixture is also perfect for using to crumb chicken breast or fish fillets.

serves 6

what you need

4 slices wholemeal bread, torn

½ cup basil leaves

½ cup flat-leaf parsley leaves

1 lemon, zest finely grated, juiced

pinch of sea salt

freshly ground black pepper, to taste

100g feta, crumbled

4 apples, peeled, cored and each cut into 6 wedges

1 tbsp extra virgin olive oil

1 tbsp butter

1 tbsp rapadura sugar

2 eggs

½ cup (125ml) milk

6 pork cutlets (1-2cm thick), trimmed of excess fat and skin

olive oil to cook cutlets

lemon wedges, to serve

what you do

1. Preheat the oven to 160°C (140°C fan forced). Place the bread, herbs, lemon zest, salt and pepper into a food processor. Process until the mixture forms coarse crumbs. Mix the feta through the breadcrumbs.

2. Combine the apples, lemon juice, oil, butter and sugar in a small saucepan. Cook uncovered over high heat for 5 minutes, stirring occasionally, until sugar is dissolved and apples are golden brown. Reduce the heat to low, cover and cook a further 10 minutes.

3. Spread the breadcrumb mixture onto a flat tray. Whisk the egg and milk in a large bowl until combined. Dip the pork cutlets in the egg mixture, then press them into the breadcrumbs to coat .

4. Heat a large frying pan over high heat, and cover the base of pan with a thin layer of oil. Cook the cutlets in 2 batches, for 2 minutes each side, until golden brown. Transfer the cutlets to a baking tray lined with non-stick baking paper and finish cooking in the oven for about 15 minutes (time in oven depends on the thickness of the meat). Serve cutlets with warm apples and a wedge of lemon.

Note: For information on rapadura sugar see page 18.

GF option: Use a gluten-free bread for bread crumbs.

apples are delicious and in season are a crunchy and juicy fruit. They contain a long list of essential nutrients, are low in kilojoules and high in dietary fibre. Apples contain good quantities of vitamin C and beta-carotene, and are a good source of B-complex vitamins such as riboflavin (vitamin B2), thiamine (vitamin B1), and pyridoxine (vitamin B 6). Is it any wonder they say "an apple a day keeps the Doctor away?"

beef and bean nachos with guacamole

A healthier take on your traditional nachos, it's great for a casual nibble or as an easy, nutritious family favourite - everybody loves this nachos!

serves 6

what you need

1 tsp cumin seeds

1 tsp coriander seeds

½ tsp cloves

1 tbsp olive oil

1 onion, finely diced

1 garlic clove, crushed

2 large green chillies, deseeded and finely sliced

1 tsp paprika

500g beef mince

2 tbsp tomato paste

400g can diced tomatoes

400g can red kidney beans, drained

½ cup flat-leaf parsley leaves, finely chopped

to serve

230g bag corn chips

2 cups guacamole
(see basics page 13)

1 cup (250ml) mild tomato salsa
(see basics page 13)

½ cup (125ml) natural yoghurt
(european or greek style)

2 green shallots, finely sliced, to serve

what you do

1. Place the cumin seeds, coriander seeds and cloves into a dry frying pan. Cook over medium heat for 2-3 minutes, tossing frequently, until toasted and fragrant. Cool slightly, then grind the spices using a mortar and pestle or spice grinder.

2. Heat the oil in a large deep frying pan over medium heat. Add the onion, garlic and chilli, and cook for 2-3 minutes, stirring constantly.
Add the ground spices and paprika to pan, cook for a further 2 minutes. Add the beef mince, increase the heat to high and cook until browned, breaking up any lumps with a wooden spoon as it cooks.

3. Add the tomato paste and cook a further 2 minutes, stirring constantly. Add the tomatoes, kidney beans, parsley and one cup (250ml) water. Reduce the heat to low, and simmer uncovered for 30 minutes, stirring occasionally.

4. To assemble the nachos, arrange a bed of corn chips onto individual serving plates or a large platter. Layer the beef and bean mixture over the corn chips, then top with the guacamole, salsa, yoghurt and shallots. Serve straight away.

Note: If you want more kick in the beef mixture leave the chilli seeds in, or for extra heat, use 2 small red chillies with seeds. You can use one cup (200g) dried kidney beans, soaked overnight then boiled for 30 minutes, in place of the canned beans, if you like. The beef mixture can be made up to 2 days in advance and stored in the fridge in an airtight container.

V option: Omit the beef and double the kidney beans.
Add kernels from 3 raw corn cobs for the last 10 minutes of cooking.

GF option: Use gluten-free corn chips.

kidney beans with their shape and dark red skin, are named for their visual resemblance to a kidney. Dried beans, have the highest protein content of all plant-based foodstuffs, offering many benefits, including the absence of fat, which helps prevent heart disease and obesity. Extremely rich in fibre, like all of its cousins in the bean family, kidney beans also have a high level of iron, magnesium, phosphorus and folic acid (vitamin B9). High in potassium and low in sodium, kidney beans have natural diuretic properties. Raw or dried kidney beans contain a toxin which is destroyed by boiling for at least ten minutes, therefore the beans must be boiled prior to slow cooking to avoid poisoning.

basil pesto pasta with chicken

A simple combination of flavours, dominated by beautiful fresh basil.
This is delicious served hot, or cold as a pasta salad.

serves 6

what you need

1 chicken breast fillet
(about 250g)

500g wholemeal penne or
spiral pasta

1 cup (250ml) basil pesto
(see basics page 15)

1 cup (150g) semi-dried tomatoes
(or 250g halved cherry tomatoes)

50g parmesan, shaved

½ cup basil leaves, torn

freshly ground black pepper,
to serve

what you do

1. Bring a saucepan of water to a gentle simmer. Add the chicken breast, cover the pan and simmer over low heat for 15 minutes. Remove from the water and set aside to drain on a plate. Cool slightly, then cut into thin slices.

2. Meanwhile, cook the pasta in a large saucepan of boiling water according to packet directions, or until 'al dente' (see below). Drain into a colander, and rinse with hot water to remove excess starch, drain well.

3. In a large bowl combine the pasta with the pesto, chicken and tomatoes. Serve sprinkled generously with parmesan shavings and fresh basil leaves. Season with pepper as desired.

V option: Substitute roast sweet potato chunks for the chicken.

GF option: Use gluten-free pasta.

'al dente' *is an Italian expression used to describe the desired texture of cooked pasta. It loosely translates as 'to the tooth', meaning the pasta is cooked through but still has a slight resistance to the bite - not too soft. Pasta that is cooked 'al dente' has a lower glycemic index than pasta that is cooked until very soft.*

spiced red lentil and vegetable soup

Using lentils makes for the most delicious soups and they're budget friendly too. This is a great soup for people who are in need of healing - the ginger and spices give it real warmth. For me it is essential to serve it with a dollop of natural yoghurt.

serves 6

what you need

2 tbsp olive oil

1 large onion, finely chopped

2 carrots, diced

2 celery stalks, diced

1 tbsp ginger, grated

2 red chillies, deseeded and finely chopped

1 tsp ground turmeric

pinch ground allspice

1 tsp ground sweet paprika

1½ cups (285g) red lentils, rinsed

1 litre vegetable stock (see basics page 21)

400g can diced tomatoes

pinch of sea salt

natural yoghurt (european or greek style) and coriander leaves, to serve

V GF

what you do

1. Heat the oil in a large saucepan over medium heat. Add the onion, carrot, celery, ginger, chilli, turmeric, allspice, sweet paprika and lentils. Sauté for 2 minutes, stirring constantly.

2. Add the stock, 2 cups (500 ml) water and the tomatoes. Cover and bring to boil, then uncover and cook for 10 minutes, stirring occasionally.

3. Reduce the heat and simmer for a further 20 minutes. Season with sea salt to taste.

4. Serve with a dollop of natural yoghurt and a sprinkling of coriander leaves.

ginger is a spice consumed either fresh, or dried and ground. It is spicy-hot in flavour and can only be consumed in small quantities. Fresh ginger is one of the main spices used when making pulse and lentil curries and other vegetable dishes. Also known for its medicinal properties, ginger is most commonly known for its effectiveness as a digestive aid, and is used widely to make a lovely warming ginger tea, said to be a natural remedy for the common cold. Fresh ginger is also used to break down high protein foods such as meats and beans and helps to lessen the effects of uric acid in the body from these foods.

pumpkin and basil gnocchi with tomato and feta

Making your own gnocchi is not as hard as you may think! This is a nutritious and budget friendly meal, which is a lot of fun to make together with children or a group of friends. Many have tried this simple, flavoursome recipe, with delicious results.

serves 4

what you need

500g '00' flour, plus extra for rolling out dough (see note)

½ tsp freshly ground nutmeg

1⅓ cups (300g) mashed pumpkin, cooled

1 small garlic clove, crushed

2 eggs

50g butter, softened

¼ cup (20g) grated parmesan

handful basil leaves, finely chopped

2 cups (500ml) tomato sauce (see basics page 15)

¼ cup (60g) crumbled feta

extra basil leaves, and freshly ground black pepper, to serve

V

what you do

1. Pile the flour onto a clean dry bench, sprinkle with nutmeg, then make a well in the centre. Add the pumpkin, garlic, eggs, butter, parmesan and basil to the flour. Mix with your hands to make a sticky dough. Dust with a little extra flour if it is too sticky to work with. Gather the dough into a ball.

2. Cut the dough into 4 even pieces. Roll each piece into a long sausage shape about 30cm long. Using a floured butter knife, cut each sausage into 15 evenly sized pieces. Cut each piece in half crossways. Place the gnocchi pieces onto a tray lined with non-stick baking paper.

3. Bring a large saucepan of water to the boil. Meanwhile, warm the tomato sauce in a separate saucepan.

4. Place half the gnocchi pieces into the rapidly boiling water. Gently stir to stop them sticking to the bottom of the pot. Once the pieces begin to float to the surface, remove with a slotted spoon and place into a colander to drain. Repeat with remaining gnocchi.

5. Place the hot gnocchi onto a warmed plate, and cover with the warmed tomato sauce. Serve topped with feta, basil leaves and pepper as desired.

Note: '00' flour is a finely ground, high protein flour ideally suited to making pasta. You will find it at most large supermarkets.

GF option: Use spelt flour. For information on spelt flour see page 49. Many people who have wheat allergies can tolerate spelt, use your own discretion.

nutmeg *is a spice, wonderfully rich in fragrance, which is known for its aromatic, aphrodisiac and curative properties. Nutmeg trees are evergreen, native to the rainforest of the Indonesian Moluccas Islands, also known as the Spice Islands. Nutmeg is the actual seed of the tree, and is light brown in colour and roughly egg-shaped. It is used for flavouring many dishes, usually ground or even better, freshly grated.*

brown rice risotto with peas, chilli and prawns

Here I happily break with tradition by using brown rice for risotto,
which adds more nutrition and fibre, plus a nutty flavour to the dish.
The parmesan cheese gives the creamy texture you're looking for in risotto.

serves 4

what you need

2 litres (8 cups) chicken stock
(see basics page 21)

3 tbsp olive oil

1 onion, finely chopped

1 garlic clove, crushed

500g (2½ cups) brown rice
(preferably short or medium
grain)

1 cup (150g) fresh green peas

1 chilli, seeded and finely chopped

1 tbsp butter

1 tbsp mint leaves, finely chopped
plus extra to serve

juice of 1 lemon

1 cup (80g) parmesan,
finely grated

500g green prawns,
peeled and deveined

pinch of sea salt

GF

what you do

1. Heat the chicken stock in a saucepan until almost boiling. Keep hot over a very low heat.

2. Heat 2 tablespoons of the oil in a large pot. Add the onion and garlic, and sauté for 2-3 minutes over medium heat until soft but not coloured. Add the brown rice and stir for 2 minutes, to coat in the oil and begin to soften the rice.

3. Increase the heat to high. Add a large ladleful of the hot chicken stock (about 200ml). Cook, stirring occasionally, until the stock is absorbed. Repeat this process, until all the stock is added. Add the peas and chilli with the final ladle of stock.

4. Once the stock is absorbed, stir in the butter, mint, lemon juice and parmesan. Turn off the heat and place a lid on the pot. Stand for 5 minutes.

5. Heat the remaining oil in a large frying pan. Add the prawns and cook over high heat for 2 minutes each side. Season risotto with sea salt to taste. Serve risotto topped with prawns, and sprinkled with remaining mint.

V option: Substitute prawns with ½ cup (90g) toasted whole almonds.

parmesan *is a hard cow's milk cheese which originated in and around the Parma region of Italy. The cheese is made and placed in cheesecloth-lined moulds for two days. It is then salted in brine for a month, then allowed to mature for up to two years in very humid conditions. It is a part of the Italian national cuisine and is used in many traditional recipes or served grated or shaved over the finished dish.*

green split pea and herbed meatball soup

A hearty soup, high in protein, iron and dietary fibre. This soup was inspired by my husband's love for both pea and ham soup, and a meatball soup his mother used to cook for him. I have sort of combined the two to give you a soup every meat-eating man will love!

serves 6

what you need

2 litres vegetable stock
(see basics page 21)

1 cup (200g) dried green
split peas

1 onion, finely diced

2 carrots, finely diced

2 celery stalks, finely diced

1 cup (100g) green cabbage,
finely shredded

6 green shallots, finely sliced

parmesan, grated, to serve

meatballs:

500g beef mince

1 cup (40g) wholemeal
breadcrumbs

2 eggs

1 tsp tomato paste

1 garlic clove, crushed

1/3 cup flat-leaf parsley, chopped

pinch of sea salt

freshly ground black pepper,
to taste

what you do

1. Combine the stock, split peas, onion, carrot, celery (and potatoes if using V option) in a large saucepan over medium heat. Bring to the boil, reduce the heat slightly and simmer uncovered for 30 minutes, stirring occasionally.

2. Add the cabbage and shallots, simmer for a further 15 minutes.

3. To make the meatballs, combine all the ingredients in a large bowl, and use your hands to mix until evenly combined. Shape heaped teaspoons into balls. Add to the soup and simmer for 10 minutes, until meatballs are cooked through. Serve with finely grated parmesan.

V option: Substitute chunks of potato for the meatballs.

GF option: Use rice crumbs instead of breadcrumbs in the meatballs.

Note: For information on rice crumbs see page 151.

split peas *are the dried, peeled and split seeds of a pea plant. They come in yellow and green varieties. The peas are round when harvested and dried. Once dry, the skin is removed and the natural split in the seed is mechanically separated, to encourage faster cooking. They are a lean and healthy food, as they are a great source of protein and are very low in fat. The green variety are most commonly used in soups, the yellow also in soups and to make dhal.*

lamb, guinness and potato pie

There is something so comforting about eating a hot savoury pie. This is the perfect winter dish, suitable for a cosy Sunday lunch or as a casual dinner with friends on a chilly evening. I like to serve mine with mashed green peas and a nice glass of organic red wine.

serves 6

what you need

2 sheets frozen butter puff pastry, thawed

1 tbsp olive oil

2 large onions, diced

2 large or 4 small carrots, diced

3 garlic cloves, thinly sliced

1kg diced lamb

2 tbsp roughly chopped rosemary

2 tbsp plain flour

440ml can Guinness

1 cup (150g) peas
(fresh or frozen)

6 large potatoes, chopped in to evenly sized chunks

1 tbsp butter

¾ cup (180ml) milk

pinch of sea salt

1 tbsp olive oil, extra

what you do

1. Preheat the oven to 180°C (160°C fan forced). Grease a 28cm × 18cm (base measurement), 5cm deep (about 8 cup capacity) pie dish. Overlap the pastry sheets slightly and press to join. Line the dish with the pastry. Lay a sheet of non-stick baking paper over the pastry, and fill with dried rice or beans, to stop the pastry rising as it cooks. Bake for 10 minutes, then remove paper and rice and bake a further 10 minutes, until lightly golden. If the pastry has puffed up, gently press it back down with a clean tea towel. Set aside to cool.

2. Heat the olive oil in a large saucepan. Add the onions, carrots and garlic, and sauté over medium heat for 3 minutes. Increase the heat to high, add the lamb and rosemary, and cook for 5 minutes, stirring occasionally, until browned.

3. Reduce the heat to medium and sprinkle the flour over. Cook, stirring, for one minute. Gradually add the Guinness, stirring constantly. Bring to the boil, then reduce the heat to low and simmer uncovered for 20 minutes. Stir in the peas and cook a further 10 minutes.

4. Meanwhile, cook the potatoes in a large saucepan of boiling water for 20 minutes, or until tender. Drain and return the pan to the stove over low heat to evaporate any excess water. Add the butter, milk and salt and mash to a creamy texture.

5. Transfer the lamb mixture to the pastry shell, and top with mashed potato. Brush with the extra olive oil and bake for 15 minutes, then place under the grill for 5 minutes, to brown the top.

GF option: Use gluten-free pastry and rice flour.

guinness *is a type of beer, an Irish stout to be exact. Arthur Guinness started the St James Gate Brewery in Dublin back in 1759 and developed the beer himself. A unique feature of the beer is the burnt flavour which is derived from the use of roasted unmalted barley. Guinness is a darker colour than other ales and when poured develops a creamy head. Research has found that antioxidant compounds in the Guinness are similar to those found in certain fruits and vegetables.*

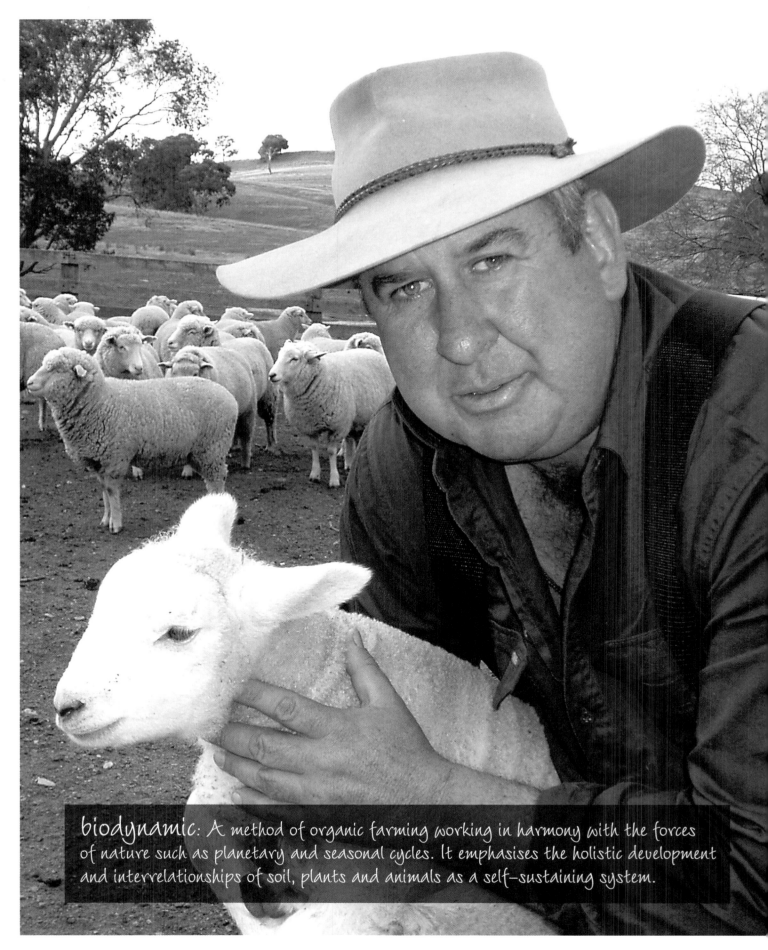

biodynamic: A method of organic farming working in harmony with the forces of nature such as planetary and seasonal cycles. It emphasises the holistic development and interrelationships of soil, plants and animals as a self-sustaining system.

meet the people...

I first met Vince Heffernan from Moorlands Lamb at the Eveleigh Farmers' Market in 2011. I purchased some of his tender biodynamic lamb that day and took home a flyer that he handed me, promoting the idea of ordering a whole lamb once a month at a great price. After tasting the lamb I bought that morning, it wasn't long before I was ordering my first whole lamb. It comes direct from Vince's Moorlands Lamb farm in Dalton, which is between Goulburn and Yass in the southern tablelands of NSW. Sheep and lamb have been their family business for over 160 years. Their combined organic/biodynamic approach, coupled with rotational grazing, produces succulent lamb which is healthier for both your family and the environment.

Moorlands Demeter certified biodynamic lamb is produced using sustainable farming techniques without using pesticides, antibiotics or growth-promoting hormones. Biodynamics is an enhanced organic approach. Biodynamic practices focus on producing healthy, living, well-structured soil, as the basis of growing healthy plants and animals. Biodynamics ensures that the full interrelationship of soil to plants to animals is considered in the care of the land and livestock. The result is farming that is ecologically friendly and produce that is organic and premium quality.

Vince says *"None of the lambs are fed hay made from GM canola, or exposed to fungicides, or fed grain. No insecticide, artificial fertiliser, weedicide, chemical drench, vaccine, chemical dips or pesticides are applied to the soil, the plants or the animals on Moorlands. The lambs have a smorgasbord of grass varieties on which to graze - pasture fed - nothing artificial or forced. We are fully trained in stress-free stock handling techniques. Ethical considerations are foremost in our minds. Not only is this kind to our beautiful sheep but it results in tender meat.'*

Moorlands Lamb is also affordable since it comes to you directly from the farmer. Dealing directly with the farmer means you save as much as 40% over shop prices. Typically once a month a load of fresh, never frozen, lamb comes to markets in Sydney and Canberra where you can pick up your order.

moorlands lamb

Vince Heffernan

t: 61 2 6242 9979

www.moorlandslamb.com.au

roast vegetable lasagne

A delicious array of flavours and textures in this vegetable lovers' delight!
This recipe can easily be prepared and assembled the day before and refrigerated,
then baked an hour before meal time. Any leftovers are tasty served cold for the
next day or two, with a simply dressed garden salad.

serves 6
what you need

1 large or 2 small eggplant, cut
into 1cm slices (salting may be
necessary, see below)

500g sweet potato,
cut into 1cm slices

2 large green zucchini,
thickly sliced lengthways

1 tbsp extra virgin olive oil

2 bunches english spinach,
trimmed and washed

250g fresh ricotta

½ cup (125ml) basil pesto
(see basics page 15)

2 x 400g cans diced tomatoes

375g packet fresh lasagne sheets

1 cup (80g) parmesan, grated

V
what you do

1. Preheat the oven to 180°C (160°C fan forced) and line 2 large baking
trays with non-stick baking paper. Arrange the eggplant, sweet potato and
zucchini onto the trays, and drizzle with oil. Bake for 30 minutes, turning
halfway through cooking. Set aside to cool.

2. Steam the spinach until wilted. Refresh in cold water, then drain and
squeeze dry. Spread out the leaves. Combine the ricotta and pesto in
a bowl.

3. Brush a 30cm x 20cm x 6cm deep (or similar with a 12 cup capacity)
ovenproof dish with oil. Spread one cup (250ml) of the tomatoes over the
base of the dish. Arrange a layer of lasagne sheets over the tomato, trimming
to fit if necessary. Top with a neat layer of zucchini and sweet potato.

4. Make another layer of lasagne sheets, and spread with another one cup
of tomatoes, then the spinach leaves. Make another layer of lasagne sheets,
followed by the eggplant slices, the remaining tomato and a final layer of
lasagne sheets. Finish with the ricotta mixture, and sprinkle with parmesan.

5. Place a sheet of non-stick baking paper, then a piece of foil over the
baking dish (this stops the foil sticking to cheese). Bake for one hour.
Remove the baking paper and foil, and cook for a further 15 minutes
or until golden brown on top.

GF option: Use gluten-free lasagne sheets.

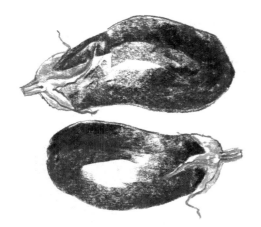

eggplant *also known as aubergine, grows on a small bushy plant. The fruit
is fleshy, with a meaty texture. It contains numerous small, soft seeds, which
are edible but have a bitter taste. To counteract the bitterness of the seeds,
generously sprinkle the sliced fruit in sea salt, let it sit for half an hour, then
rinse off salt with cold water, dry with paper towel and use as required. This is
only necessary with older, larger fruit which contains many seeds. The thin skin
is also edible, so peeling is not necessary. The raw fruit becomes tender when
cooked and develops a rich, unique flavour.*

roast chicken with apricot and pine nut stuffing

I often talk with people who are overwhelmed at the thought of doing a roast,
like it is some massive event! It really is a simple joy to roast a chicken, and once it is in
the oven you are released from the kitchen to do as you wish. On your return you'll enjoy
a very satisfying meal you cooked from scratch. Slow cooked succulent roast chicken with
a delicious apricot stuffing, is perfect for Christmas day - or any day really!

serves 6

what you need

1.7kg - 2kg whole chicken

¼ cup (60ml) extra virgin olive oil

pinch of sea salt

stuffing:

2 tsp olive oil

½ red onion, diced

2 slices wholemeal sourdough
bread, roughly chopped

150g fresh apricots, deseeded
and roughly chopped

¼ cup basil leaves, finely chopped

¼ cup (40g) pine nuts, toasted

2 eggs, lightly beaten

pinch of sea salt

freshly ground black pepper

gravy:

¼ cup (35g) plain flour

1 cup (250ml) chicken stock
(see basics page 21)

what you do

1. Preheat the oven to 200°C (180°C fan forced).

2. To make the stuffing, heat the oil in a small frying pan, and cook
the onion over medium heat for about 3 minutes, until soft.
Combine the onion with the remaining stuffing ingredients and mix well.

3. Open the cavity of the chicken wide and fill with the stuffing mix,
pressing in firmly. Close the skin over the stuffed cavity, and secure
with 2 small bamboo skewers. Rub the whole exterior of the chicken
with the oil, and sprinkle with salt.

4. Place the chicken into a roasting pan, breast side up. Roast for 30 minutes,
then reduce the heat to 160°C (140°C fan forced) for a further 1½ hours.

5. Remove from the oven. Carefully turn the chicken over, cover with
foil and rest for 30 minutes. Turning the chicken ensures the moisture is
retained in the breast.

6. To make the gravy, transfer the chicken to a serving platter. Warm the chicken
stock in a separate saucepan. Place the roasting pan over medium heat, to
heat the pan juices. Sprinkle the flour over the pan juices and cook, stirring
for 1-2 minutes, until smooth. Add the warmed chicken stock a little at a time,
stirring until smooth between each addition, until all the stock has been added.
Bring to a simmer and cook for 2 minutes. Strain into a warm jug to serve.

7. Carve the chicken or cut into portions, and remove stuffing.
Serve meat with a slice of stuffing and gravy.

Note: When apricots aren't in season, use 75g chopped dried apricots instead.

GF option: Use gluten-free bread in the stuffing.

apricots *are a stone fruit that grow on a small tree. They are a small peach
shaped fruit, yellow to orange in colour, often tinged red on the side most exposed
to the sun. Eating in season means they are only available for three to four months
of the year, in late Spring and Summer. They can be eaten raw, cooked or sun dried.
Apricots are low in kilojoules and are a rich source of dietary fibre, vitamins and
minerals.*

tandoori lamb and chickpea curry

This dish was created as a way of starting to add more pulses and legumes to our everyday diet. Up until a few years ago I had never really cooked much with these foods, and it has been a great education, as well as a tasty and nutritious addition to our mealtimes. This curry is serious comfort food, tender lamb with an abundance of spice and the added goodness of chickpeas. It is preferable to marinate the lamb for at least an hour, or overnight, to maximise flavour.

serves 6

what you need

1kg diced lamb

2 tbsp olive oil

1 onion, diced

2 garlic cloves, crushed

2 large tomatoes, cored and diced

400g can diced tomatoes

400g can chickpeas, rinsed and drained

400ml can coconut milk

1 cup (150g) peas
(fresh or frozen)

handful of flat-leaf parsley or coriander, chopped

steamed brown rice, to serve

tandoori marinade:

1 heaped tbsp tandoori paste

2 heaped tbsp natural yoghurt
(european or greek style)

1 tsp ground turmeric

1 tsp paprika

GF

what you do

1. To make the marinade, combine the ingredients in a shallow glass dish.

2. Add the lamb, and turn to coat thoroughly. Cover and refrigerate for at least one hour or overnight.

3. Heat the oil in a large saucepan, and cook the onion and garlic over medium heat for about 2 minutes, until transparent. Add the marinated diced lamb and cook for 5-7 minutes, stirring often, until coloured.

4. Add the fresh tomatoes, cover and bring to a simmer. Cook, covered, for 15 minutes. Stir in the canned tomatoes, chickpeas and coconut milk. Simmer uncovered for 30 minutes.

5. Add the peas, cover and cook for 5 minutes. Sprinkle with parsley or coriander leaves, and serve with brown rice.

Note: You can use one cup (200g) dried chickpeas, soaked overnight then boiled for 30 minutes, in place of the canned beans, if you like.

chickpeas (also known as garbanzos) are a type of pulse, with one seedpod containing two or three peas. They are grown in the Mediterranean, western Asia, the Indian subcontinent and Australia. Mature chickpeas can be pre-cooked and eaten cold in salads, or included in curries and stews. They can be ground into a flour called gram flour (also known as chickpea or besan flour), minced, shaped into balls and fried as falafel, or cooked and ground into a paste called hummus. They also make a great snack when roasted and spiced. Chickpeas are a helpful source of zinc, folic acid (vitamin B9) and protein and are very high in dietary fibre.

spiced chicken with quinoa

Great flavours come together to make this warming dish with a healthy twist.
Many people have asked me *"What do you do with preserved lemons?"*.
They can be used in both savoury and sweet dishes. Here is an easy,
slow cooked chicken dish to get you started. Although I cook this in the oven,
if you have a slow cooker this recipe would be suitable.

serves 4-6

what you need

6 chicken thighs

1 litre chicken stock
(see basics page 21)

100g preserved lemon

1 tbsp olive oil

1 onion, finely sliced

2 garlic cloves, sliced

1 tbsp tomato paste

4 large potatoes, cut into quarters

12 black olives, halved and pitted

2 bay leaves

1 cup (200g) quinoa

steamed green beans, to serve

spice rub:

1 tbsp sweet paprika

1 tbsp freshly grated ginger

¼ cup thyme leaves,
roughly chopped

2 tbsp extra virgin olive oil

GF

what you do

1. Preheat the oven to 200°C (180°C fan forced).

2. To make the spice rub, combine all the ingredients in a large bowl.
Add the chicken and massage the spice rub into the skin and flesh until
well coated.

3. Heat 750ml of the stock in a small saucepan. Remove the white pith and
any flesh from the lemons and discard. Rinse the rind under cold water, drain.

4. Heat the olive oil in a large flameproof casserole dish, and cook the
chicken over medium heat, turning to brown all over.

5. Add the onion, garlic and tomato paste. Cook, stirring constantly, for one
minute. Add the hot stock, preserved lemon, potatoes, olives and bay leaves.
Stir to combine.

6. Place the lid on the casserole dish, and bake for one hour. Reduce the
heat to 160°C (140°C fan forced) and cook for a further 30 minutes.

7. Combine the remaining stock (250ml) with one cup (250ml) water in a
medium saucepan and bring to the boil. Add the quinoa, cover and return
to the boil. Reduce the heat to low and simmer uncovered, stirring
occasionally, for 10 minutes, until all the liquid is absorbed and the quinoa
is soft and translucent.

8. Serve the chicken casserole with the quinoa and steamed green beans.

Note: Preserving lemons was done to utilise an abundance of fruit in season
and keep them for another day. When using preserved lemons you should
always discard the white pith and rinse the rinds in water to reduce the
saltiness. You can also soak the rinds in water with a little honey to add
some sweetness. For information on quinoa see below.

quinoa *(pronounced 'keen-wah'), is a grain-like crop, grown mainly for its edible
seeds. Recently becoming more popular in the western diet, it is being hailed a
super food because it is so good for you. Nutritionally quinoa contains a
balanced set of essential amino acids for humans, making it a complete protein
source. It is a good source of dietary fibre and phosphorus, and is high in
magnesium and iron. Quinoa is gluten-free and considered easy to digest. It has
a light, fluffy texture when cooked, and its mild, slightly nutty flavour makes it a
delicious alternative to white rice or couscous.*

marinated lamb leg

Roast lamb is enhanced with this fresh marinade and is perfect served with pan juices, smashed potatoes and steamed greens. Leftover sliced meat, served the next day in a sandwich with mustard pickles and salad leaves, is a winner.

serves 6
what you need

1kg - 1.5kg easy-carve leg of lamb (see note)

extra thyme leaves, to serve

garlic and thyme marinade:
finely grated zest of 1 lemon
¼ cup thyme leaves, chopped
2 garlic cloves, crushed
¼ cup (60ml) extra virgin olive oil

GF
what you do

1. Use a small sharp knife to make incisions into the surface of the lamb (this allows the marinade to permeate the meat).

2. To make the marinade, combine the lemon zest, thyme leaves, garlic and olive oil in a bowl. Rub the marinade all the over the lamb meat.

3. Wrap the leg of lamb in a piece of non-stick baking paper, place onto a plate and cover with plastic wrap. Refrigerate for at least one hour or preferably overnight, to marinate.

4. Bring the lamb out of the fridge at least 30 minutes prior to cooking, to allow it to come to room temperature (so it will cook more evenly). Preheat the oven to 180°C (160°C fan forced).

5. Uncover the lamb and remove the paper. Place into a roasting pan, and cook for 50-60 minutes per kg for medium result. (To test, pierce a metal or bamboo skewer into centre of the lamb, checking for clear, not pink juices.)

6. Remove the lamb from the oven, cover loosely with foil and allow to rest for 30 minutes before serving. Sprinkle with fresh thyme leaves.

Note: 'Easy-carve' means the centre H bone and upper part of leg bone have been removed, making it easy to carve the meat once cooked. Remember that the meat continues to cook as it rests, so factor this into the cooking time. If you like your lamb pink, a 1.3kg easy carve lamb leg at room temperature would cook for one hour and rest for 30 minutes; for medium to well done, cook for 1¼ hours and rest for 30 minutes.

thyme is a soft leaf, woody stemmed, aromatic culinary herb. It is often used to flavour meats, soups and stews; it goes especially well with lamb, tomatoes and eggs. Thyme is available both fresh and dried, fresh being more flavoursome. The best way to have it on hand is to grow your own in a pot or in the garden.

mild sweet chicken curry pies

This recipe began as a way to use up my leftovers of mild chicken curry and has ended up as a family favourite! This quantity will make you enough for two meals, curry for the family one night and then enough leftovers to make the homemade pies later in the week.

makes curry for 6, plus 6 meal-sized pies or 12 mini pies

what you need

2 cups (500ml) chicken stock (see basics page 21)

50ml extra virgin olive oil

2 onions, diced

1 carrot, diced

2 celery stalks, diced

1kg chicken thigh or breast, roughly chopped

2 tbsp mild curry powder

1 garlic clove, crushed

1/3 cup (50g) plain flour

400g sweet potato, finely diced

1/2 cup (75g) peas (fresh or frozen)

1 tbsp roughly chopped coriander leaves

steamed basmati or brown rice, to serve

for the pies:

4 1/2 sheets frozen butter puff pastry, thawed

2 tbsp milk

what you do

1. To make the curry, heat the stock in a small saucepan. Heat the oil in a large saucepan, and cook the onion, carrot and celery for 5 minutes. Add the chicken and cook a further 5 minutes, until lightly coloured, stirring occasionally.

2. Add the curry powder and garlic, and cook, stirring, for one minute. Sprinkle the flour over and cook, stirring, for one minute.

3. Add the hot stock a little at a time, stirring until smooth after each addition, until all the stock has been added and a smooth thick sauce has formed.

4. Add the sweet potato, reduce the heat to low and simmer uncovered for 20 minutes, stirring occasionally. Add the peas and cook for a further 10 minutes, then stir in the coriander.

5. Serve half the curry with basmati or brown rice. Cool the remaining curry, and refrigerate until required.

6. To make the pies, preheat the oven to 180°C (160°C fan forced). Grease six pie dishes or mini springform tins (one cup capacity). Cut the whole pastry sheets into quarters, and the half pastry sheet into half. Use 6 of the pieces to line the bases of the tins. Cut 6 of the pieces each into 3 strips, and use to line the sides of the tins, pressing gently to seal the joins to each other and to the base. Refrigerate remaining quarters until needed.

7. Place crumpled pieces of non-stick baking paper over the pastry in the tins, and fill with dried rice or beans, to stop the pastry rising as it cooks. Bake for 10 minutes, then remove the paper and rice and bake a further 10 minutes.

8. Increase oven to 200°C (180°C fan forced). Fill the pastry cases with curry. Top with the remaining pastry quarters, press to seal, folding over any excess pastry. Brush with milk. Bake for 30 minutes, until the pastry is golden brown and the filling is heated through. Stand in the tins for 10 minutes, then run a knife around the pies to loosen before releasing the sides.

Note: The pastry is easiest to work with if still quite cold when thawed. Keep in the fridge until needed, so it doesn't become too soft.

Variation: You could make 12 smaller pies in muffin tins. You will only need 3 sheets of pastry. Grease tin and line each one with 1/4 of a pastry sheet for each. Fill with curry and fold the overhanging pastry over to enclose the filling. Brush with milk and bake for 15 minutes.

GF option: Use gluten-free pastry. Substitute rice flour for the plain flour.

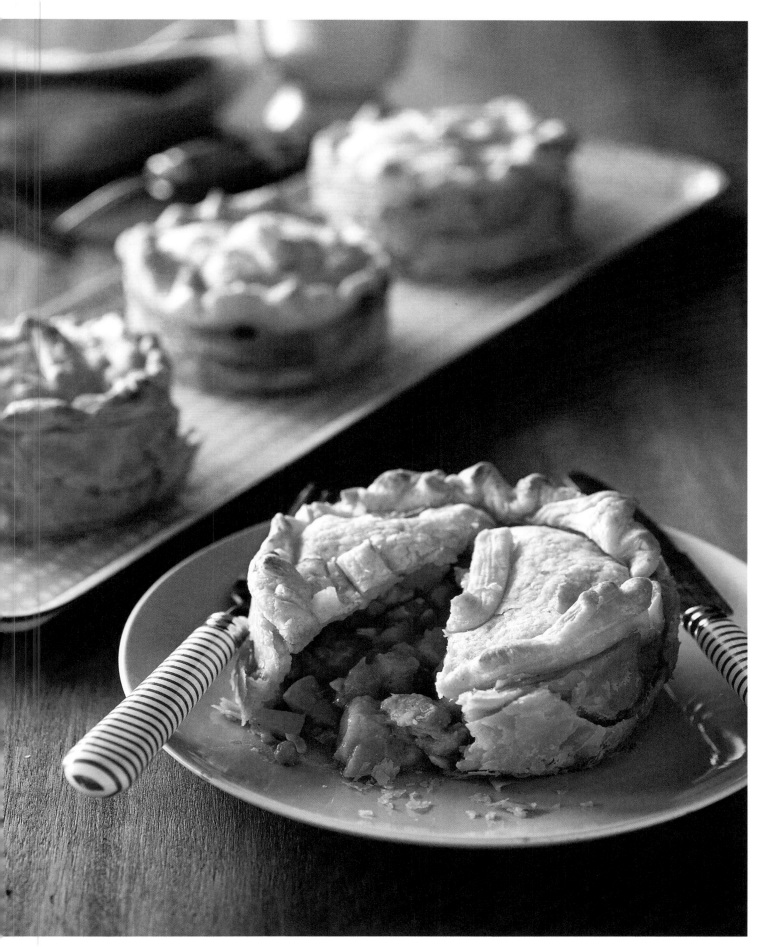

gourmet pizzas

It's not rocket science making your own pizzas, and if you have the time you can quite simply make your own bases too! It is a great way to introduce children to cooking, and the quality of ingredients and taste is far superior to anything you'll have delivered to your door. Here I have given you three different toppings to choose from.

makes four 30cm bases
what you need

1 quantity pizza dough
(see basics page 18)

1 cup (250ml) tomato sauce
(see basics page 15)

tandoori chicken pizza:
(quantity for 2 bases)

1 chicken breast fillet, finely sliced

1 tsp olive oil

1 tsp tandoori paste

½ bunch fresh coriander, roughly chopped (keep ¼ cup of fresh coriander leaves to serve)

1 small red capsicum, finely sliced

2 green shallots, finely sliced

100g semi-dried tomatoes, halved

½ cup (125ml) natural yoghurt (european or greek style)

1 cup (100g) finely grated mozzarella

50g snow peas, trimmed and finely sliced, to serve

V

potato and rosemary pizza:
(quantity for 1 base)

1 large potato, finely sliced

1 garlic clove, finely sliced

1 tbsp rosemary, roughly chopped

1 small red onion, finely sliced

½ cup (40g) finely grated parmesan

freshly ground black pepper. to serve

tomato and bocconcini pizza:
(quantity for 1 base)

½ cup fresh basil leaves, plus extra to serve

10 grape or cherry tomatoes, halved

100g baby bocconcini cheese, halved

½ cup (50g) finely grated mozzarella

what you do

1. For the tandoori chicken pizza, coat the chicken in the tandoori paste and marinate in the fridge for 30 minutes. Heat the oil in a frying pan and cook the chicken over low heat, covered, for about 10 minutes, until cooked through. Transfer to a plate to cool.

2. To make all the pizzas, preheat the oven to 200°C (180°C fan forced). Roll the pizza dough out and place onto pizza trays. Spread with tomato sauce, leaving 1cm around the edge for the crust.

3. For the tomato and bocconcini pizza, arrange the basil leaves, tomatoes, and bocconcini over the base, and sprinkle with mozzarella.

4. For the potato and rosemary pizza, arrange the potato, garlic, rosemary and onion over the base, and sprinkle with the parmesan.

5. For the tandoori chicken pizza, arrange the cooled chicken, coriander, capsicum, shallots and semi-dried tomatoes over the remaining 2 bases. Dollop the yoghurt here and there, and sprinkle with mozzarella.

6. Bake all the pizzas for 15 minutes, until golden brown. Top the tomato and bocconcini pizza with fresh basil leaves, and the tandoori chicken pizza with the snow peas and reserved coriander. Grind pepper over the potato and rosemary pizza. Cut into wedges to serve.

GF option: Use gluten-free ready made pizza base.

feature recipe...

Agape is Sydney's largest certified organic licensed restaurant and bar, serving tapas, spelt pizza, mains and dessert. It is certified by the Organic Food Chain (OFC), and proudly supports Australian farmers, using the best certified organic, sustainable and natural produce.

Executive Chef Simon Lawson started cooking at a very early age in his grandmother's kitchen and this was where he started a lifelong passion for food. He has a great ability for marrying flavours and creating dishes which are delicious and nutritious. He has worked in Sydney's top restaurants. After cooking professionally for over fifteen years, he realised his dream to open a restaurant with his sister, stylist and entrepreneur Lyn Yu.

Agape is breaking down the perception that organic food is expensive. By using local ingredients, buying smartly and in season, Simon manages to keep his prices reasonable.

We love to dine at Agape and especially delight in their amazing spelt pizzas. Chef Simon Lawson has shared two of his lovely ancient grain recipes.

Agape Organic Restaurant and Bar is fully licensed and is open for dinner Tuesday to Saturday from 6pm and for lunch Friday and Sunday 12pm – 3pm.

agape organic restaurant and bar

1385 Botany Road,
Botany NSW 2019

t: 61 2 8668 5777

www.agaperestaurant.com

slow braised beef brisket with swiss brown mushrooms and ancient grains, with salsa verde

This recipe is courtesy of Chef Simon Lawson from Agape Organic Restaurant and Bar in Botany, NSW. Simon is passionate about cooking with ancient grains such as quinoa and amaranth, and he uses Gundooee organic wagyu beef at his restaurant. This dish is a lovely combination of both, a sample of the delightful dishes you'll enjoy at Agape.

serves 4-6

what you need

100ml rice bran oil

500g beef brisket, cut into 2cm pieces

2 onions, diced

6 garlic cloves, peeled and left whole

1 bunch thyme, finely chopped

6 juniper berries

250g swiss brown mushrooms, halved

1 cup (250ml) red wine

3 cups (750ml) beef stock

1 bunch purple carrots, peeled

4 sebago potatoes, cut into large chunks

100g white royal quinoa

100g amaranth

pinch of sea salt

freshly ground black pepper, to taste

salsa verde:

1 bunch flat-leaf parsley, finely chopped

1 bunch mint, finely chopped

finely grated zest of 1 lemon

2 garlic cloves, finely chopped

100ml olive oil

GF

what you do

1. Heat half the rice bran oil in a large flameproof casserole dish over medium high heat. Add the beef and seal on all sides until golden brown. Remove the beef from the pan and set aside.

2. Add the remaining rice bran oil to the pan, and reduce the heat to medium. Cook the onion, garlic, thyme and juniper berries for 4 minutes, or until the onions are golden. Add the mushrooms and cook for another 2 minutes.

3. Pour in the red wine and stock, add the carrots and potatoes, and return the beef to the pan. Cover and bring to the boil. Reduce the heat to low and simmer for 2 hours, stirring occasionally, until the beef is tender and falling apart. Add the quinoa and amaranth and cook for a further 15 minutes. Season generously with salt and pepper.

4. For the salsa verde, combine all the ingredients in a small bowl. Serve the slow braised brisket sprinkled with the salsa verde.

Note: For information on quinoa see page 183. Amaranth is a healthy grain, which is very high in protein. Adding it to slow cooked dishes and when baking, boosts the dish's nutritional content.

my story...jane cooks live

The Jane COOKS classes were designed for up to twelve guests in a session, therefore creating a more personal experience for those who attend. The guests enjoy watching a demonstration of five recipes and receive generous tastings of each dish. They have their questions answered as we go, and then take home the recipes to cook for family and friends.

After just a few months of running the cooking classes, opportunities began to open up for me to speak and cook in front of larger audiences, which is something I really enjoy. Lights, cameras and action...I found myself doing demonstrations for up to 500 people, inspiring them to cook and eat well, using simple healthy recipes. Gatherings for women, community and corporate events, Health and Lifestyle Expos, seniors' events and educational sessions known as 'Food for thought', designed for both primary and secondary students in local schools.

Most people, whether they be young or old, need to be educated or re-educated, inspired and equipped to embrace the idea of a healthier diet. One of my favourite things to do is to speak to and cook for primary school kids, I count this part of what I now do as an absolute privilege. Children are more eager to learn than most adults realise, and many children I have encountered have really grasped the concept of looking after their bodies and eating well. Funnily enough I often receive emails from children, sending me photos of the food they have cooked after attending my sessions, as well as emails from mothers, recounting to me that their child came home and purged the pantry, exclaiming *"Do you ever read the labels on the food you buy, Mum? This stuff is really not good for my body!"*

I love to explain to the children the different impact on their bodies, of eating a raw carrot rather than drinking a can of cola, and to my surprise by the end of the session the majority all have their hands raised to eat the carrot. What a responsibility we have to the next generation to help them discover naked food, the way food was meant to be, rather than the highly processed, brightly packaged convenience food, that is not really food, that they are bombarded with at every turn.

Thus from the seed of an idea, starting with Jane COOKS cooking classes teaching others to cook and eat well, another branch has grown, which I like to call Jane COOKS LIVE.

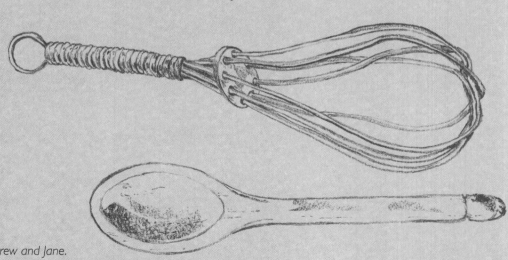

top right: Wendy Kendrew and Jane.
bottom right to left: Jane COOKS LIVE for Everywoman Sydney, Jane does a 'Food for thought' session for primary school children.

is there any dessert?

dessert; *the sweet course eaten at the end of the meal*

This is the daily question, coming from our third child Jake, asked towards the end of the evening meal…*"Is there any dessert?"*

These recipes are my attempt to provide a nutritious answer to this persistent question. Incorporating fruit and vegetables as healthy alternatives, to such staples in the western diet as refined white sugar and refined white flour, I have come up with these cakes, crumbles and cookies, that taste great and are good for you too.

My mum was always baking cakes throughout my childhood and it seems to be an art that is being lost, rather than continued through the generations. Our daughter Molly loves to bake and finds it fascinating that some think you can only bake from a packet mix. These recipes will help you to discover the joy of cooking from scratch, using fresh eggs, fresh spices and wholefoods in season.

Baking brings people together and children love to be involved, as there is always a mixing bowl or beaters to lick! The aroma of freshly baked goods fills the home and the neighbourhood. These recipes also make excellent treats for birthdays, lunchboxes and an answer to those other persistent daily questions, most parents face… what to put into the lunchbox and then later in the day…
"What is for afternoon tea?"

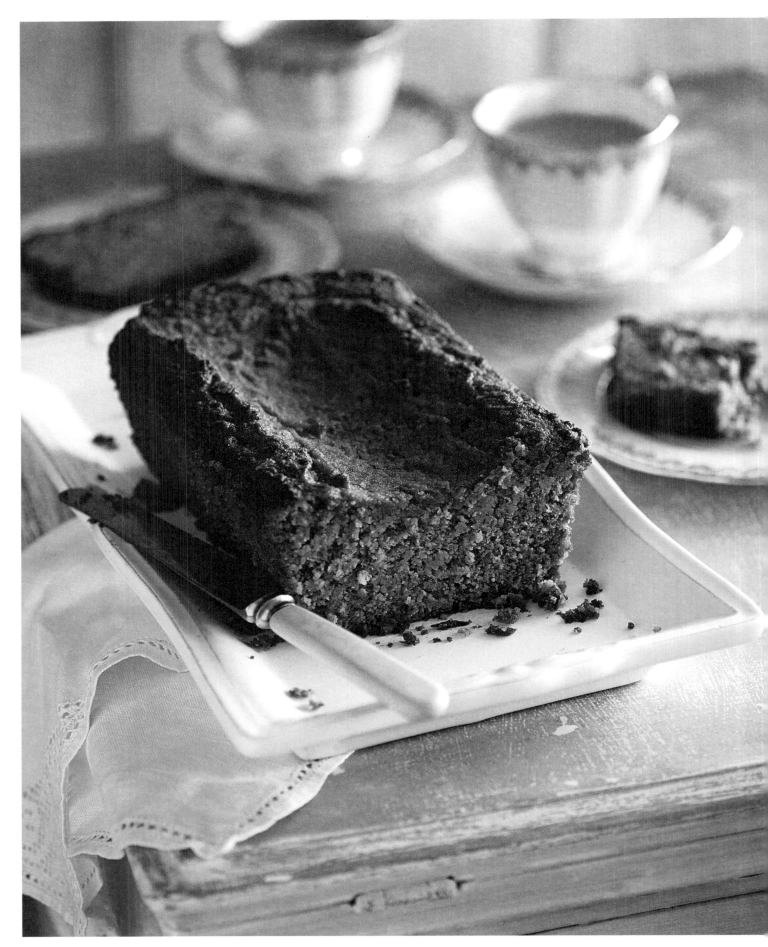

flourless pear and date cake

This wholesome gluten-free cake just happened one day.
I was having a bit of an almond meal obsession, putting it in everything I cooked,
plus I had some ripe pears and fresh dates on the kitchen bench needing to be used.
Turns out it works well and served as a dessert with vanilla bean ice cream, it's a hit.

serves 8

what you need

200g fresh dates, pitted and roughly chopped

2 pears, peeled, cored and roughly chopped

125g butter, at room temperature, chopped

¼ cup (45g) rapadura sugar

1 tsp finely grated lemon zest

1 tsp ground cinnamon

pinch of sea salt

2 eggs

2 cups (240g) almond meal

1 tsp baking powder (gluten-free)

V GF

what you do

1. Preheat the oven to 160°C (140°C fan forced) and lightly grease a 19cm x 9cm (base measurement) loaf tin and line the base with non-stick baking paper, extending over the two long sides of the tin.

2. Place the dates, pears and 200ml of water into a small saucepan over high heat. Bring to the boil, then reduce the heat slightly and cook for 10 minutes, stirring occasionally, until very soft. Mash or blend the mixture to a paste, and leave to cool.

3. Using electric beaters, beat the butter, sugar, lemon zest, cinnamon and salt until light and creamy. Add the eggs, and beat to combine.

4. Fold in the almond meal and baking powder until evenly combined, then fold in the date mixture.

5. Transfer to the prepared tin, and bake for one hour. Stand in the tin for 30 minutes, then lift out onto a board.

6. Serve warm as a dessert with vanilla ice cream, or cool and serve sliced.

Note: For information on rapadura sugar see page 18. The cake will sink a little on cooling.

Storage: Keep in an airtight container in the fridge for up to 5 days, but is best eaten at room temperature.

pear *is the fruit of a medium sized tree and is very similar to the apple in cultivation, propagation and pollination. Pears and apples cannot always be distinguished by the form of the fruit; some pears look very much like some apples. One major difference is that the flesh of pear fruit contains stone cells (also called "grit"). Pears may be stored at room temperature until ripe and are ripe when the flesh around the stem gives to gentle pressure. Ripe pears are optimally stored refrigerated, uncovered in a single layer, where they have a shelf life of 2 to 3 days. Pears are eaten fresh, canned, as juice, and dried. The juice can also be used in jellies and jams, usually in combination with other fruits or berries. Pears are a good source of dietary fibre and vitamin C, most of which is contained within the skin of the fruit.*

spelt and sweet potato scones

The combination of the lightness of spelt flour with the sweetness of the sweet potato makes for a sensational scone experience. Served with my home-made organic strawberry jam this is an unbeatable offering for morning or afternoon tea!

makes 9

what you need

1 tbsp butter, softened

¼ cup (45g) rapadura sugar (or brown sugar)

pinch of sea salt

1 egg

1 cup (200g) mashed sweet potato, cooled

2 cups (220g) wholemeal spelt flour

2 tsp baking powder

butter or jam and cream, to serve

(see basics strawberry jam page 29)

V

what you do

1. Preheat the oven to 210°C (190°C fan forced) and line an oven tray with non-stick baking paper, and dust the paper with spelt flour.

2. Beat the butter, sugar and salt with a wooden spoon until well combined. Mix in the egg and mashed sweet potato, then stir in the flour and baking powder. Gather the dough together with your hands.

3. Transfer the dough to the prepared tray, and shape into a square. Use a floured knife to score the dough into 9 pieces. Bake on the top shelf for 20 minutes, until golden brown.

4. Cool slightly then break or cut into 9 portions. Serve warm with butter or jam and lightly whipped cream.

Note: For information on rapadura sugar see page18 and for spelt flour page 49. Scones are best eaten on the day they are made.

GF option: Many people who have wheat allergies can tolerate spelt, use your own discretion. Use gluten-free baking powder.

the scone is a small British quick-bread, traditionally originating in both Scotland and south west England. It is usually made from wheat, barley or oatmeal, with baking powder as a raising agent. The scone is the core component of the English cream tea or Devonshire tea. Popular variations include adding raisins, currants, cheese or dates to the standard dough. In Australia pumpkin scones rose to fame during the period when Flo Bjelke-Petersen was in the public eye.

fruit mince tarts

Everybody loves a little fruit mince tart to celebrate Christmas, and these will melt in your mouth. They are quite simple to make and I often give home baked goods like these, packaged in a clear cellophane bag with a ribbon or jute string, as a gift at Christmas time.

serves 24
what you need

shortcrust pastry:

2 cups (300g) plain flour

150g butter, softened

1 tbsp rapadura sugar
(or caster sugar)

pinch of sea salt

¼ tsp caster sugar,
to glaze

fruit mince:

200g sultanas

100g raisins

100g fresh apricots, pitted

50g currants

1 tbsp freshly grated ginger

1 tsp freshly grated nutmeg

1 tsp ground allspice

1 tbsp finely grated orange zest

¼ cup (60ml) fresh orange juice

¼ cup (60ml) maple syrup

V
what you do

1. Preheat the oven to 180°C (160°C fan forced) and lightly grease 24 shallow patty pans.

2. To make the pastry, combine the flour, butter, rapadura sugar and salt in a food processor and process in short bursts, (alternatively combine in a bowl and use your fingertips to rub together) until crumbly. Add 100ml cold water and mix gently until evenly moistened.

3. Gather the dough together into a ball, and divide into 2 equal portions. Wrap each piece in non-stick baking paper and refrigerate while you prepare the fruit mince.

4. Combine all the fruit mince ingredients in a food processor and chop to form a moist fruit mince.

5. Using a rolling pin, roll a portion of pastry on the baking paper sheet it was wrapped in, to about 3mm thick. Use a 7cm round cutter to cut 12 rounds from the pastry. Ease them into the tins. Fill each pastry shell with a heaped teaspoon of fruit mince.

6. Roll out pastry scraps, and use a 2cm star cutter to cut out 12 stars. Place on top of the fruit mince. Repeat with remaining pastry and fruit mince to make 24 tarts.

7. Dissolve the caster sugar in one teaspoon warm water, and use to glaze the stars. Bake for 20 minutes, until just golden brown. Leave in the tins for 5 minutes, then lift out onto wire racks to cool.

Note: For information on rapadura sugar see page 18.

Storage: Store in an airtight container in the pantry for up to 5 days.

GF option: Use a ready made gluten-free pastry.

dried fruit is fruit where the majority of the original water content has been removed either naturally, through sun-drying, or through the use of specialised dryers or dehydrators. Dried fruits retain most of the nutritional value of fresh fruits. Sulphur dioxide is used as an antioxidant in some dried fruits to protect their colour and flavour and while harmless to most, sulphites can induce asthma when inhaled or ingested by sensitive people. Consequently, the law says the presence of sulphites must be clearly indicated on the label. Although they can be more expensive, purchasing organic dried fruits means there is no use of sulphur dioxide, this eliminates related health concerns.

mum's christmas cake

My mum is a great cook and every year since I can remember she has made a Christmas cake or two! It is always a big event - the soaking of the fruit a few days before, hours in the oven on baking day, the rum poured over it as soon as it comes out of the oven, and then the hours it must spend cooling down, to be wrapped and stored! This is her recipe.

serves about 30

what you need

750g mixed dried fruit

250g raisins

125g pitted dried dates

125g glace cherries

½ cup (110g) each chopped glace fig, glace apricots and glace peaches

¼ cup (55g) each chopped glace ginger, glace pear and glace pineapple

250g blanched almonds

⅓ cup (80ml) brandy

250g butter, at room temperature, chopped

125g brown sugar

125g caster sugar

6 eggs

1 tbsp golden syrup

250g plain flour

30g self-raising flour

1 tsp cocoa powder

½ tsp each ground cinnamon and nutmeg

pinch of salt

200ml rum

V

what you do

1. Soak the dried fruits, glace fruits and half the almonds in the brandy, at least 24 hours prior to baking the cake.

2. Preheat the oven to 180°C (160°C fan forced) and line a 22cm (base measurement) square cake tin with 2 layers of foil, leaving a decent overlap to be used later to wrap the cooked cake.

3. Using electric beaters, beat the butter and sugars in a large bowl until light and creamy. Add the eggs one at a time, beating well after each addition. Beat in the golden syrup. Sift the flours, cocoa powder, spices and salt over, and mix well.

4. Add the soaked fruit mixture, and stir through until evenly dispersed. Transfer to the prepared tin, and smooth the surface. Decorate the top with the remaining almonds.

5. Bake for one hour, then reduce the heat to 130°C (110°C fan forced) and bake for another 4 hours. Remove the cake from the oven and pour the rum over the hot cake. Leave in the tin to cool for 2 hours, then fold the foil over to cover the top surface. Wrap the cake (still in the tin) in 2 sheets of newspaper and 2 clean tea towels, and leave overnight to cool completely.

Note: If you can't find any of the glace fruit types, you can substitute with a different glace fruit, or increase one of the others up to the total amount.

Storage: Remove the tea towels and newspaper, then lift the cake from the tin, still in the foil lining. Store in an airtight container in the pantry. The cake will keep for up to 3 months — but rarely will it remain uneaten for this length of time!

GF option: Substitute brown rice flour for the flours and add one teaspoon gluten-free baking powder.

glace fruit also known as crystallised fruit or candied fruit, has been around since the 14th century. Whole fruit, small pieces of large fruit, or pieces of peel are placed in a heated sugar syrup, which absorbs the moisture from within the fruit and eventually preserves it.

organic orange and almond cake

This recipe is from Chef James Limnios of
The Peasants Feast Organic Restaurant, Newtown NSW.
At the restaurant they use all certified organic ingredients.

serves 8-10

what you need

3 medium oranges

300g raw almonds

290g xylitol (natural sugar)
or caster sugar

1½ tsp baking powder

2 eggs

3 egg whites

yogurt sauce:

250g plain yogurt

2 tbsp raw honey

½ tsp ground cinnamon

V GF

what you do

1. Place the oranges into a saucepan and cover with cold water. Bring to a simmer, and cook for 45-60 minutes, until soft. Lift out with a slotted spoon, and leave to cool.

2. Preheat the oven to 220°C (200°C fan forced). Grease a 20cm (base measurement) round cake tin, and line the base with non-stick baking paper.

3. Place the almonds into a food processor and process until finely ground. Remove and set aside.

4. Slice the oranges into 8 pieces each, remove and discard any seeds. Place orange pieces (skin included) into the food processor and puree until smooth. Add the almond meal, xylitol, baking powder, eggs and egg whites, and process until combined.

5. Transfer the mixture to the prepared tin, and bake for 25 minutes. Reduce the temperature to 190°C (170°C fan forced) and cook for a further 25 minutes, until browned and just firm to a light touch in the centre. Leave in the tin for 10 minutes. Run a knife around the cake to loosen, then release the side and leave to cool completely.

6. To make the sauce, whisk the ingredients together in a bowl. Serve slices of cake with a drizzle of sauce.

Note: Xylitol is a natural sugar, made from a natural substance found in fruit and vegetables, as well as corn cobs and various hard wood trees, including birch. Xylitol has a sweetness equal to sugar and in most cases can replace sugar in equal amounts. It is available from health food or organic food stores.

ancient grain rice pudding with caramelised figs and almond biscotti

This recipe is from Chef Simon Lawson of
Agape Organic Restaurant and Bar in Botany, NSW.
Simon suggests serving the pudding cold with figs, vanilla bean ice cream and almond biscotti.

serves 8
what you need

biscotti:

220g raw sugar

2 eggs

300g spelt flour

½ tsp baking powder

150g almonds

pudding:

1 litre milk

2 tsp ground cinnamon

1 vanilla bean, split in half lengthways

350g white short or medium grain rice

100g white quinoa

20g amaranth

200g raw sugar

vanilla bean ice cream to serve

caramelised figs:

8 figs

2 tbsp raw honey

3 tbsp raw sugar

V

what you do

1. To make the biscotti, preheat the oven to 170°C (150°C fan forced). Line a large baking tray with non-stick baking paper. Whisk the eggs and sugar together until pale and creamy. Fold in the sifted flour, baking powder, and the almonds.

2. Gather the dough together and shape into 2 logs about 20cm long and 10cm wide. Place onto the prepared tray, and bake for 20-25 minutes, until lightly golden and firm to the touch. Transfer to a wire rack to cool completely.

3. Reduce the oven to 140°C (120°C fan forced). Using a bread knife, cut the loaves into 1cm thick slices. Arrange onto 2 baking trays, and bake for 15-20 minutes, until crisp and golden.

4. For the rice pudding, place the milk, cinnamon and vanilla bean into a large saucepan and bring slowly to the boil. Add the rice, quinoa and amaranth, and return to the boil. Reduce the heat to low and simmer for 20 minutes, stirring occasionally, until the rice is soft.

5. Stir in the sugar and cook for another 2 minutes to dissolve. Remove from the heat, transfer to a bowl, and place in the fridge to set for 30 minutes.

6. For the caramelised figs, cut the figs in half and place cut side up onto a foil-lined oven tray. Drizzle the cut surfaces with honey, and sprinkle with sugar. Place under a hot grill for 2 minutes, or until golden.

7. To serve, spoon the rice pudding into serving bowls and top with caramelised figs. Serve with almond biscotti and vanilla ice cream.

Note: For information on spelt flour see page 49, quinoa see page 183 and amaranth see page 192.

Storage: Biscotti will keep for up to one month in an airtight container. Leftover pudding will keep for up to 2 days in the fridge.

my story...the cookbook

It began with building a website and doing the Jane COOKS cooking classes. The blog and monthly e-newsletter 'Cooking from Scratch' followed, then the road trips, market tours and Jane COOKS LIVE. Many people attending both the cooking classes and the Jane COOKS LIVE events began to ask if I had a cookbook containing all my recipes. Of course my response was (with absolutely no idea of the hard work involved) ... *"I do plan to write one soon!"*

Often I hear things coming out of my own mouth and think to myself, I can't believe I just said that! If I hear the same thing come out of my mouth many times, I start to realise it could happen, if I put some action to my words.

After two years of running the cooking classes and about eighteen months of telling people I was going to put together a cookbook, it really was time to make it happen. I have a sign on a wall in our home bearing words which resonate deep within me, reflecting a trait I saw in my parents and have also admired in my husband. It reads... *"Some people want it to happen, some wish it would happen, others make it happen"*.

I started by attending two courses at the Sydney Writer's Centre, one 'How to get published' and the other 'How to self-publish'. I approached two publishers, neither of whom were willing to take me on, and so after talking to a few people who had already done it, I decided to self-publish the cookbook. I realised I needed to set myself a deadline or this dream of writing a cookbook could go on forever. I was attending a business women's group at the time and these ladies helped me to set realistic goals to see the cookbook process begin and end by my deadline. It never ceases to amaze me how when you just take a step to begin something, things begin to happen and beautiful talented people, just the people you need, are there.

I remembered a mum from the preschool my children had attended years before and vaguely recalled she had something to do with cookbooks. Less than a month after I set my deadline and began moving forward, I ran into her at the local shopping centre. We exchanged business cards and that was the beginning of working with recipe editor and food stylist Tracy Rutherford. If there was anything Tracy couldn't do for me, she certainly knew someone who could. My graphic designer Nicky Kukulka, who I had worked with over the previous two years, bravely agreed to take on the role as the book designer. One of the most daunting days for me, along with the day I discussed with Paul if we could actually finance this dream, was when I booked (four months in advance) Nicky to do the design, Tracy to do the recipe editing and food styling and Steve Brown to do the food photography. I was no longer just talking about it, now I was getting professional people involved and making commitments to them. It was no longer a nice idea, it was now a reality, it was now really happening.

It took just short of twelve months to see the cookbook completed and arrive in my hands from the printer. It was a stretching experience, exhausting and exciting all at once. The cookbook really is the culmination of three years of working hard at building the Jane COOKS business. What you hold in your hand is the result of a group of people who are very good at what they do, who worked hard as a team.

And so three and a half years after the words first came out of my mouth, back in May 2009, *"I think I might start a cooking school and teach others my passion to cook and eat well"*, I offer you *Naked Food - the way food was meant to be*. I hope you enjoy it.

top left: Nicky Kukulka, Tracy Rutherford, Steve Brown
top right: Wendy Kendrew, centre right: Rhona Scotter
bottom left to right: Nicky Kukulka, Tracy and Richo Rutherford, Jan Saville

thank you...

This book began as my idea, a piece of my dreams....to choose to self-publish was a huge step of faith, and has only come together because of the team around me who helped to make it happen. Nothing of any worth is ever achieved alone, and doing things with others means you can share the load and also share the reward.

Firstly, I thank my family - my incredible husband Paul and our delightful children Tom, Molly and Jake. I know that the process of 'the book' stretched us for many days, so thanks for persevering and helping me to be able to do this in the midst of our already full lives.

Secondly, without the talent and willingness of the following people (in no particular order!) I would never have made it past the idea stage. My gratitude and appreciation for you all goes beyond words…but you know me, I'll have a shot at expressing myself!

Tracy Rutherford, for your initial guidance in the planning stages which was invaluable to me. For your amazing recipe editing, for your gorgeous food styling and prop organising (without a budget!) and for introducing me to photographer Steve Brown. To you and your husband Richo, for the liberal use of your lovely Ingleside home as the location of the photo shoot. For all the little extra things you both did, custom painting and building backgrounds, sourcing unusual ingredients, lighting fires and pushing through on the days you were feeling poorly!

Steve Brown for your wonderful food photography and for being such a nice guy, along with Tracy you both made my 'naked food' look better than I ever have! Thanks Steve for going the extra mile, driving across town each day for the shoot and willingly offering to take extra shots outside of location for me.

Nicky Kukulka, the bravest graphic designer I know. We both took on this project as rookies - but your creativity and willingness to try something new just about daily has so helped us to pull it off, you inspire me. Thanks for believing in me when it all began over three years ago, and sticking with me as the Jane COOKS journey has progressed. For all your clever design layout ideas and introducing me to your friend Nicky, the beautiful illustrator. For continuing to push for making the book 'tell a story' and eating your 'not so tasty hat' when required! For making me laugh on location, bringing your 'compact' PC to the shoot daily, continually eating my food and acting as my chief wardrobe advisor.

Wendy Kendrew, my faithful friend and kitchen assistant, you are the ultimate in selflessness. You have given way beyond what was reasonable. As you have walked with me over the past three years, your company and hard work has made the Jane COOKS journey do-able and more enjoyable. I do appreciate you, I have said it before and I'll now put it in print…"You make me look good!" Please forgive me if I have included too many photos of you in the book without your permission!

Jan Saville, another gorgeous friend and great cook, for your faithful 'under-cover' recipe testing over the previous year, your kitchen assistance on the photo shoot and your continual ability to rise to any challenge and find a solution.

Rhona Scotter, my wonderful friend and another photo shoot kitchen assistant, you attended every one of my Jane COOKS cooking classes in their inaugural year, what an encouragement that was to me. Obviously I am a great teacher, as you have now graduated to a kitchen assistant… thank you for your joyful approach in everything you do. I love doing life with you, and for reasons known only to us…I dedicate the photo of the radicchio salad recipe to you!

Nicky Hodgson, you are a very talented illustrator. Your amazing drawings are so beautiful and have added another dimension to my cookbook. I am so thrilled you agreed to be involved.

Silvia Noble, my lovely creative friend who allowed me to come and raid her home and barn for all things old and beautiful to feature in the photo shoot. Thanks for cheering me on, as we have dreamed together of doing the things in our hearts, which most days seem beyond natural possibility.

Friends, Ben and Maryline Norsa, and Tracy's neighbours, Rob and Ruth Kennedy for the generous use of your homes for the photo shoot, thank you for sharing. Jane Collins for willingly lending us many props for Tracy to use in the food styling. Penny Dalton, Wendy Brodhurst and Justeen Kinchington for agreeing to proof read the final draft of the cookbook, prior to going to print, your input and attention to detail is appreciated.

Amy Willisee and Katie Rivers for your inspiration and camaraderie, and for willingly answering my questions on self-publishing, after your own experience self-publishing your delightful *Locavore* book.

Kerry Lynch, my neighbour who introduced me to Lettuce Deliver Organics, and inspired me to turn my sunny front yard into a vegie patch of my own. For your constant encouragement and friendship and for generously doing our hair and make up for the final photo shoot day.

Ben and Emma Slade, Bob and Cheryl Stuart and family, and all the team at Lettuce Deliver Organics, who have sponsored Jane COOKS with farm fresh organic produce for the past three years, your generosity and passion for what you do and how you run your business, is reminiscent of the days when a person's word and a hand-shake was enough.

Toni Salter aka 'The Veggie Lady' for doing what you do and answering my continual vegetable garden questions, and for introducing me to the Mosman Mastermind Business Group. These lovely women helped me to set goals and work towards them, keeping me accountable, offering strategy for my challenges and helping me work towards a win.

Dr Phil Pringle and gorgeous Ps Chris Pringle, Ps Greg and Julie French, Ps Mark and Bernie Kelsey, Ps Jeff and Tracey Berry of C3 Church Sydney, thank you for your persistence in thinking bigger, believing the impossible and then putting your faith into action. You have all encouraged, challenged and inspired me to follow my dreams and live my best life. Thank you Everywoman Sydney for constantly believing in me and embracing the Jane COOKS LIVE events.

To all who agreed to contribute delicious feature recipes to this cookbook, Chef Simon Lawson and Lyn Yu from Agape Organic Restaurant and Bar, Dr Robert Warlow and Chef James Liminios from The Peasants Feast Organic Restaurant, Chef Dave Campbell and Nicole Campbell from Hungry Duck Restaurant and Sevtap Yuce from Beachwood Café, thank you for doing what you do and sharing your talent with me.

Many thanks to all the amazing people who agreed to be featured in 'meet the people', who contributed photos and allowed me to visit and see firsthand how passionately they do what they do, so we can enjoy the fruits of your labour.

To my mum Annabell, for always loving and encouraging me, for sending me texts to cheer me on each morning of the photo shoot and for allowing me to cook and print her Christmas cake recipe in the book for all to share.

Ron and Janet Hughes who employed me for many years and trained me to be a chef, you planted in me a level of excellence in my trade and a passion to eat seasonally and to cook from scratch.

Mike Petty from Splitting Image Colour Studio for the colour management of the photos and making it so much easier for Nicky and I to do something for the first time, when we really knew nothing about what we were doing!

Tiffany Johnson from 1010 Printing International for enthusiastically taking on the printing of my project and graciously and patiently leading me through the initial decisions, when I didn't even know 'HB' meant hardback!

To the other contributing photographers Kate Heaslip, Rylstone Olive Press, Toni Salter, Rebekah Brauman, Katie Rivers, Sydney Fish Market, Pasture Perfect Pork, Rosie Francis, Lyn Yu, Stacie La Greca and Barambah Organics.

Finally to my extended family and many friends, I cannot mention you all by name, I know you know who you are, you have believed in me, listened to me, encouraged me, walked with me, prayed for me and remained excited for the long time it has taken to see this book finally land in your hands. Some days your words of hope, faith and love to me were just what got me through to see 'the book' completed...thank you.

where to shop and eat local sydney

About Life
31-37 Oxford Street, Bondi Junction
t 61 2 9389 7611

605 Darling Street, Rozelle
t 61 2 8755 1333

Agape Organic Restaurant and Bar
1385 Botany Road, Botany
t 61 2 8668 5777

Always Organics
682 Pittwater Road, Brookvale
t 61 2 9939 1913

Armchair Collective
9A Darley Street East, Mona Vale
t 61 2 9999 2871

Avalon Organics
25 Avalon Parade, Avalon
t 61 2 9918 3387

Billy Kwong
Shop 3/355 Crown Street,
Surry Hills
t 61 2 9332 3300

Brasserie Bread
1737 Botany Road, Banksmeadow
t 1300 966 845

Claudio's Quality Seafood
Sydney Fish Market
Bank Street, Pyrmont
t 61 2 9660 5188

**Cleaver's The Organic
Meat Company**
Shop 6/The Grove
174-176 Military Road, Neutral Bay
t 61 2 8969 6982

Dare Food
Shop 25/Stockland Balgowlah
cnr of Sydney Road and
Condamine Street, Balgowlah
t 61 2 9949 4436

Earth Food Store
81A Gould Street, Bondi
t 61 2 9365 5098

Fatima's Lebanese Restaurant
294-296 Cleveland Street,
Surry Hills
t 61 2 9698 4895

**Fish & Co The Sustainable
Seafood Café**
41 Booth Street, Annandale
t 61 2 9660 5575

Granny Smith Natural Food Market
6 Princes Street, Turramurra
t 61 2 9988 3787

7th Heaven Wholefoods
122 Belmore Road,
Randwick
t 61 2 9326 5006

Honest to Goodness
Unit 5, 6-8 George Place, Artarmon
t 61 2 9420 3761

Iku Wholefoods
Shop 2/The Grove (rear)
168 Military Road, Neutral Bay
t 61 2 9953 1964

Lakeside Fish Market
1485 Pittwater Road,
North Narrabeen
t 61 2 9913 8318

Lettuce Deliver Organics
Unit 8/177 Arthur Street,
Homebush
t 61 2 9763 7337

Livoti's Deli Café
Shop 7/13-15 Francis Street,
Dee Why
t 61 2 9981 3550

Love.fish
580 Darling Street, Rozelle
t 61 2 9818 7777

Mezza Grill Lebanese Restaurant
1767 Pittwater Road, Mona Vale
t 61 2 9997 6588

Naturally Organic Meat and Poultry
Big Bear Shopping Centre
Shop 14 /116 Military Road,
Neutral Bay
t 61 2 9904 3333

Nourish
17 Avalon Parade, Avalon
t 61 2 9973 3233

Organic Avenues Market Place
2/1 Bilambee Avenue, Bilgola
t 61 2 8919 0279

Organicus Kitchen and Pantry
Shop B/2-8 Darley Road, Manly
t 61 2 9977 0201

Pure Wholefoods
Shop 5/10 Darley Road, Manly
t 61 2 8966 9377

Red Lantern
545 Crown Street, Surry Hills
t 61 2 9698 4355

Sam the Butcher
129 Bondi Road, Bondi
t 61 2 9389 1420

Taste Organics
25 Falcon Street, Crows Nest
t 61 2 9437 5933

The Boathouse Palm Beach
Barrenjoey Boathouse,
Governor Phillip Park,
Palm Beach
t 61 2 9974 3868

The Cooks Larder
Shop 1/21-23 Old Barrenjoey Road,
Avalon
t 61 2 9973 4370

The Organic Food Network
14-16/84 Old Pittwater Road,
Brookvale
t 61 2 9938 2364

The Organic Food Co
15 Robertson Road, Newport
t 61 2 9997 3530

**The Peasants Feast
Organic Restaurant**
121A King Street, Newtown
t 61 2 9516 5998

TJ's Quality Meats
319 Darling Street, Balmain
t 61 2 9810 2911

Tokyo Mart
Shop 27/Northbridge Plaza
79-113 Sailors Bay Road,
Northbridge
t 61 2 9958 6860

Warriewood Health Shop
Shop 5/Centro Warriewood
12 Jacksons Rd, Warriewood
t 61 2 9913 1505

Wholefoods House
3/9 Danks Street, Waterloo
t 61 2 9319 4459

109 Queen Street, Woollahra
t 61 2 9363 9879

where to shop and eat out of town

Bakehouse on Wentworth
105 Wentworth Street,
Blackheath NSW 2785
t 61 2 4787 6744

208 The Mall,
Leura NSW 2780
t 61 2 4784 3588

Beachwood Café
22 High Street,
Yamba NSW 2464
t 61 2 6646 9781

**Berry Woodfired Sourdough
Bakery and Café**
23 Prince Alfred Street,
Berry NSW 2535
t 61 2 4464 1617

Blue Mountains Food Co-Op Shop
1&2 Jones House, Ha'penny Lane
(under Post Office),
Katoomba NSW 2780
t 61 2 4782 5890

**Common Ground Bakery
and Café**
1580 Remembrance Drive,
(Old Hume Hwy),
Picton NSW 2571
t 61 2 4677 0633

Contadino - The Olive Farm
1106 Princes Highway
(cnr Peterson Road),
Falls Creek NSW 2540
t 61 2 4447 8791

Cullen Wines
4323 Caves Road,
Wilyabrup WA 6280
t 61 8 9755 5277

Flour Water Salt Bakery Café
374 Bong Bong Street,
Bowral NSW 2576
t 61 2 4861 7900

Hominy Bakery
185 Katoomba Street,
Katoomba NSW 2780
t 61 2 4782 9816

Kombi Café
226 Naturaliste Terrace,
Dunsborough WA 6281
t 61 8 9779 9977

La Tartine Organic Bakery
2/111 Wisemans Ferry Road,
Somersby NSW 2250
t 61 2 4340 0299

Lyrebird Ridge Organic Winery
270 Bugong Road, Budgong
NSW 2540
t 61 2 4446 0648

Manfredi at Bells
107 The Scenic Road,
Killcare Heights NSW 2257
t 61 2 4349 7000

Merry Maiden's Veggies
Shop 9/65 Princes Highway,
Milton NSW 2538
t 61 2 4454 0142
t 0423 207 219

North Street Café and Bar
5 North Street,
Batemans Bay NSW 2536
t 61 2 4472 5710

Organic Plus
1 Bonnal Road,
Erina NSW 2250
t 61 2 4365 0978

Pilgrim's Wholefoods
Shop 8 & 9/The Settlement,
Princes Highway,
Milton NSW 2538
t 61 2 4455 3421

**Raw and Wild Market
and Café**
250a Bong Bong Street,
Bowral NSW 2576
t 61 2 4861 2838

Rosnay Wines and Olives
444 Rivers Road,
Canowindra NSW 2804
t 1300 767 629

South Coast Providores
89 Queen Street,
Berry NSW 2535
t 0418 223 464

**The Blue Swimmer
at Seahaven**
19 Riverleigh Avenue,
Gerroa NSW 2534
t 61 2 4234 3796

The Bogbean Health Food Store
122 Wentworth Street,
Blackheath NSW 2785
t 61 2 4787 5777

The Hungry Duck Restaurant
85 Queen Street,
Berry NSW 2535
t 61 2 4464 2323

The Organic Wholefood Store
9/47 Bowral Street,
Bowral NSW 2576
t 61 2 4861 1322

The Robertson Cheese Store
107 Illawarra Highway,
Robertson NSW 2577
t 61 2 4885 1133

Thistle Hill Wines
74 McDonalds Road,
Mudgee NSW 2850
t 61 2 6373 3546

**Wharf Rd Restaurant
and Bar**
10 Wharf Road, Nowra
NSW 2541
t 61 2 4422 6651

**Wholly Smoked
Organic
Butchery Shop**
7/130 Jonson Street,
Bryon Bay NSW 2481
t 61 2 6685 6261

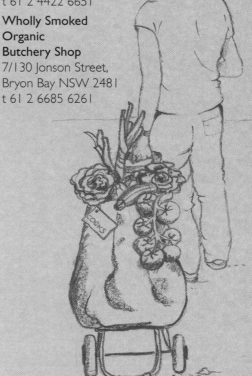

local markets sydney

Avalon Village Growers' Market
Dunbar Park, Old Barrenjoey Road,
Avalon
t 0415 753 773
Last Friday of the month
9am – 2pm

**Bondi Junction Organic Food and
Farmers' Market**
Oxford Street Mall, Bondi Junction
t 61 2 9999 2226
Thursdays and Fridays 9am – 5pm

**Chatswood Organic Food and
Farmers' Market**
Chatswood Public School, cnr of
Pacific Highway and Centennial
Avenue, Chatswood
t 61 2 9999 2226
Saturday 8.30am – 1pm

Eveleigh Farmers' Market
243 Wilson St, Darlington
(Adjacent to Carriageworks)
t 61 2 9209 4220
Saturday 8am – 1pm

**Frenchs Forest Organic
Food and Farmers' Market**
Parkway Hotel,
35 Frenchs Forest Road East,
Frenchs Forest
t 61 2 9999 2226
Sunday 8am – 1pm

**Sydney Morning Herald
Growers' Market**
Pyrmont Bay Park,
Pirrama Road, Pyrmont
t 61 2 9282 3518
1st Saturday of the month
7am – 11am

Sydney Sustainable Markets
Farmers' Market at Taylor Square,
Bourke and Flinders Street,
Darlinghurst
t 0416 525 244
t 0412 214 844
Saturday 8am - 1pm

**Hornsby Organic Food and
Farmers' Market**
Hornsby Mall,
cnr Florence Street and
Hunter Street, Hornsby
t 61 2 9999 2226
Thursday 8am – 4pm

Leichhardt Organic Market
Orange Grove Public School, cnr
of Perry Street and Balmain Road,
Leichhardt
t 61 2 9999 2226
Saturday 8am – 1pm

North Side Produce Market
cnr McLaren Street and Miller
Street, North Sydney
t 61 2 9922 2299
3rd Saturday of the month
8am – 12 noon

Manly Farmers' Market
Central Avenue Intersection,
Sydney Road, Manly
t 61 2 9977 4969
Saturday 10am – 5pm

Marrickville Organic Market
Addison Road Community Centre,
142 Addison Road, Marrickville
t 61 2 9999 2226
Sunday 8.30am – 3pm

The Beaches Market
Pittwater Rugby Park,
1472 Pittwater Road, Warriewood
t 0414 809 916
t 0477 223 655
Friday 8am - 2pm

regional markets nsw

Avoca Growers' Market
Hunters Park, cnr Avoca Drive
and Vale Street, Avoca
t 0415 863 398
1st Sunday of the month
8am – 12noon

Bangalow Farmers' Market
Bangalow Hotel Carpark,
1 Byron Street, Bangalow
t 61 2 6687 1137
Saturday 8am – 11am

Bathurst Region Farmers' Market
Bathurst Showgrounds,
Durham Street, Bathurst
t 0420 669 701
4th Saturday of the month
8am – 12 noon

Bellingen Growers' Market
Bellingen Showground,
Black Street, Bellingen
t 61 2 6655 1279
2nd and 4th Sunday of the month
8am – 1pm

Blackheath Growers' Market
Blackheath Community Centre,
cnr Great Western Highway and
Gardiner Crescent, Blackheath
t 61 2 4572 6260
2nd Sunday of the month
8am – 12noon

Bowral Public School Market
Bendooley Street, Bowral
t 0428 771 179
2nd Saturday of the month
8am – 1pm

Byron Farmers' Market
Butler Street Reserve, Byron Bay
t 61 2 6687 1137
Thursday 7am – 11am
Bangalow Hotel, Byron Street
(behind the Bangalow Hotel)
Saturday 7am – 11am

Coffs Coast Growers' Market
City Square, Coffs Harbour Drive,
Coffs Harbour
t 61 2 6648 4084
Thursday 8am – 4pm

Hawkesbury Harvest Farmers and Fine Food Markets
t: 0406 237 877

Castle Hill Showground
Doran Drive,
Harvey Lowe Pavillion, Castle Hill
2nd Saturday of the month
8am – 12noon

Outside Penrith Plaza near library,
High Street, Penrith
Saturday 8am – 1pm

Richmond School of the Arts
cnr West Market and March Streets,
Richmond
2nd Saturday of the month
8am – 12noon

Kiama Produce Markets
Black Beach, Shoalhaven Street,
Kiama
t 61 2 4232 0464
4th Saturday of the month
8am – 1pm

Kingscliff Farmers and Friends Market
On the beachfront, Marine Parade,
Kingscliff
t 0406 724 323
2nd and 4th Saturday of the month
7am – 1pm

Lismore Farmers' Market
Lismore Showground,
Alexandria Parade, Lismore
t 0418 622 336
Saturday 8am – 11am

Mudgee's Farmers' Market
St Mary's Church grounds,
cnr Market & Church Streets,
Mudgee
t 61 2 6372 6594
3rd Saturday of the month
8.30am – 12.30pm

Orange Region Farmers' Market
Orange Showground,
Leeds Parade, (May – Oct)
or
Orange Regional Gallery, cnr Byng
and Peisley Streets, (Nov – April)
Orange
t 0425 259 350
2nd Saturday of the month
8.30am – 12noon

Rainbow Region Organic Market
Lismore Showground
Alexandra Parade, Lismore
t: 61 2 6628 1084
Tuesday 7.30am – 11am

Wagga Wagga Farmers' Market
Civic Centre Gardens, Tarcutta
Street, Wagga Wagga
t 61 2 6922 9221
2nd Saturday of the month
8am – 1pm

favourite books...

The Cook's Companion by Stephanie Alexander (Viking Penguin Books Australia Ltd, 1996)

The Return of the Naked Chef by Jamie Oliver (Michael Joseph Ltd / Penguin Books Australia Ltd, 2000)

Jamie's America by Jamie Oliver (Michael Joseph Ltd / Penguin Books England Ltd, 2009)

Jamie Does...Spain, Italy, Sweden, Morocco, Greece, France: Easy twists on dishes inspired by my travels
(Michael Joseph Ltd / Penguin Books England Ltd, 2010)

Jamie's 30 Minute Meals: A Revolutionary Approach to Cooking Food Fast
(Michael Joseph Ltd / Penguin Books England Ltd, 2010)

Bills Food by Bill Granger (Murdoch Books Australia, 2002)

Bills Open Kitchen by Bill Granger (Murdoch Books Australia, 2003)

The Miracle of Fasting: Proven Throughout History For Physical, Mental and Spiritual Rejuvenation
by Patricia Bragg and Paul C Bragg (Health Science, USA)

Changing Habits Changing Lives by Cyndi O' Meara (Penguin Group (Australia), 2007)

In the Defence of Food: The Myth of Nutrition and the Pleasure of Eating by Michael Pollan
(Penguin Group (USA), 2009)

The Omnivores Dilema: The Search for a Perfect Meal in a Fast-Food World by Michael Pollan
(Bloomsbury, 2006)

Food Rules: An Eaters Manual by Michael Pollan (Penguin Group (USA), 2009)

Gwinganna...from Garden to Gourmet: Organic Recipes for life from Gwinganna Lifestyle Retreat
(Gwinganna Lifestyle Retreat, 2007)

It Tastes Better by Kylie Kwong (Penguin Lantern, 2010)

Locavore: A Foodies Journey through the Shoalhaven by Amy Willesee and Katie Rivers
(Katie Rivers and Amy Willesee, 2010)

Italian Food Safari: A Delicious Celebration of the Italian Kitchen by Maeve O'Meara with Guy Grossi
(An SBS Book / Hardie Grant Books, 2010)

Green Food Generation: a Culinary Adventure by Hayden Wood (Drink Australia Pty Ltd, 2010)

The Urban Cook: Cooking and Eating for a Sustainable Future by Mark Jensen (Murdoch Books Pty Ltd, 2011)

Turkish Flavours: Recipes from a Seaside Café by Sevtap Yuce (Hardie Grant Books, 2012)

Explore Australia's Coast by Margaret Barca and Ingrid Ohlsson
(Explore Australia Publishing Pty Ltd in association with Australian Geographic Pty Ltd, 2004)

Explore Australia's Outback by Margaret Barca and Ingrid Ohlsson
(Explore Australia Publishing Pty Ltd in association with Australian Geographic Pty Ltd, 2005)

Great Gourmet Weekends in Australia by Sally Hammond (NSW), Tricia Welsh (VIC), Quentin Chester (SA),
Carmen Jenner (WA), Liz Johnston (QLD), Sue Medlock (TAS) (Explore Australia Publishing Pty Ltd / Hardie
Grant Publishing Pty Ltd, 2010)

The Foodies Guide to Sydney by Elizabeth Meryment and Kate Gibbs (Hardie Grant Books, 2011)

The Sydney Morning Herald Good Food Guide by Terry Durack and Joanna Savill
(Penguin Group (Australia) 2010)

Organic: Don Burke's Guide to Growing Organic Food by Don Burke (Reed New Holland, 2009)

index

Jane Grover is passionate about food and cooking it well, using wholefoods, locally grown, in season and where possible organic and biodynamic produce.

Jane is a qualified chef, she runs Jane COOKS Cooking Classes, Jane COOKS LIVE Cooking Shows and Fresh Produce Market Tours.

Jane lives happily on the Northern Beaches of Sydney, with her husband Paul and their three teenage children Tom, Molly and Jake.

Naked Food the way food was meant to be is her first cookbook.

www.janecooks.com.au
http://janecookslive.blogspot.com.au/

Aussie Helpers Ltd is a non-profit registered charity that has been operating since 21 May 2002, to help fight poverty in the Australian bush. Started and run by Brian and Nerida Egan, who themselves lost their own farm in the 1990's, due to a combination of drought and Brian's own personal depression. The charity is operated by some forty volunteers working to help farmers in Queensland, NSW, Victoria, South Australia and have also assisted farmers in Tasmania and Western Australia. They have created a charitable association that is strongly supported by local communities, many of whom have donated and supplied goods and services, to enable Aussie Helpers to achieve its goal of "helping to fight poverty in the bush". The assistance they offer includes, counselling, visits, excursions, human food, toiletries, stock feed and work with unwanted homeless people and elderly people in the country areas. Their work builds and strengthens the families in the bush and the farming communities.
A percentage of all the profits of this book will be donated to Aussie Helpers.
To learn more go to www.aussiehelpers.org.au or call 1300 665 332
Registered Charity: CH-1376

AUSSIE HELPERS LTD

First published in 2012 by Jane Cooks Pty Ltd

PO Box 595, Narrabeen NSW 2101, Australia
jane@janecooks.com.au
www.janecooks.com.au

Written by Jane Grover
Design by Nicky Kukulka © Kukulka Design
Photography by Steve Brown
Recipe editing and food styling by Tracy Rutherford
Illustrations by Nicky Hodgson

Additional Photography:
Kate Heaslip: p46 MTP The 1910 Bottling Co (full page, top left, bottom left)
Rylstone Olive Press: p93,94 MTP Rylstone Olive Press (all images)
Toni Salter: p101 My Story (top left), Rebekah Brauman p101 My Story (bottom left)
Katie Rivers Photography: p119 Feature Recipe Hungry Duck (bottom centre)
Sydney Fish Market: p121,122 MTP Sydney Fish Market (all images)
Pasture Perfect Pork: p141,142 MTP Pasture Perfect Pork (all images)
Rosie Francis: p175,176 MTP Moorlands Lamb (all images),
Lyn Yu: p191 Feature Recipe Agape Organic Restaurant and Bar (bottom centre, bottom right)
Stacie La Greca of Stacie_petraphotography: p195 My Story (top left, top right, centre right, bottom left)
Barambah Organics: p207,208 MTP Barambah Organics (all images)
Jane Grover: p12 My Story (b&w images), p33,34 MTP Lettuce Deliver (full page, top left, bottom left),
p35 My Story (top right, centre left, bottom left), p46 MTP The 1910 Bottling Co (centre left)
p56 MTP La Tartine (top left, centre left), p67 Feature Recipe Beachwood Café (bottom left, bottom right),
p72 My Story (top left, top right, centre left, centre right, bottom left, bottom right),
p73 MTP Eveleigh Farmers' Market (full page), p83,84 MTP Kurrawong Organics (top left, bottom left, bottom centre),
p101 My Story (top centre, top right, centre left, centre right, bottom centre, bottom right),
p119 Feature Recipe Hungry Duck (bottom right),
p124 My Story (top left, top centre, centre right, bottom left, bottom centre),
p125 Chapter Opener Fast Food (full page), p195 My Story (bottom right)
p227 Photo Collage (centre, bottom centre) p228 Photo Collage (top left, centre left, bottom left)

Colour Reproduction by Splitting Image Colour Studio Pty Ltd, Clayton, Victoria
Printed and bound in China by 1010 Printing International Limited.

National Library of Australia
Cataloguing-in-Publication entry

Author: Grover, Jane

Title: Naked Food: the way food was meant to be / Jane Grover
with photography by Steve Brown.

Edition: 1st ed.

ISBN: 9780646575766 (hbk.)

Notes: Includes index

Subjects: Nutrition
Natural foods
Cooking (Natural foods)

Other Authors/Contributors: Brown, Steve

Dewey Number: 641.563

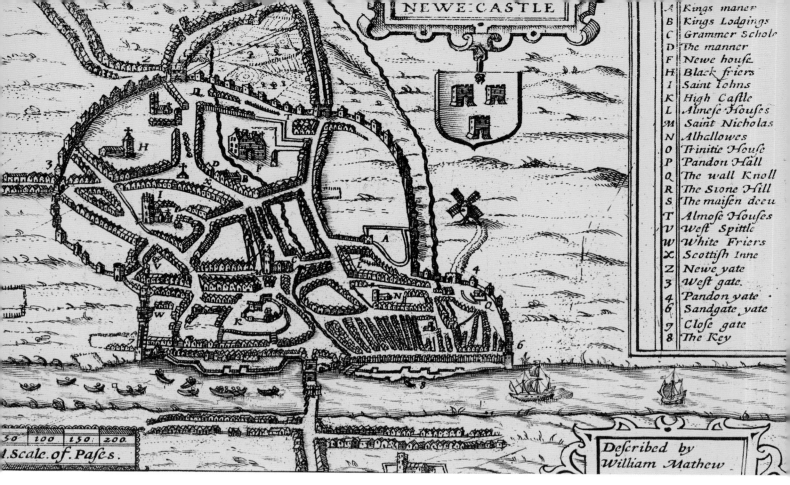

NEWE-CASTLE

A	Kings maner
B	Kings Lodgings
C	Grammer Schole
D	The manner
F	Newe house
H	Black friers
I	Saint Iohns
K	High Castle
L	Almese Houses
M	Saint Nicholas
N	Alhallowes
O	Trinitie House
P	Pandon Hall
Q	The wall Knoll
R	The Stone Hill
S	The maisen deeu
T	Almose Houses
V	West Spittle
W	White Friers
X	Scottish Inne
Z	Newe yate
3	West gate
4	Pandon yate
6	Sandgate yate
7	Close gate
8	The Key

Scale of Paces.

Described by William Mathew

▶ Timeline

AD C122	The Romans establish Pons Aelius (a fort and bridge) on the banks of the Tyne – creating a fortress that would later become Newcastle
AD 122–126	Hadrian's Wall is built
AD 410	The Romans leave Britain
1080	A 'new castle' is built on the site of the Roman Fort by Robert Curthose, who is the son of William the Conqueror. It is from this castle that the city takes its name
1139–1157	The town falls into Scottish hands
1172	The city's castle is rebuilt in stone
1248	The old Tyne Bridge is destroyed in a fire

1265

A tax is levied to start building the town walls

1539

Under the reign of Henry VIII the town's five friaries and other religious institutions are closed as the King severs links with the church in Rome

1646

Charles I is held as a prisoner in Newcastle during the English Civil War. Despite this, the town's leaders were sympathetic to the Royalist cause

1649

Gray's *Chorographia* is published

1650

It is recorded that 14 witches were executed in Newcastle

1741

Thomlinson library first opened to the public

1771

On 17 November the Great Flood destroys the medieval bridge over the Tyne

1772

John Scott, later Lord Eldon and Lord Chancellor of England, elopes with Elizabeth 'Bessie' Surtees, daughter of an influential town banker. She escapes from the first floor window of her father's house with the help of a ladder, provided by John. The pair marry in Scotland

1797

Local artist Thomas Bewick publishes the first volume of his acclaimed *History of British Birds*

1823

World's first purpose built locomotive manufacturing works established by George and Robert Stephenson in Newcastle

1835–1839

Modern Newcastle begins to take shape as the city centre is re-vamped in the Classical style by builder Richard Grainger and architect John Dobson

1838

Grey's Monument is erected in honour of the Northumberland-born Charles, Earl Grey who became Prime Minister in 1830 and in 1832 steered through the Great Reform Bill

1847

William George Armstrong sets up W.G. Armstrong and Co

1853

A severe outbreak of cholera kills around 1,500 in the city

1854

The Great Fire of Newcastle. Started in Gateshead, the blaze spread across the river killing at least 50 people and destroying much of the city's quayside

1862

Tyneside anthem 'The Blaydon Races' is first sung by entertainer Geordie Ridley in Balmbra Music Hall. It celebrates a horse racing meeting held on an island in the middle of the Tyne

1876

Armstrong's Swing Bridge completed and opened

1880

At the same time as Thomas Edison is inventing the light bulb, Joseph Swan demonstrates his incandescent electric light bulb at the Newcastle Literary and Philosophical Society. The pair eventually team up to form The Edison & Swan United Electric Company

1882

Newcastle officially becomes a city and St Nicholas' church becomes its Cathedral

1884

The first steam turbine is patented on Tyneside by Charles Parsons

1928

The Tyne Bridge is opened by King George V

1929

North East Coast Exhibition held in Newcastle. This was the largest single public event in the history of the city, attracting over four million visitors

1941

Newcastle suffers air raids during the Second World War. On 1 September 100 bombs fall on Newcastle and its suburbs, killing 50 people and injuring around 200

1955

Newcastle United wins the FA cup. It was to be their last major domestic title of the century

1980

The city's Metro service begins

2000

The NewcastleGateshead Initiative is created to promote the city and its regenerated quayside. During the previous decade, the city's waterfront witnessed dramatic changes as investment poured into the area. The resulting prosperity attracted more businesses, bars, restaurants and arts projects to the area, helping to turn Newcastle into a tourist destination and cultural centre

Chapter 1 ⊙ Twin Cities Rich in History

left: view of conurbation
from Kibblesworth
right: all the bridges across
the Tyne
photography by Sally Ann Norman

The great thing is that river and that gorge, that one visual sweep – a more dramatic entrance than any [other] English city ... and below you see something in time, layers of history. Very few cities have that dramatic approach Sir Terry Farrell[1]

Both first-time traveller to Tyneside and returning native become momentarily speechless, awestruck, by the magnificence of the entry to Newcastle and Gateshead, high above a Tyne transformed from industrial sewer to the finest salmon river in England. The variety of buildings below – old and new, Modernist and sometimes brash – adds to the excitement: the cluster of medieval structures near Newcastle Quayside mingling with sturdy 19th-century offices, functional yet bland 1990s buildings and more recent adventurous developments. They range from Norman Foster's undulating stainless-steel and glass Sage Gateshead concert hall and music centre, opposite the Newcastle Quayside in Gateshead, to the post-Art Deco solidity of the BALTIC Centre for Contemporary Art, alongside and the sheer variety, splendour and – yes – engineering genius of seven bridges close together. Breathtaking!

Capturing that emotional attachment to the river gorge, deep in the psyche of people the country has come to know as 'Geordies', the late playwright, poet and novelist Julia Darling vividly remembered that arriving in Newcastle and Gateshead for the first time in the late 1970s was 'like falling in love'.[2]

Along with many others, she found the grandeur overpowering: 'It was an overwhelming place with its soaring bridges, and train lines that run through ancient castles – the new and the old entangled with one another. The moment I got there I knew I would never leave ...'.

Can any city – heck, let's label them 'twin cities' and be done with it! – evoke such passion, nostalgia, a sense of belonging and pride, with a history stretching back 2,000 years? Whether arriving by rail or by road from the south – the warm embrace of Antony Gormley's towering, steel *Angel of the North* sculpture, on Gateshead's southern edge, initially lifts the spirits – crossing the Tyne gorge a few minutes later is an exhilarating experience. It might be over the iconic Tyne Bridge, opened in 1928; the top-rail deck of Robert Stephenson's ingenious High Level Bridge, 160 years old and still going strong; the more functional King Edward VII rail bridge (1906); or strolling, perhaps cycling, over the graceful, arching and tilting Gateshead Millennium Bridge (2001), linking the reborn south bank, rebranded 'Gateshead Quays', with a redeveloped Newcastle Quayside. Whichever way, the crossing is an unforgettable experience. Julia Darling had one priceless anecdote about that gorge. 'Once, on a crowded train, a teenage girl shouted "everyone lift your feet and have a wish" – and we did!', she enthused.

The setting of Newcastle and Gateshead, then, is not only world class; it is also one of the great crossroads of Britain, where the principal north–south route along the coastal plain meets the east–west corridor formed by the Tyne and the Solway. The origins of Newcastle and Gateshead lie in these cross-river urban twins – now strong partners culturally and, increasingly, economically

on colliery wagon-ways, presented Newcastle
and Gateshead with the greatest challenges and
opportunities: a locomotive works, opened by George
Stephenson and his son Robert in 1823 at South
Street, Newcastle – just behind the subsequent
central railway station – had already become a
world first in manufacturing. Finally abandoned at
the beginning of the 20th century, the building –
an industrial gem – remains partly intact as a fine
exhibition space, with the original cast-iron columns

supporting heavy timber trusses.

Aside from locomotive manufacturing, the
Stephensons were a considerable engineering force.
For years, various schemes had been proposed for
a rail crossing over the Tyne gorge to complete a
continuous rail route to Scotland, and – it must
be said – to sideline Gateshead, which, through
necessity, had become a railway terminus. Up to
this point, the challenge of a high-level crossing of
the Tyne capable of accommodating a railway had

above: Newcastle's Central Station
photograph by Sally Ann Norman

appeared daunting even to the most adventurous – but not to the Stephensons.

Enter Robert Stephenson. His eventual plan for a twin-decked, iron bridge – rail on the top, horse-drawn carriages (subsequently motor traffic) and pedestrians below – undoubtedly constituted one of the 19th century's greatest engineering achievements. Built on three piers, with foundations driven into the river bed by newly patented steam hammers, the bridge, still fully functional today after recent restoration, was remarkable in scale: 230 m across the river, and 40 m above it at low tide. Not for nothing did George Hanks, the Mayor of Gateshead, whose firm had undertaken the ironwork contract, praise what he termed the 'labours of the skilful and industrious workmen by whom I am surrounded'.

However, the High Level Bridge, opened in 1849, was but one part of a wider plan; in turn, it would take Anglo-Scottish rail traffic into a new central station, designed by John Dobson as another equally ambitious project and still one of the crowning architectural glories of Newcastle. Opened by Queen Victoria and Prince Albert in 1850, its incorporation of glass and iron roof ribs over a sweeping curve along its entire length, and its towering, Classical entrance portico, still represent a masterpiece of engineering

and design. Today, it seems inconceivable that anyone would want to threaten this, one of Europe's finest 'cathedral stations' – yet in the late 1960s British Rail, fresh from demolishing the Euston Arch in 1962, was preparing to flatten the structure for a more modern transport 'hub'. The city council partly concurred, with the proviso that the portico remained! Thankfully common sense eventually prevailed.

Not surprisingly, with fine designs matching world-beating engineering skills, Newcastle and Gateshead were both being celebrated nationally as industrial pace-setters, taking Britain into a new age of manufacturing. William Gladstone, then Chancellor of the Exchequer, was clearly impressed on a visit in 1862: 'I know not where to seek ... so extraordinary and multifarious a combination of the various great branches of mining, manufacturing, trade and shipbuilding and I greatly doubt whether the like can be shown upon the whole surface of the globe.'

This was no hyperbole. Sir Ambrose Crowley's ironworks at Winlaton and Swalwell in Gateshead became one of the largest 'manufactories' in Europe in the early 18th century, while across the river a century later George Stephenson, and son Robert, built the world's first steam engines, including the

famous *Rocket*; Charles Parsons invented the first steam turbine, buying his patents back from his former employers, Clarke Chapman, of Gateshead, before founding C. A. Parsons at Heaton, Newcastle, in 1889 – and creating the Newcastle and District Electric Lighting Company in the same year; and Joseph Swan, who lived at Low Fell in Gateshead, first demonstrated his world-beating electric lamp at Newcastle's Literary and Philosophical Society around the same time.

Founded in 1793, the still-functioning 'Lit and Phil' – the largest private library outside London – represented in the breadth of its membership a remarkable fusion of engineering and invention with the arts and architecture. It certainly played its part in the transformation of Newcastle from medieval town into England's most ambitious urban centre – boasting offices, shops, housing, warehouses, major public buildings and almost a hectare of covered market – with the help of John Dobson and his remarkable partnership with Richard Grainger (both key 'Lit and Phil' members) and an equally entrepreneurial town clerk, John Clayton. This was truly 'comprehensive, mixed-use redevelopment' on a grander scale than anywhere else, well before the term became common planning currency.

Grainger, builder-cum-developer and ultimate risk taker, 'changed the appearance, nature, the commercial heart and the external perception of Newcastle ... he gave a nucleus to the developing conurbation from which a great Victorian city grew'.[11] His vision was probably bolder than that of city council leader T. Dan Smith – renowned, or notorious, depending on your point of view – and his planning supremo, Wilfred Burns, 130 years later. But there was one difference: Grainger, unlike Smith, stayed the course, although his financial 'engineering' and questionable links with the ambitious John Clayton might have raised eyebrows today!

Unencumbered by a seemingly inflexible planning system which was to emerge a century later, Grainger, joiner's apprentice turned influential builder and property developer, saw through his plans with breathtaking speed, employing a workforce of 2,000 in construction alone. Not long after the city's common council approved his ambitious scheme, the first buildings were completed by February 1835. Inspired by Edinburgh's New Town, as well as earlier 19th-century 'metropolitan improvements' in London undertaken by John Nash, Grainger and his team of architects created grand, Classical stone frontages. First came Eldon Square, designed by John Dobson

previous page: view from Grey's Monument
below: Grey's Monument from Blackett Street
right: Grey's Monument
photography by Sally Ann Norman

many years, all honeyed sandstone with a century and more of grime removed, it has effectively gone 'back to the future' by re-embracing Grainger's initial concept of a mix of prestigious shops, offices and housing. For many it remains the pinnacle of Newcastle architecture – curving gently southwards towards the river from Grey's monument, with fine views of Gateshead beyond – but it should be so much better. Lauded more recently by the government's Commission for Architecture and the Built Environment (CABE) as the finest thoroughfare in the country, Grey Street – sadly – has surrendered to the motor car. It is littered with parking bays, often choked with traffic.

Overall, however, the grandeur of this part of central Newcastle cannot be contested, in this country at least. As the historian Judge Lyall Wilkes noted in the 1960s, Grainger's unique planning and developments, and his partnerships with town clerk Clayton, made Newcastle 'the first city [in Britain] with an elegantly planned commercial centre ... in scale and beauty it has never been equalled in this country'.

Aside from a string of planning blunders in the 1960s – and they reached a nadir when two-thirds of Eldon Square was demolished – it is remarkable how enduring the Grainger-Clayton city centre has proved. Events, however, could easily have taken a different course: from the 1960s to the 1990s, much of the area was fast deteriorating as the city council pushed through plans for a brasher shopping complex, taking the misguided view – in the words of one official at the time – that 'the older areas can look after themselves'. They clearly could not: much of Grainger's city centre was falling into disrepair. Limited demolition, and redevelopment, seemed a strong possibility.

Thankfully, by early 1997 a more pragmatic Labour city council persuaded a Conservative government to intervene, with a new state-sponsored regeneration agency known as English Partnerships (EP). The 'Grainger Town' Initiative was born in honour of the master developer and speculator. This saw EP investing £40 million of government money in order to 'lever' a further £160 million from the private sector. The impact was fairly immediate: over 120 buildings were brought back into use, creating (on some estimates) 286 new businesses.

In British terms, this project proved to be an exemplar; truly, regeneration on a scale rarely seen in other cities. As we shall discover

and Thomas Oliver, of which only the east side now remains, the central and western portions having fallen victim to an incongruous but successful 1970s shopping centre (ironically labelled 'Eldon Square'!). This was followed by Leazes Crescent and Leazes Terrace; then the Royal Arcade in Pilgrim Street, also subsequently demolished (in 1963), this time to make way for an urban motorway and an office block, Swan House. A new covered market became the biggest and best in Britain, lit by gaslight with 14 entrances and 243 shops; still thriving today, Grainger Market remains an architectural and engineering masterpiece.

Ever keen to press forward in the shortest possible time, Grainger raised the money to buy a large open space within the old city walls, the site of a former convent and friary, in order to complete his planned 'new town within a town' – in the process, as author and local historian Ian Ayris points out, delivering 'the foremost architecturally designed and planned developments of the day'.[12] The city soon had a new centre: 'Seven Dials Circus', now familiar as the Monument, with a 41 m-high Roman Doric column topped by a 4 m-tall statue of Earl Grey (of Howick Hall, Northumberland), who was instrumental in pushing through the Great Reform Act in 1832. Below the circus, the gentle sweep of what Nikolaus Pevsner labelled 'one of the best streets in England' unfurled.

From its outset, Grey Street set new standards in urban elegance. Now looking fresher than it has for

much of the city centre, cheek by jowl with 19th-century Neoclassicism and medieval Newcastle – mixing old and new, harsh concrete with honeyed sandstone – was not to everyone's taste.

This emerging urban hybrid was hailed by some as a 'Brasilia of the North', although the description, suggestive of tearing down everything and building anew, was to prove a rather inappropriate and clumsy comparison with Oscar Niemeyer's new capital of Brazil, begun from scratch in open country.

Smith, 'one of the most provocative figures to grace English local government',[6] ran a painting-and-decorating concern and other businesses. While firmly rooted on the Left, he had a taste for the good life. Full of contradictions, he owned a Jaguar limousine with a personalised number plate. He went to Europe for the best architects, boasting that he held talks with, among others, Le Corbusier and Arne Jacobsen (who designed an ill-fated hotel for Eldon Square): 'two of the best architects in the world ... I had the capacity to attract and organise people'.[7]

In a remarkable series of previously unscreened interviews, undertaken by Newcastle's Amber Films,

Smith insisted his main concern was providing better housing – and not just by building new homes. He wanted to renovate older property throughout the city, in a plan called 'Operation Revitalise'. This was vetoed by the late Conservative housing minister, Sir Keith Joseph, who would only provide government funds for new properties, preferably system-built flats. Smith, filmed in 1987, was still outraged by Joseph's intransigence.

With considerable foresight, he created the country's first planning department and appointed the late Sir Wilfred Burns as its head. A civil engineer-turned-planner, Burns, who went on to become England's chief planner in a new Department of the Environment, had experience of rebuilding a war-ravaged Coventry. Soon, council leader and chief planner became a classic double act. Smith could sometimes be seen, pen in hand, making rough sketches for Burns and his team to finesse; he even took some credit for the basic outline of Newcastle's imposing Civic Centre, designed by George Kenyon, the council's then chief architect, and officially opened by King Olav V of Norway in November 1968.

As Faulkner, Beacock and Jones point out, the Nordic monarch was probably an appropriate choice.[8] Unusually expensive facing materials – marble, Portland stone and Norwegian Otta slate externally, for instance – gave the building distinctly Scandinavian overtones with a resemblance to both Oslo and Stockholm city halls, along with some references to Newcastle's medieval past. Historically, Tyneside had always boasted strong Nordic links, with (until recently) direct ferry services to Scandinavia.

Work on the Civic Centre, opposite Newcastle University's traditional (late 19th-century) 'quad' and its cluster of more modern buildings, began in 1958 and continued in stages for ten years. Including a handsome banqueting hall – walls incised with the names of mayors and sheriffs dating back to 1216 – it incorporated a considerable amount of contemporary art into the finished structure to form 'a kind of democratic art gallery'.[9] Even at historical prices, the cost – almost £4.9 million – still seems high.

The imposing Civic Centre, in short, symbolised T. Dan Smith's vision of fusing the traditional and the contemporary, grafting a Modernist city centre into a Neoclassical core. However, Smith had wider ambitions for the council to become the city's biggest land and property owner. 'We were buying land ... left, right and centre,' he recalled, 'I was buying up all the city centre ... no development would be allowed unless the council had an equity in it.'[10] Partly as a result, the council today owns almost a

third of the city centre, over 120 hectares, and has a 40 per cent stake in its covered, central shopping complex, inspired by Smith and known, rather ironically, as Eldon Square.

Meanwhile, Burns was busily preparing his city plan. In retrospect, his first report to the planning committee, in March 1961, had an ominous ring, with its grudging admiration for the city's fine Neoclassical centre.[11] Extolling the virtues of 'revolution rather than evolution', he warned councillors that 'redevelopment' – for some, a euphemism for large-scale demolition – was needed immediately. 'The majority of buildings in the city centre were built in the 19th century and many of them are now in a state where redevelopment has become a matter of great urgency,' the report cautioned, 'The total age of the city centre undoubtedly creates the conditions for wholesale redevelopment [for] a virtually new centre within a short period.'

Over in Gateshead, municipal minds were similarly exercised. In 1963, a local newspaper headlined a provisional plan 'Gateshead is really going to town with vast new shopping complex',[12] while another noted that the borough council had 'lived within the shadow of big brother [Newcastle] for too long'.[13] The resulting shopping centre, Trinity Square – Brutalist in the extreme, costing £2 million at mid-1960s prices and designed by the Owen Luder Partnership – soon emerged, with indoor market, 104 shops, two

department stores, a multi-storey car park – made famous by a car chase in Michael Caine's cult 1971 gangster movie, *Get Carter* – and partly covered walkways. Luder himself told councillors that his design 'exploited the natural fall of the site towards the Tyne ... with vertical as well as horizontal movement'. He also acknowledged: 'we were pushing at the frontiers of design and planning'.

Even 'Northlight', the anonymous architectural critic of the *Journal*, the local morning newspaper (formerly the *Newcastle Journal*), thought it had the potential to steal a march on Newcastle, describing the precinct as 'one of the best buildings north of the Trent'. He was wide of the mark; three years after opening, only 15 of the 50 shops in the central square of the precinct alone had been let; supply simply exceeded extremely limited demand.

'Uncompromisingly stark ... fallen into a state of severe dilapidation'[14] is today probably the most flattering description of the Gateshead centre. The nickname 'concrete elephant' soon became common parlance. Unsurprisingly, the whole complex – car park and all – has now been demolished. In the summer of 2010, the engaging Owen Luder, now in his early 80s, returned to the car park on the day demolition began to lament the passing of his creation. Clearly sentimental, yet remarkably sanguine, he recalled 'a certain amount of amazement' when the structure was completed.

with traditional industries – coal, shipbuilding, engineering – in decline, it is reasonable to speculate how Newcastle's economy would have fared without the new, brash covered retail offer of 'Eldon Square' when Gateshead's rival edge-of-town Metrocentre shopping extravaganza was opened 16 years later. The new Eldon Square and its adjoining car parks, never pleasing to the eye, still represent a canny investment for the council. Its 40 per cent stake yields around £6 million annually for the city.

As the crow flies, the Metrocentre probably lies a mile southwest of Eldon Square across the Tyne. A sprawling complex surrounded by 10,000 car-parking spaces beside the A1 on the western approaches to Gateshead, it signalled a turnaround for the local economy. Initial plans for the concept, forerunner of other similar developments throughout the country, did not seem auspicious: much of the 55-ha site was waterlogged, bogged down with ash from a former power station. However, with the country in recession in the early 1980s the then Conservative government pioneered a series of 'enterprise zones' around Britain to stimulate employment. These offered 100 per cent capital allowances on building work and, equally crucially, a three-year rate-free period for businesses. Throw in other inducements, such as a special Whitehall grant to clear up derelict sites and the cost of vital access roads linking the centre to the A1 western bypass, and the way was open for a local property entrepreneur to exploit the site's potential. Enter Sir John Hall, a former National Coal Board surveyor, son of a miner from nearby Ashington in Northumberland, with an ambition to bring North-American-style shopping malls to Britain.

As one of the first major out-of-town shopping centres in England, the Metrocentre set the trend for others to follow. However, Sir Les Elton, former Chief Executive of Gateshead Council, recalls that it could all have been very different. Initially, the concept embraced a series of retail 'sheds' at what was then known as the 'Cross Lane' development, but in 1984 the council helped host an exhibition in a local hotel to publicise the scheme. Top high-street retailers showed interest. Then Marks and Spencer, up to that point committed to town-centre development, broke with tradition and signed up as an 'anchor' tenant. This provided the incentive for others to follow. Hall's vision would soon become reality, but Elton recalls that Hall faced opposition from regional property surveyors, who were advising clients against moving to such a development.

The Church Commissioners, the Church of England's paymasters, agreed to fund the project and, when the first phase opened in 1986, Hall – who was later to transform Newcastle United into a top Premier League club – proudly proclaimed that he had beaten a Northeast Establishment, which saw him as an upstart. 'My greatest critics were professional people in the early days, the establishment,' he recalled, 'I was not part of the scene.'[19]

Today, with 350 retail tenants, 5.5 kilometres of shop frontage and a total of 6,000 employees collectively, the Metrocentre – again, functional but hardly pleasing to the eye, and, with hindsight, over-dependent on the motor car – is one of the largest private employers in North East England. In 2004, it expanded further by adding 22 more shops and 1,100 extra car-parking spaces. Alongside this, a bus and

below: Volvo parts being craned off a ship on Newcastle Quayside, 1965
courtesy of Newcastle City Library

rail interchange has been built, providing frequent services to nearby Newcastle city centre as well as regular stops on the Newcastle–Carlisle rail line.

Blessed with an adventurous council, high on ambition, Gateshead's confidence was growing as the 1980s progressed, its land area considerably extended by local-government reorganisation in 1974 and the absorption of Felling, Whickham and Blaydon urban districts. The result is that half of Gateshead now comprises undulating countryside, green and pleasant, with mature woodlands, meadows, farms and walking trails – and a spectacular, rolling 182-ha National Trust estate, Gibside. Overlooking the River Derwent, a tributary of the Tyne, it was created by a local coal 'baron', George Bowes, between 1729 and 1760. It seems a world away from industrial Tyneside, barely five kilometres northwards and the site of the 1990 National Garden Festival.

Five years of land restoration saw the festival site – a former coke and gas works, plus railway

sidings – transformed into 80 hectares of parkland, incorporating a nature reserve with two million new trees and shrubs. The festival, in turn, alerted the country to Gateshead's growing reputation as a sponsor of public art, with a programme which began four years before the event. Installations on streets, several of the stations on the Tyne and Wear Metro, a riverside sculpture park and a string of other locations are testament to this ambitious programme.

Gateshead was determined to erase the memories of jibes and petty insults from commentators and essayists, notably Bradford-born J. B. Priestley. Giving credit to Newcastle's 'sombre dignity' while dismissive of Tyneside generally, he famously – or infamously – characterised Gateshead as a town which seemed to have been carefully planned 'by an enemy of the human race'.[20]

Priestley was not alone. Over 80 years ago, a visiting academic, Dr Henry A. Mess, noted that local people had a 'singular blindness to the almost

Gateshead closer together,' enthuses Lord John
Shipley, former leader of Newcastle City Council, who
stood down in summer 2010, to enter the House of
Lords.

By 2000, a formal, over-arching concord – the
Gateshead-Newcastle Partnership – was cemented
between both councils. They decided that more could
be achieved by formal cooperation, joint marketing
and branding than by acting individually.

For marketing purposes and branding, the merging
of the twin cities – NewcastleGateshead, without
a hyphen – is no accident. The prize that they
sought together was the possibility of being named
European Capital of Culture in 2008. Although the
twin cities were pipped at the post (by Liverpool),
cooperation has proved so enduring that a stronger
partnership has been forged with the creation of a
joint marketing organisation, originally to pursue
a joint bid to become European Capital of Culture.
This was followed by a joint housing partnership and
then, in 2008, by a joint City Development Company,
known as 1NG. Other ventures could follow. 'We
simply recognised that we couldn't compete with
bigger cities unless we co-operated,' recalls Mick
Henry, leader of Gateshead Council, 'This talk of
rivalry is a myth. When I was a lad, growing up in
[Lobley Hill] Gateshead, going to "town" meant going
to Newcastle.'

The waters of the Tyne, restored in health to their
former glory, now represent the beating heart, the
spiritual essence, of an emerging cross-river 'twin-
city' embracing the centres of NewcastleGateshead.
Blessed with a new central-area plan, born out
of mutual respect between a Labour leader of
Gateshead Council (Mick Henry) and a Liberal
Democrat leader of Newcastle City Council (John
Shipley), who knows what the future might bring?
'We have to recognise that Newcastle has a strong
identity that brought national recognition and we, in
turn, have brought the skills of cultural regeneration
to the table,' says Henry.

Shipley, recently ennobled, and thus replaced
as council leader by David Faulkner is equally
magnanimous, noting that Gateshead has certainly
led the way culturally. He is a great fan of the reborn
south bank, 'Gateshead Quays', declaring: 'I was
always in favour of it. I do not see myself competing
with Gateshead in the slightest. This is a much
stronger partnership than two political parties.'

Changed times, indeed!

NOTES:

1: Alan Hull, 'All Fall Down', Hazy Music, The
Famous Charisma Label, 1972.
2: *Ibid.*
3: *NewcastleGateshead 1Plan. An economic and
spatial strategy for NewcastleGateshead*, 1NG
Limited, Gateshead, 2010.
4: *Ibid.*
5: *Ibid.*
6: Nigel Todd, *Water Under The Bridges;
Newcastle's Twentieth Century*, Tyne Bridge
Publishing, Newcastle upon Tyne, 1999.
7: T. Dan Smith, interviewed in 1987 by Amber
Films. Part of 'City State' exhibition, Newcastle
Literary and Philosophical Society, 5 September–
11 October 2009.
8: Thomas Faulkner, Peter Beacock and Paul
Jones, *Newcastle and Gateshead: Architecture
and Heritage*, The Bluecoat Press, Liverpool,
2006.
9: *Ibid.*
10: *Op. cit.*, Amber Films interview, 2009.
11: *First report of city planning officer*,
Newcastle Corporation, March 1961.
12: *The Journal*, formerly the *Newcastle Journal*,
July 1963.
13: *Evening Chronicle*, June 1961.
14: *Op. cit.*, Faulkner, Beacock and Jones.
15: *The Journal*, January 1969.
16: Wilfred Burns, *Newcastle: a study in re-
planning*, Leonard Hill, London, 1967.
17: *Op. cit.*, Faulkner, Beacock and Jones.
18: John Pendlebury, *Alas Smith and Burns?
Conservation in Newcastle upon Tyne city
centre*, 1959-68, Planning Perspectives,
April 2001.
19: Fred Robinson (ed.), *Post Industrial
Tyneside*, Newcastle Libraries, Newcastle upon
Tyne, 1988.
20: J.B. Priestley, *English Journey*, 75th
anniversary edition, Great Northern Books,
Ilkley, 2009.
21: Henry A. Mess, *Industrial Tyneside – A Social
Survey*, Ernest Benn Ltd, London, 1928.
22: *Op. cit.*, Robinson.

Chapter 3 ◐ Transforming the City

Few UK cities contain an architectural heritage as rich as that of NewcastleGateshead. It ranges from medieval through to fine Georgian, Victorian and Edwardian buildings, a touch of Art Deco, and subsequent Brutalism-cum-Modernism – a mid-20th century aberration best forgotten – to the adventurism of the millennium. In short, the twin cities have a diverse mixture of styles representing – as Sir Terry Farrell has noted – layers of history creeping up from the quayside areas.

The challenge in selecting case studies for this chapter, which, at their best, have transformed the twin cities, is how to marry old and new, modern and traditional, eye-catching and enduring, into a selection which represents some of the best architecture in NewcastleGateshead. The case studies have been grouped into categories which are most representative of the transformation in recent years of NewcastleGateshead.

The first of these categories, 'connectivity', celebrates the rich variety of bridges, and the Metro light-rail network, which is partly underground – in British terms, a rarity in a relatively small conurbation – and incorporates attractive city centre stations, giving the twin cities a distinctly mainland European 'feel'.

Naturally, the variety of housing in the twin cities is highlighted, from conversions of listed buildings such as the Wills Building, to the adventurous new developments such as the Staithes South Bank. The buildings which have driven the cultural and artistic revival of the twin cities are also highlighted.

Many of these buildings, such as The Sage Gateshead, have helped give NewcastleGateshead a fresh, modern identity.

Although NewcastleGateshead has its share of Brutalist office blocks, blighting small parts of the twin cities, more modern developments, around Gallowgate and near Newcastle Quayside, provide a welcome antidote to the concrete building spree of the 1960s – and, consequently, have been selected as case studies.

And finally, the importance of higher education to the economy and culture of the twin cities cannot go unrecorded, with 55,000 full and part-time students adding considerably to the vitality of NewcastleGateshead. As a result of careful planning since the 1960s, Newcastle has a 'university quarter' which spreads around its Nordic-style Civic Centre. Opposite the Civic Centre stands Newcastle University's new Kings Gate building, blending well in height and scale with the streetscape. Further eastwards, Northumbria University is fast expanding with a new east campus while, across the river, near the BALTIC Centre for Contemorary Art , Gateshead can boast a fine, new college of further education.

◐ Connectivity

Bridges define and connect Newcastle and Gateshead. From Newburn and Blaydon, towards the west of the twin-cities' boundary, to the ingenious Gateshead Millennium Bridge downstream eastwards, a remarkable variety of no less than ten crossings provide road, rail and pedestrian links across the river.

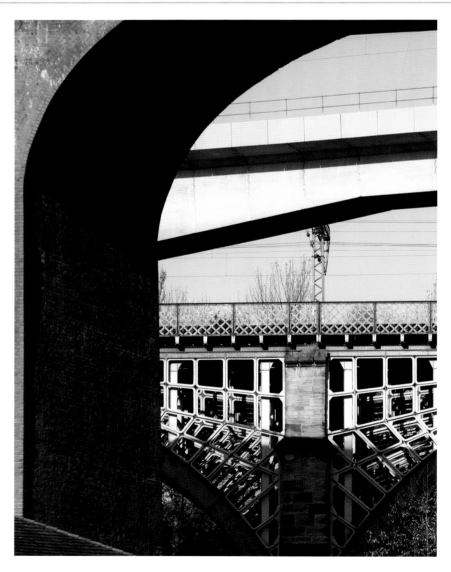

So crucial are these crossings – this, after all, is one of Britain's great east–west and north–south 'gateways' – that they have underpinned both the history of Newcastle and Gateshead and, more recently, the popular image of Tyneside. After all, for visitors and Geordies alike, the Tyne Bridge is still the enduring image of NewcastleGateshead, although the new Gateshead Millennium Bridge, Stirling Prize winner in 2001 and probably the first in the world to tilt, is a close contender.

At such a gateway, the Romans – bridge-builders and engineers par excellence – were naturally the first to exploit the river crossing. Beside the Emperor Hadrian's Pons Aelius (meaning the bridge of Hadrian), finished in AD 122, they built the first settlement in what is now Newcastle; there is also evidence of a Roman fort at Bottle Bank, in Gateshead.

A wooden structure, resting on stone piers, supported this Roman structure which was erected close to the current Swing Bridge, built by the late 19th-century Tyneside industrialist and benefactor, Lord Armstrong.

The first Roman bridge was eventually replaced by the medieval crossing, built in the late 12th century. Incorporating towers, houses, shops and at least one small church, this was finally swept away in floods in 1771 to be replaced by a Georgian bridge (1781–1866), which was regarded as impossibly narrow. Its Swing Bridge replacement (1876 and still going strong) was both wider and more robust – but more crossings were needed to cope with the

62   all photography on this spread by Sally Ann Norman

demands of rail and commerce. In came Robert Stephenson's High Level Bridge (1849), incorporating road and rail traffic on separate decks; then the King Edward VII railway bridge (1906), accommodating the main north–south rail link; and, subsequently, the Tyne Bridge (1928).

Newcastle and Gateshead, then, can boast more river crossings than most cities. And that's before subsequent ventures – the Queen Elizabeth II Bridge (1981), carrying the Tyne and Wear Metro; and the Gateshead Millennium Bridge (2001) – are taken into account.

'on many occasions, disputes over city boundaries meant that the bridges were often a source of division, [however] in recent years joint ventures and partnerships mean they have become symbols of collaboration and friendship.'

The Tyne Bridge, designed by Mott, Hay & Anderson and built by Dorman Long of Middlesbrough, undoubtedly remains the best known, a symbol of the twin cities internationally and often regarded – wrongly – as the model for the Sydney Harbour Bridge designed by the same company. In fact, work began on the much larger Sydney structure in March 1924, eight months before that on the Tyne Bridge, although it

opened four years later than the latter.

With a 2,000-year history of bridge-building across the Tyne, you might have thought that formal, business and personal relationships between Newcastle and Gateshead had remained strong for centuries, cemented by all those crossings. You would be wrong.

As a fascinating 'Building Bridges' exhibition in Gateshead's Shipley Art Gallery late in 2009 underlined: 'on many occasions, disputes over city boundaries meant that the bridges were often a source of division, [however] in recent years joint ventures and partnerships mean they have become symbols of collaboration and friendship.'

Such collaboration, through a Tyneside passenger transport authority created in the 1960s, ensured the development of a conurbation-wide light-rail network (now the Tyne and Wear Metro, since its subsequent extension to Sunderland) with an underground section in Newcastle, from which Metro trains emerge to cross the Queen Elizabeth II Bridge before heading briefly back underground into Gateshead. The Metro system also included a new, elegant viaduct, largely parallel to the main east coast rail line across the Ouseburn at Byker, just east of the city centre.

Like the region's bridges in the 19th, 20th and 21st centuries, the Metro emerged as a national pace-setter and the most extensive light-rail network outside London when it was built in the early 1980s, partly by updating an existing suburban railway. Station design was determined

by consultant architects Faulkner Brown, Watson Hendy and Stoner (now FaulknerBrowns), a national practice based at Killingworth near Newcastle. With white and yellow vitreous interior panels; large, bold signage; and brown and red brickwork, the stations have proved remarkably enduring.

Jesmond Metro Station, for instance, where the system goes underground, still has a modern and fresh appearance. Designed in a pavilion style, extensively glazed with public art outside the north entrance, it remains – like its city-centre counterparts – a powerful symbol for a system which received Royal Assent in 1973 and opened its first section seven years later. The Tyne and Wear Metro is now in the throes of substantial upgrading.

Thirty years on, the system and its stations – the envy of other conurbations – retains a contemporary mainland European 'feel', adding considerable value to both the image and 'connectivity' of the twin cities across a relatively modern Metro bridge, now painted bright blue.

all photography on this spread by Sally Ann Norman

Gateshead Millennium Bridge

Gateshead/Newcastle

Construction value **£22 million**
Date of completion **September 2001**
Project type **New-build**

INTRODUCTION

The elegant, curving lines of this ground-breaking tilting bridge, perfectly reflecting the symmetry of the Tyne Bridge upstream, have become the symbol of the regenerated quaysides on both banks of the river and of the twin cities of Newcastle and Gateshead themselves. Winner of the 2002 RIBA Stirling Prize, the outline of this £22 million crossing for pedestrians and cyclists has now become the logo, officially or otherwise, for countless organisations; for some, its new-found stature even rivals the much larger Tyne Bridge, for so long the enduring image of Tyneside.

While linking both cities, the Gateshead Millennium Bridge was the brainchild of an ambitious Gateshead Council, which needed a new crossing to directly link the BALTIC Centre for Contemporary Art with Newcastle quayside. Dramatic when static and exciting in motion, combining simplicity and sophistication – thus adding to its worldwide reputation as a tourist attraction in its own right – it is essentially two graceful curves, one forming the deck and the other supporting it, spanning between concrete bases on both banks. When open, the bridge's two matching curves form what has been labelled an open or 'blinking' eye, unique in bridge construction.

Completed in September 2001, in truth the bridge represents a fusion of architecture and engineering with both Wilkinson Eyre Architects and engineers Gifford being given equal status.

CLIENT'S BRIEF

Significantly, commissioning the bridge and organising a design competition became the responsibility of Gateshead Council's Engineering Department. Its brief was demanding, driven by the imperative that any scheme must not detract from the famous view of the existing six Tyne crossings while being accessible at quayside level to pedestrians and cyclists. In addition, the scheme could not be allowed to restrict shipping capable of travelling under the nearby Tyne Bridge upstream, and hence through the lower level Armstrong's Swing Bridge; a key requirement, therefore, was that a clear navigation channel must be retained – 25 m high and 30 m wide – for river traffic. Perhaps unsurprisingly some sceptics in the Port of Tyne Authority, responsible for river traffic, had to be brought on board through gentle diplomacy.

Nevertheless, in spite of these issues the clients demanded a strong architectural statement – in short, a world-class bridge – to match a significant engineering challenge: no easy task at the best of times. And time became the essence; vital Lottery funding for the adjoining BALTIC Centre for Contemporary Art was dependent on a new bridge.

It has been acknowledged as one of the most successful of the millennium projects, with its landmark status enhanced by spectacular night-time lighting.

Newcastle and Gateshead: Architecture and Heritage
Faulkner, Beacock and Jones

all photography on this spread by Sally Ann Norman

DESIGN PROCESS

The opening movement of the new bridge is both its design and engineering highlight. Bridges that open offer a spectacle, yet are rarely spectacular in themselves. This one, in contrast, has sculptural presence in its static position, giving way to a sense of theatre and power in operation. The idea is simple: a pair of arches – one forming the deck, the other supporting it – pivot around their common springing point to allow shipping to pass beneath. The motion is simple, efficient and rational, yet provides a drama rarely seen in other such mechanisms. Hydraulic rams, located in each end, provide motive power to the base of the bridge's arch. The whole bridge tilts, and as it does so the entire composition undergoes a metamorphosis into a 'grand arch'; the 4 1/2-minute operation evokes the action of a closed eye slowly opening, hence the structure being initially labelled the 'blinking eye' bridge.

The bridge provides an important low-level link, much needed within the context of the Tyne's existing crossings. Its location opens up an area of Gateshead quays by linking with Newcastle quayside and allowing the all important 'foot fall' to access the new development on Gateshead's regenerated quayside. The design is a mixture of the robust and the slender, its overall lightness contrasting with the visual mass of the adjoining Baltic Flour Mills (now the BALTIC Centre for Contemporary Art). The 45 m-high arch provides an instant visual reference to the Tyne Bridge beyond but presents a slender profile against the skyline, interpreting and updating the structural and aesthetic order of its historic neighbour.

The bridge spans 105 m between two caissons, each of which houses public viewing decks and a crystalline all-glass pavilion atop sub-aqua plant rooms and hydraulic enclosures. The crossing features two parallel decks, separated by level and intermittent screening in order to differentiate pedestrian and cycle paths.

Pedestrians are allowed clear views over the lower cycle deck, and seating and other amenities promote the bridge as a place as well as a crossing point.

The parabolic arch comprises a kite-shaped cross-section tapering in both plan and elevation, fabricated from steel plate up to 25 mm thick. The main pedestrian deck is a similarly fabricated steel box, parabolic in plan and narrowing from the quaysides towards the centre of the river. The lower cycle deck features a lightweight open-grille aluminium surfacing supported from the main deck on cantilevered arms.

The lighting design balances function and spectacle in order to highlight the bridge's structural form. It incorporates computer-controlled colour-change spotlights, illuminating the main arch with a dramatic and constantly varying scripted display that transforms the bridge by night.

The complex steel superstructure was transported in sections to nearby Wallsend, where the arch and deck pieces were welded together and painted, lying flat, before being raised and joined. The entire superstructure was transported intact for the 9.5 km journey to its final position in Gateshead in November 2000, using the giant Asian Hercules II floating crane.

PROJECT EVALUATION

The bridge was conceived as being in the great tradition of engineering on Tyneside, and represents the revitalisation of the Gateshead riverfront. This truly unique design has realised an iconic landmark for both Gateshead and Newcastle – indeed, it has become a new symbol of the twin cities, as famous as the nearby Tyne Bridge – and has proved highly popular since its public opening in September 2001. Faulkner, Beacock and Jones note in their *Newcastle and Gateshead: Architecture and Heritage* book that it has been acknowledged as one of the most successful of the millennium projects, with its landmark status enhanced by spectacular night-time lighting.

One success amongst many is the highly faithful realisation of the competition-winning design, which has been achieved through an exceptional team effort across disciplines and a strong belief in the quality of the original concept.

 all photography on this spread by Sally Ann Norman

Client Gateshead Council
Architect Wilkinson Eyre Architects
Main Contractor Harbour & General Works Ltd
Structural Engineer Gifford & Partners
Services Engineer Bennett Associates

Lighting Designer Jonathan Speirs and
Associates

High Level Bridge restoration

Quayside,
Newcastle upon Tyne/Gateshead

Construction value **£42 million**
Date of completion **May 2008**
Project type **Refurbishment/renovation**

CONNECTIONS

INTRODUCTION

Designed by Robert Stephenson, son of the railway pioneer George Stephenson, the Grade I listed High Level Bridge linking Gateshead with Newcastle remains one of the engineering and design marvels of the mid-19th century. It provided the first rail crossing over the Tyne gorge, thus delivering an uninterrupted rail link between London and Edinburgh – previously London trains terminated at Gateshead – and heralding Newcastle's magnificent Central Station.

Opened by Queen Victoria in September 1849, the ingenious cast-iron bridge comprises an upper deck for rail traffic and a lower one for road vehicles. Even by today's standards, the bridge was built with remarkable speed, with the main arches completed in less than a year. Not for nothing did the then mayor of Gateshead, George Hawks, whose family firm undertook the ironwork, praise the labours of 'skilful and industrious workmen'.

As the oldest of the Tyne bridges, it is undoubtedly one of the most treasured historic structures on the British rail network – thankfully saved from closure, by a £42 million repair and strengthening project, to ensure its continuation as a major link for the local and national rail networks as well as a significant Tyneside landmark.

CLIENT'S BRIEF

The age and historical value of the structure made the two-year restoration project particularly challenging. Following a commission by Network Rail, and the preparation of a detailed conservation plan, an inspection and assessment by the main contractor and structural engineer in 2006 found many elements needing repair and strengthening in order to extend life expectancy. This became a major structural project in its own right, embracing strong elements of conservation to preserve a listed structure of national significance.

The contract involved the complete replacement of the lower road deck (while keeping the top level open for rail services) by installing an alternative, heavy steel 'load path' to replace worn-out cast-iron girders. It also involved selective replacement of corroded sections of wrought-iron suspension hangers, 'like-for-like' replacement of all steel cross-girders, new drainage and deck waterproofing, improved inspection and maintenance facilities, and restoration and electrification of the original lamp standards – in addition to extensive metalwork repairs and complete repainting of the structure to match the original colour scheme.

Although essential repair work was funded by Network Rail as part of its commitment to maintaining a national infrastructure, restoration and electrification of the cast-iron lamp standards on the road deck was funded in partnership with the Railway Heritage Trust, Newcastle City Council and Gateshead Council.

To keep the High Level true to its origins, great pains were taken to restore the final finish in keeping with the traditions and practices of the mid-19th century.

all photography on this spread by Sally Ann Norman

DESIGN PROCESS

Structural engineers worked closely with the architects up to planning stage, with designers subsequently developing the detailed design which consists of two main elements: a 'motorway' span and a span crossing the Tyne and Wear Metro.

The latter element consists of a 1.3 m-deep plate-girder-supported deck, resting on new abutments at each end. A concrete underpass, consisting of a box structure and retaining walls, was constructed to maintain access to the car park.

The motorway span consists of a 20 m-high inclined pylon with three pairs of cables holding up a steel deck. Two backstays, each comprising three cables, support this pylon. The west end of the deck is underpinned by modifying the existing retaining wall, and at the east end the wall of the concrete underpass is used as an abutment. The backstays are anchored into the abutment for the Metro bridge span. In order to avoid inducing lateral forces on the pile foundations, an ingenious method was used: two large concrete beams connected the pylon base to the backstay anchorage and were used as compression struts, forming a closed triangle which kept all tension forces within it. The reuse of the existing structure and the dual use of new foundations kept the substructure design economical and efficient.

The bridge was designed to cope with both dynamic and static effects. The pre-planning structural analysis led to the use of tuned mass dampers for the two separate, resulting types of vibration.

The construction process had to take complex site factors into account. Heavy plant was needed next to a busy live motorway and Metro line; owing to space constraints, careful coordination of deck steelwork delivery was needed. In addition, the very large Pandon sewer passed through the site at a depth of 28 metres. The two steel decks were lifted into place using an 800-tonne crane. A prop was constructed in the centre of the motorway to support the deck whilst the cables were being connected to the pylon.

Extensive coordination between the construction team, Newcastle City Council and the Metro operators ensured that the entire construction process took place according to a tight time-limited programme, with minimal disruption to traffic.

A cement replacement, GGBS (ground granulated blast-furnace slag), was used in the concrete in order to reduce carbon emissions. Stainless-steel handrails were chosen to eliminate painting and for their long design life.

The lighting design considered cost, lifespan and long-term maintenance. Weighing these factors against each other resulted in the use of LED fittings. This ensured the most sustainable possible end product – and one that was visually stunning, too.

New embankments were constructed, largely of 'fill' material left over from a nearby construction site. The landscape design added new areas of grass, trees and other greenery, making an environmentally friendly and pleasing backdrop to the bridge.

PROJECT EVALUATION

Bridges which provide direct and continuous access between eminent and widely used landmarks encourage people to walk or cycle in order to reach their destination. The Northumbria University East Campus Bridge therefore plays its part in reducing car use within the city and in encouraging walking and cycling.

The location of the new bridge has been a key factor in its success. It provides street level access both sides for pedestrians and cyclists by its position at the bottom of the motorway slip roads where the main carriageway drops under the New Bridge street roundabout.

The footbridge project is a structurally ingenious addition to the campus, bringing together its west and east sections. It contributes to the long-term sustainability of both the academic community and, to an extent, of nearby residential neighbourhoods – whilst also ensuring the growth necessary for the development of the University. Outstanding working relationships and communication between the city council, the Metro operators and the design team contributed to the project being delivered to schedule and within its challenging budget, with minimum inconvenience to the public. In addition, the bridge makes a powerful visual statement for the university itself.

all photography on this spread by Sally Ann Norman

Client **Northumbria University**
Architect **WSP and Atkins**
Main Contractor **VolkerStevin**
Quantity Surveyor **Turner & Townsend plc**

Structural Engineer **WSP**
Services Engineer **WSP**
Project Manager **Gardiner and Theobald LLP**
Landscape Architect **Insite Architecture**

CONNECTIVITY

Air Traffic Control Tower, Newcastle International Airport (now re-named The Emirates Tower)

Woolsington,
Newcastle upon Tyne

Construction value **£4.4 million**
Date of completion **August 2007**
Project type **New-build**

INTRODUCTION

This project coincided with Newcastle International Airport's ongoing infrastructure development to accommodate its sustained growth in traffic. The building of a new 46 m-high tower followed an industry-wide design competition.

The latticework structure, named 'The Emirates Tower' – in recognition of the commencement of flights to Dubai and onwards to over 90 destinations – has been labelled 'technically innovative and incredibly efficient, rivalling those of major airports across the world'.

Delivered on time and to budget, the scheme fulfilled many functions on a highly secure site: offices, workshops and operational accommodation. The design, based on research with industry experts, involves innovative materials such as the new Kalzip product – described by its makers as 'the world's leading aluminium standing seam roofing and wall-cladding system' – and a highly economical mesh screen, which changes in appearance under different lighting conditions.

CLIENT'S BRIEF

It was important that the project created a positive image, in keeping with the environment and – equally importantly – that a tight budget should not compromise building quality. Replacing an outdated 1960s control tower with an iconic design that reflects a modern image for the airport was a key priority, while, crucially, creating a functional solution encompassing the necessary technical requirements and improving the 'sight lines' for air traffic controllers. The building had to be both durable and cost-effective, with minimum requirements for maintenance. In addition, it was decided that extra income could be generated by sub-letting additional office space.

image courtesy of Hufton and Crow

'A monumental improvement in facilities at the airport'.

Chris Davis, *Air Traffic Control Manager at Newcastle International Airport*

image courtesy of Hufton and Crow

right: photography by Keith Paisley

– began an Art on the Riverside programme with landmarks such as River God by the sculptor Andre Wallace.

With the help of artists in residence, and international sculptors, Gateshead had soon created more than 80 works of public art – topped, of course, by Antony Gormley's towering *Angel of the North* by the town's southern entrance. Celebrated as the country's largest sculpture when erected in 1998, its influence on wider cultural-led regeneration cannot be overerestimated.

Gateshead was on a roll. The creation of National Lottery funding helped the (then) borough punch well above its weight, and soon its capital works programme – that slice of funding devoted to big projects – overshadowed that of its neighbour across the Tyne for the first time. Roger Kelly, Chief Executive of Gateshead Council, likes to call it 'serendipity' – on the grounds that Lottery funding, by happy coincidence, came along as his council was planning its riverside transformation. In its bid to assemble land for cultural redevelopment, the ambitious council at one notable time in the 1990s had the distinction of assembling more compulsory purchase orders than any other English local authority.

In many respects, the council was able to cope with this workload because, unlike other authorities, it still had a well-staffed and functioning architecture and engineering department capable of managing large projects.

Across the river, in Newcastle, the city was benefiting from the masterplanning of Terry Farrell and Partners. The practice was

commissioned to breathe new life into the Quayside area following a competition by the former Tyne and Wear Development Corporation. As Faulkner, Beacock and Jones note, in their 2006 book, *Newcastle and Gateshead; Architecture and Heritage*, Sir Terry Farrell – trained at Newcastle University School of Architecture – is 'just as interested in the spaces between buildings as the buildings themselves'. Consequently, sculptures, new public spaces and squares – wonderful venues for open-air events – all formed part of his design concept. It was to prove the ideal complement to Gateshead Quays opposite, as the area incorporating the BALTIC Centre for Contemporary Art and The Sage Gateshead is now known.

In Newcastle, the city council, theatres, arts organisations and universities are no less short on ambition: a recently rebuilt Northern Stage theatre is proving a pivotal element of a new cultural quarter, near the Great North Museum and incorporated into Newcastle University; Live Theatre, near the Quayside, is one of the country's leading centres of new writing and production; Newcastle's City Library is a pace-setter for a new wave of lending institutions; and a rebuilt Tyneside Cinema can justly claim to be one of the country's finest art-house cinemas.

Sir Terry Farrell – trained at Newcastle University School of Architecture – is 'just as interested in the spaces between buildings as the buildings themselves'. Consequently, sculptures, new public spaces and squares – wonderful venues for open-air events – all formed part of his design concept.

Faulkner, Beacock and Jones, *Newcastle and Gateshead; Architecture and Heritage*, 2006

The Sage Gateshead

St Mary's Square,
Gateshead Quays

Project cost **£70 million**
Date of completion **December 2004**
Project type **New-build**

INTRODUCTION

In its relatively short existence, The Sage Gateshead can justifiably claim to have become a regional music centre-cum-concert hall of international standing, with around half a million visitors each year. It forms the heart of an exciting project to regenerate Gateshead's river frontage – known as Gateshead Quays – and lies, alongside the BALTIC Centre for Contemporary Art, roughly between the great arch of the Tyne Bridge and the curving Gateshead Millennium Bridge.

Beneath the shell-like form of stainless steel and glass, the building contains three auditoria in addition to a series of public spaces, including cafés, bars and restaurants; a music-education centre; and a base for the Northern Sinfonia Orchestra and Folkworks, a project largely dedicated to traditional Northumbrian music. The last-named represent the two founding artistic partners of the North Music Trust, which operates the centre.

The largest of the three performance spaces is an acoustically state-of-the-art concert hall seating up to 1,700. The second hall, intimately ten-sided and tiered on three levels – providing a studio or cabaret-style atmosphere – can be arranged to suit performances ranging from folk and jazz to chamber music, and seats up to 400. The third is both a rehearsal hall for Northern Sinfonia and a smaller multi-purpose space, accommodating music performance and education. The concourse incorporates the ticket office, a flexible performance space, and a restaurant and café with an informal atmosphere and unrivalled views across the Tyne to Newcastle a few hundred metres away.

CLIENT'S BRIEF

In the late 1990s, Gateshead Council saw the potential of transforming Gateshead Quays into a new cultural quarter. When a home was being sought for an international centre for music, the Quays emerged as the perfect location. In July 2002, sponsorship arrangements were announced between the Tyneside-based international software company, The Sage Group plc, local music charities and Gateshead Council to give what had been a plain 'music centre' a permanent name and identity: The Sage Gateshead was born. The aim was to generate a widespread and lasting enrichment of music through performance, learning and participation in a new kind of venue dedicated to all forms of music, from classical to traditional Northumbrian, from jazz to pop.

The brief evolved from an initial concept for two concert halls – one large, one small – and a music-education centre, together with associated offices and back-of-house facilities. Architects were then asked to consider the possibility of a third performance space – now the Northern Rock Foundation Hall – which became increasingly important as the design developed. The building was to be open and inviting – inclusive, rather than a 'temple' to high culture. This led the team to add a further, important, ingredient to the brief: a large public concourse, which has emerged as an enclosed, inviting public square and popular meeting place.

The Sage Gateshead fills a 'gap on the map' for music venues in the North East, and has consolidated Tyneside's position as an arts destination, drawing tourists from around Britain and abroad.

DESIGN PROCESS

The location, along the southern bank of the Tyne gorge, was derelict and windswept. From medieval times, it had been occupied by a variety of industries and fishing interests, as well as being the departure point for coal brought from local mines for shipping to other parts of Britain.

The original concept was to position the building immediately adjacent to the Baltic Flour Mills, now transformed into a contemporary art centre, in order to create a 'critical mass' of cultural facilities. However, a location between the Tyne Bridge and the Gateshead Millennium Bridge was soon thought more appropriate, bringing it closer to Gateshead town centre and helping to stimulate further development along the river.

The site drops steeply towards the river. This relatively steep, banked site for the music centre became a key influence on the design, allowing the building to be arranged on several levels with the auditoria and the associated loading facilities crucially staying on the same level, beside a service road, to maintain operational efficiency.

A Sage Gateshead Access Panel was established in 2000 to ensure that disabled people contributed to the design process; indeed, during the design and construction period, 14 panel meetings and four site visits eventually had a significant impact on the final designs. One of the most valuable results of this consultation was the subtle use of visual definition on steps, counter edges and on ironmongery and material selections to help visually-impaired people.

At the beginning of the project, the key consultant team – including members of Northern Sinfonia, Gateshead Council and Folkworks – toured some of the best concert halls and performance spaces in Britain and Europe. This proved an important influence for the brief, and led to the decision to adopt a 'shoebox' auditorium format for the main hall rather than a tiered design.

A basic organisational diagram then emerged, whereby three acoustically separate volumes were arranged in parallel along the top of the bank – with foyers and a public concourse linking the halls and facing the splendid views of Newcastle and the Tyne bridges. Taking advantage of the slope, the music-education centre was then tucked underneath. A single, flowing roof unifies the three separate auditoria, back-of-house facilities and the public concourse – its shape inspired in part by the iconic arches of the Tyne Bridge. The independent volumes of the three halls, each with its own particular shape, can be easily distinguished.

The concourse, with views across to Newcastle Quayside and cityscape beyond, is the public focus of the building. It is open 16 hours a day, with cafés, bars, shops, box office and, most importantly, informal performance spaces. The concourse is also part of a major pedestrian route linking the low-level swing bridge to the west with the new Gateshead Millennium Bridge to the east, thus forming a 1.5 km-long circular tour along the quaysides of Newcastle and Gateshead.

PROJECT EVALUATION

The Sage Gateshead fills a 'gap on the map' for music venues in the North East, and has consolidated Tyneside's position as an arts destination, drawing tourists from around Britain and abroad. Performers in Hall One, from symphony orchestras to jazz ensembles, frequently comment on its high acoustic standards as well as the sense of intimacy it encourages between audience and artistes. The building, a world-class venue, is firmly placed on the national and international circuit for leading performers, placing The Sage Gateshead alongside major concert halls from London to Birmingham, Manchester and Glasgow. It is already a local landmark, has provided a further catalyst for the regeneration of Gateshead's riverside and has created more than 400 new jobs. Despite its relatively small catchment area, sales figures taken during an evaluation in 2008 were impressive.

The front-of-house space has proved to be flexible, and still looks fresh and new. The Sage Gateshead continues to explore new ways of maximising access for disabled people, winning awards which recognise it as a leader in this field. In terms of environmental performance, the use of underfloor heating has been reduced by taking advantage of solar gain, thus lowering energy demands; in its first five years, energy use has been cut by a quarter. The building continues to act as an economic regenerator – attracting not just music lovers (and explorers) but also major international conferences.

all photography on this spread by Sally Ann Norman
drawings supplied by the architect

Client Gateshead Council
Architect Foster + Partners
Main Contractor Laing O'Rourke
Quantity Surveyor Davis Langdon
Structural Engineer Mott MacDonald and
Buro Happold
Services Engineer Mott MacDonald

Project Manager Gateshead Council
Acoustician Arup Acoustics
Access Consultant Burdus Access
Management
Theatre Consultant Theatre Projects
Consultants

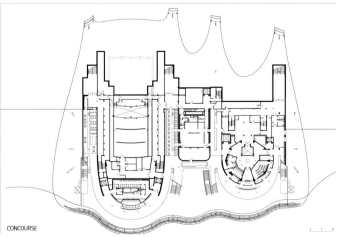

CONCOURSE

Angel of the North

A1/A167 Motorway Interchange,
Gateshead

Construction value **£800,000**
Date of completion **February 1998**
Project type **Public art commission**

INTRODUCTION

As a symbol of Gateshead's cultural resurgence, the *Angel of the North* is unsurpassed. Britain's largest sculpture when built in February 1998, it not only put Gateshead on the map nationally but provided the drive for the arts-led regeneration of the south bank of the Tyne. A triumph of both art and engineering, it was created by the sculptor Antony Gormley – indeed, he fashioned the Angel on his own body! – fabricated in nearby Hartlepool and engineered by Arup, who literally made this 20 m-high structure, with a 53 m wingspan, stand up.

Conceived by Gateshead Council as a landmark on the city's southern approach, it lies on the site of the former Teams Colliery – visible from both the main A1 north–south highway and the East Coast Main Line – and marks a dramatic extension of an ambitious programme of public art, which began in the early 1980s and was subsequently given a boost during the 1990 National Garden Festival in Gateshead, when more than 20 temporary artworks were displayed.

Consequently, Gateshead has become a trailblazer in public art, along the Tyne banks and further afield, with a dedicated curator – all because councillors pressed ahead with an ambitious programme as Gateshead (then) had no contemporary gallery of its own. They turned to the 'great outdoors' as an alternative, with one overriding objective: namely that artworks, and the role of the artist, should enhance the urban environment, involve local people through the creative process and thus create a sense of ownership.

CLIENT'S BRIEF

Driven by the success of the 1990 National Garden Festival, Gateshead Council soon decided that an artist of international stature should be considered for a bold sculpture alongside the A1, the main southern road approach to both Gateshead and Tyneside. As a suitable location, the council's Art in Public Places Panel earmarked the area where the Teams Colliery pithead baths had once stood.

Councillors on the panel wanted an artwork that would be ambitious in scale and aspect: a landmark feature within the landscape, something of significance to symbolise the character and strength of the region.

Of his involvement, Antony Gormley has stated: 'I want to make something that we can live with and that becomes a reservoir for feelings ... feelings that we hadn't known about until this thing was there, or feelings that couldn't arise until it was.'

Reflecting on the selection process, Councillor Mick Henry, Leader of Gateshead Council, observed in 2002: 'The more I think about it, the more I realise what a step in the dark it was for the council. We thought of art before jobs, knowing that one would bring the other.'

'I want to make something that we can live with and that becomes a reservoir for feelings ... feelings that we hadn't known about until this thing was there, or feelings that couldn't arise until it was.'

Antony Gormley

DESIGN PROCESS

Dominic Williams was well aware that his design had to accommodate the needs of contemporary artists, who often require large spaces for their works. Consequently, the BALTIC's gallery floors are conceived as empty spaces which can be configured in many different ways; thus, they can be modified, internal walls altered, and – when necessary – even certain 'floorplates' can be removed.

Artworks, of course, come in all shapes and sizes. To accommodate the largest, a loading bay has been incorporated under a 'fabric wing' on the east side of the building. An 'arts lift', the size of a small house, allows very large pieces to be transported around the building.

To the west of the building, a glass link connects the gallery to the new Baltic Square, where the main public entrance is marked by riven slate and tactile markings embedded in the ground. These lead the visitor through to the first gallery at ground-floor level, opposite the lift stacks.

Orientation and information areas are located at each main public level, from which visitors can move around the building by stair or by glass lifts; and light filters down the lift void, further aided by a large, glazed west façade, offering further spectacular views of the river and the twin cities of Newcastle and Gateshead.

On Level One, a 'black-box' performance gallery is largely soundproofed and can accommodate many different functions, from performances – staging and seating is concealed in an adjacent storage wall – to serving as an intimate cinema or a lecture hall, with seating for 60 people and nearby digital video-editing facilities.

Level Two contains a gallery space as well as the main administration 'heart' for the BALTIC and subsequently developed into an education space and archive.

Level Three includes what is known as the 'close control' gallery, allowing very fragile and sensitive pieces of work to be exhibited, while Level Four incorporates a lofty gallery, daylit from high-level glazing, where larger works can be exhibited.

Above Level Four, a two-level viewing 'box' projects over the west façade of the building. This encloses a visitors' platform providing views over the River Tyne to the twin cities beyond. On Level Six, the building is surmounted by a lightweight steel-and-glass structure, a facility designed to contain a café, bar or restaurant and another potential starting or end point for a gallery visit. Conceptually, this structure 'floats' between two monolithic brick and steel walls, and at night internal lighting means it is fully visible to the surrounding areas.

PROJECT EVALUATION

Although a post-completion evaluation of the building has not been undertaken, articles in the press, and critiques, have been generally favourable.

While certain reviews have questioned the quality, and relevance, of some of the exhibits contained within, the architecture is rarely contested. Writing in the *Guardian* in 2002, for instance, the respected architecture critic Jonathan Glancey observed: 'At Baltic, the architects have demonstrated great maturity and a real love of building. And they have given a thrilling, if flawed, quayside a fresh lease of gutsy, dramatic life.'

The flexibility of the art spaces that remain true to the original concept, continue to provide an ever changing sense of art spaces that always have something new to offer the visitor.

The building provides a focus for contemporary art and has acted as a catalyst in the region, invigorating interest in cutting-edge art in other venues across the region.

all photography on this spread by Sally Ann Norman

Client Gateshead Council
Architect Ellis Williams Architects
Main Contractor HBG Ltd
Quantity Surveyor Boyden and Co.

Structural Engineer Atelier One
Services Engineer Atelier Ten
Project Manager Gateshead Council
Lighting Designer Arup Lighting

Live Theatre

27 and 29 Broad Chare,
Newcastle upon Tyne

Construction value **£4.3 million**
Date of completion **September 2007**
Project type **Restoration and refurbishment**

INTRODUCTION

Tucked into a magnificent side street a few hundred metres from Newcastle Quayside, Live Theatre is housed in a range of Grade II* listed buildings, 19th-century Georgian bonded warehouse and almshouses, converted for theatrical use in the 1980s. Rapidly becoming one of the country's foremost theatres specialising in new writing – and spawning a wealth of talent in the process – it became clear in the late 1990s that the building was outgrowing its original cabaret-style layout, becoming 'tired' and in need of better technical facilities and improved public access. With expansion a necessity, a lease was negotiated on an adjacent, empty warehouse, some of which was Grade I listed, to create a new centre of excellence for performance, rehearsal and creative writing.

The project required a range of specialist skills from the architects, selected in a design competition, with a brief embracing dramatic interior design, sensitive conservation of the Grade II* and Grade I listed structure and fabric, and robust design management alongside a team of theatre consultants in order to deliver the Heritage Lottery funded project. The client's ambitious brief and expectations would have been hard enough to meet with the design freedom of a new building on a vacant site. They were to prove acutely challenging to deliver amidst such a range of small and historically sensitive buildings.

CLIENT'S BRIEF

A complete revamp became the overarching demand, and it made the brief particularly demanding. Internally, the existing building had drawbacks for an audience in a tightly packed space, with very poor circulation between seats and sometimes no clear view of the stage. For actors it was no less challenging; access to the stage from the dressing rooms was up a flight of stairs! The only bar was located in the theatre auditorium, certainly intimate yet further adding to congestion. The single rehearsal room nearby was small, inadequate and limiting. Moreover, in a theatre where creativity was an overriding ethos, there was no dedicated space for writing.

The brief, then, included a large auditorium with better views of the stage for the audience, and a new circle; refurbished dressing rooms, with improved access to the stage for actors; and a much-improved rehearsal room at second-floor level. In addition, a new suite of theatre offices was needed, with specialist rooms for writing alongside meeting and conference rooms. A new box office was also stipulated, alongside a spacious, welcoming entrance blending old brick walls with more contemporary additions.

In all, the client demanded a creative vision to make a visit to the building a dramatic experience in itself. The works had to be designed and procured over three separate contracts to meet funding criteria stipulated by the Heritage Lottery Fund.

The design has proved successful for both audience and actors, underpinning Live Theatre's reputation as a pioneer of new writing and theatre, from which productions – notably, playwright Lee Hall's widely acclaimed Pitman Painters – *have progressed to London's theatre-land and, beyond, to Broadway.*

DESIGN PROCESS

The organisational diagram that developed from the briefing-stage discussions was simple and legible. The highest block in the complex, to the west, contains the dance studios and associated activity. The second, lower block to the north relates to dance performance (the Dance:Lab) and the third, L-shaped block contains administrative functions. These three elements come together to enclose the social space, to which all the core activities within the building relate. It is a place of arrival, sociability and the commencement of movement through the building, linking all levels with a top-lit atrium.

On one level the social space functions as a generous, light-filled circulation area but it is also the social and creative focus for the whole building, giving a heart to the entire organisation. Circulation routes to and from the different parts of the building are designed to overlap here, and built-in seats on these main routes encourage sociability. It also forms the foyer to the Dance:Lab, and has the capacity to be used for performances itself.

A form of heavy masonry construction was considered ideal for the building. 'High thermal mass' – the ability of its materials to absorb and re-radiate heat helps to establish a stable temperature in the building, making it less prone to fluctuations – an important consideration for dance buildings. Brick offered the appropriate performance characteristics as well as being cost-effective. Structural investigation of this proposal revealed that a double-skin, brick diaphragm-wall type construction could also offer acoustic benefits for the building.

This type of construction principally benefits the double-height spaces in the building – the dance studios and the Dance:Lab – but it restricted possibilities elsewhere. Discussion with the client revealed a concern that the social space was too introverted and needed to engage more with the new civic square; this view was also discussed and encouraged within the Urban Design section of Newcastle City Council. The result was the decision to utilise a steel frame for the administration block, allowing increased glazing of the southeast corner and elevations of the building, promoting views into the heart of the organisation and connecting the internal space back to its surroundings.

The building's external appearance reflects the nature of these two types of construction. The Dance:Lab and main, west-facing block are built in a Staffordshire Blue facing brick. In the dance studios the brick was painted white to increase reflective light, but elsewhere the exposed brickwork provides excellent robust surfaces. In the Dance:Lab, the dark purple/ blue characteristic of the facing brick also provides good blackout qualities.

In contrast, the framed construction to the administration block allows the possibility for greater areas of glazing and articulation where required; the café space at ground level protrudes from the main building line at the southeast corner as a 'welcoming' gesture close to the entrance.

PROJECT EVALUATION

The building opened in September 2005, at a time of renewed public interest in dance. It is used by students from Northumbria University, professional dancers and the general public, and in its first year of use the number of people attending dance classes increased by 75%. Since 2006 Dance City has expanded and developed an increasing programme of public dance performances in the Dance:Lab and currently more than 140,000 people use the building each year.

Responses to the building have been overwhelmingly positive. Staff members enjoy the engagement of their work places with the liveliness and dynamism of the social space and this 'heart' to the organisation has enabled both public and professional users of the building an opportunity to meet and communicate.

One of the challenges for the design team was to understand and ensure that the building would be able to deal very heavy use. Robust building materials such as brick and concrete for dance studios and for the public areas have worked well. Five years into its creative life the building is wearing well and internal finishes look good and provide low maintenance solutions for the organisation.

In 2007 the building won a RIBA Regional Award, a Hadrian Award and the Lord Mayors Design Award.

all photography on this spread by Sally Ann Norman
drawing supplied by the architect

Client Newcastle City Council and Dance City
Architect Malcolm Fraser Architects
Main Contractor Shepherd Construction Ltd
Quantity Surveyor Newcastle City Council
Structural Engineer Arup Scotland

Services Engineer Harley Haddow
Project Manager MDA Consulting Ltd
Acoustic Consultant New Acoustics Ltd
Access Consultant Burdus Access
Management

Saltwell Park and Saltwell Towers

Saltwell Park Road,
Gateshead

Construction value £9.2 million
Date of completion March 2005
Project type Mix of building reconstruction, refurbishment, public realm and landscape

INTRODUCTION

Close to the centre of Gateshead, Saltwell Park lies just off the old A1 route and high on the eastern slope of the Team Valley. With striking views over open countryside to the west it manages to largely obscure the sprawling Team Valley industrial estate below, reflecting the rural aspect of much of Gateshead. Parks with grandeur on this scale are of great historical significance, and Saltwell is considered to be the finest Victorian park in the North East. Its 20 hectares contain a rich mix of architecture, water features and landscapes. As a centrepiece, a once-private mansion, Saltwell Towers, built between 1850 and 1862, comprises the former home and landscaped gardens of William Wailes. The parkland to the north was designed by Edward Kemp, and the gardens to the south are the grounds of The Grove, an adjoining small estate bought by the council in 1920 to increase the size of the park. Together they form parkland and gardens in a classic mid-19th-century layout: a series of external 'rooms' all depicting different characters, from open meadow to formal Italianate garden. The park is a source of both local and civic pride, and generates a strong sense of ownership within the area; its senior staff proudly curate Gateshead Council's annual exhibit at The Chelsea Flower Show, reflecting the importance the authority attaches to its long-established gardening department.

Significantly, the park and garden are of special historic interest within a Conservation Area, and contain 12 listed buildings and monuments. However, over the passage of time the park and buildings began to deteriorate; by the late 20th century, Gateshead Council decided to act. It managed to secure Heritage Lottery funding in 1999 for three-quarters of the £9 million plus cost of an ambitious restoration programme.

CLIENT'S BRIEF

In consultation with the Heritage Lottery Fund and specialist advisors, the council's in-house architectural team – drew together a project team. This included representatives of the Tyne and Wear Building Preservation Trust, North East Civic Trust, English Heritage and The National Trust (along with specialist conservation consultant architects (Simpson Brown) and a landscape historian (Fiona Green). Together, they developed a brief to reverse the deterioration of the buildings and the overgrown landscape.

Many of the original park features are characterised by a strong landscape of peripheral trees, wooded enclosure and shrubbery. The design process focused on identifying the original concept and form; stripping out 20th-century intrusions; and removing, rebuilding and replanting to recreate the Victorian park.

Extensive reinstatement of the park's infrastructure, and repair or restoration of its monuments and pavilions, was identified as the priority. Major tree-planting and landscape-restoration work to the main parkland areas were required, together with a longer-term plan for horticultural management to re-establish the Victorian 'character'. The brief also outlined plans to refurbish the park's buildings. Saltwell Towers had suffered most since the 1960s (when it had been a museum), losing its entire interior and becoming a derelict, roofless shell; external walls had collapsed owing to exposure to the elements.

The park, which has always been a major 'resort' for local people, particularly in the summer months, has been revived and reinforced since the restoration, with visitor numbers increasing with each passing year.

all photography on this spread by Sally Ann Norman

DESIGN PROCESS

The scale of the project proved so demanding that it became necessary to handle it as a series of distinct, individual schemes. In this way, the various elements of landscape work and building repair or restoration could be prepared and designed in a focused way. This was also seen as facilitating the appointment of appropriate contractors to undertake the work – including improvements to the drive and 'broadwalk' footpaths; conservation of the monuments; and restoration of the gates, boundary walls and the 'belvedere walls'. It also embraced major tree-planting and landscape-restoration in the parkland areas and restoring the lake and the island, along with major reconstruction of the 'Dene' and reinstatement of the formal gardens and the maze. In addition, the architecture was to be restored by refurbishing the park pavilions, the stable-yard buildings, animal houses, park lodges and Saltwell Towers itself.

Each of the individual landscape elements was designed in close consultation with historic-garden and landscape consultants. This involved considerable research and investigation of records in order to reveal the form and structure of the original park and the Victorian style of planting associated with 'promenading'. Some major decisions involved removing over-mature planting, to reopen vistas and to remove well-established footpath routes which had not formed part of the original plans.

Designs for the reinstatement of the perimeter walls, fences and gates, and the monuments and other significant elements were prepared in consultation with specialist conservation architects and heritage consultants. This again involved close study of records and examination of the structures themselves. Repair and reinstatement of the various pavilions and lodges was dealt with in the same, detailed way. However the major reconstruction of Saltwell Towers and its surrounding gardens marked the most significant project within the scheme.

This involved significant restoration of the original layout to the formal gardens surrounding the centrepiece of the park, but, more importantly, the almost total rebuilding of the Towers itself to create a modern visitor facility with a café, interpretation centre and a specially commissioned architectural art-glass screen (by Bridget Jones) and furniture (by Wales and Wales). Owing to the degraded state of the remaining walls of the Towers there was concern about structural stability, and design analysis showed that a new stand-alone structure would have to be inserted to carry the new roof, new floor levels and a new eastern façade. This allowed stabilisation of the existing external walls, by structurally tying them locally at every floor and roof level. From this starting point, the design process focused on conservation and repair of as much of the remaining fabric as possible.

Close consultation with conservationists took place for restoration or replication of elements such as the original timber windows, decorative brickwork elements, stonework, roofs and spires – and for insertion of new elements, where that was the only remaining option. The original roofscape of steep pitches, turrets and spires was recreated from photographic evidence, and new modern detailing was added, with new metal windows and new metal-and-terracotta cladding, to create a sympathetic but modern eastern façade.

PROJECT EVALUATION

The restored park, and the Towers in particular, have been widely acclaimed through several national award schemes. The restored Towers won the Regional Renaissance Award 2005, judged by the Royal Institute of Chartered Surveyors, and was national winner of Civic Building of the Year 2005, awarded by the Society of Chief Architects of Local Authorities. The park received a Civic Trust Award in 2006 and won the Best Park in Britain Award 2005. It was named Best Regional Park 2006, and has received Green Flag Awards in each subsequent year.

The park, which has always been a major 'resort' for local people, particularly in the summer months, has been revived and reinforced since the restoration, with visitor numbers increasing with each passing year. A Friends Group has been established in order to help ensure its long-term future. It has truly become 'The people's park'!

In addition to its function as a visitor facility, the Towers building is also used to exhibit the work of local artists and to hold events involving the local community. It also houses an interactive exhibition, which describes the history of Saltwell Park and of its great patron, the Victorian stained glass entrepreneur William Wailes.

Client Gateshead Council
Architect Gateshead Design Services
Main Contractor Gateshead Local Environmental Services
Quantity Surveyor Gateshead Design Services
Structural Engineer Gateshead Design Services
Services Engineer Gateshead Design Services

Project Manager Gateshead Design Services
Conservation Architect Simpson & Brown Architects
Landscape Historian Fiona Green
Landscape Architect Brambledown Landscapes &
Gateshead Design Services

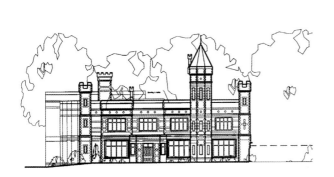

Tyneside Cinema

10 Pilgrim Street,
Newcastle upon Tyne

Construction value **£5.2 million**
Date of completion **May 2008**
Project type **Renovation and extension**

INTRODUCTION

Newcastle's Tyneside Cinema holds a special place in the history of film in the UK, as well as being an important part of the city's cultural and social life. Founded by Dixon Scott, great-uncle of legendary film directors Ridley and Tony Scott, it was built in 1937 as the Bijou Newsreel Cinema and is considered the finest purpose-built 'news theatre' in Britain that still operates as a cinema.

In its first year, the Bijou Newsreel became the home of the Tyneside Film Society, which at the time, was one of the few showcases for foreign-language films. Remarkably, by the late 1950s the society had expanded into the largest in the UK outside London. In the late 1960s it became the Tyneside Film Theatre Trust, a charity dedicated to presenting non-mainstream films.

In 2000, as a result of the English Heritage Picture Palaces Initiative, the building was listed Grade II. The listing made particular reference to the architectural importance of the double-height auditorium of the original news theatre, the entrance foyer and the superb second floor café, a thriving social hub for the city and surrounding area. Surviving elaborate plaster mouldings and panels are to be found throughout the building.

CLIENT'S BRIEF

In 2004, following years of 'benign neglect' by the previous owner, the Trust determined to restore the cinema to its Art Deco splendour and at the same time create a contemporary digital media centre for the city and region. A complete internal reconstruction was required; with only two screens, the building needed at least one more to become a sustainable cultural business operation by increasing capacity and providing programming flexibility.

Exiled 'Geordies' were contacted for help. Internationally celebrated film-maker Mike Figgis, together with musicians Neil Tennant of the Pet Shop Boys and Paul Smith of Maxïmo Park, all born locally, became patrons. They spearheaded the fundraising campaign to transform the cinema into the regional film theatre for the North East – indeed, into one of the finest art-film theatres in the country – with funding provided by the Heritage Lottery Fund, Tyne and Wear Partnership and the European Regional Development Fund. Additional funding came from trusts, foundations and many private supporters. During restoration, the cinema continued in operation, albeit across the river in Gateshead where the former town hall, conveniently located a few hundred metres from Newcastle's boundary across the High Level Bridge, became a successful temporary location.

Proposed cross-section
by Fletcher Priest Architects

'Newcastle is blessed with perhaps the finest independent cinema in the country.'

The *Guardian*

all photography on this spread by Sally Ann Norman

DESIGN PROCESS

Overcoming the restrictions of the landlocked site to provide two new screens within a distinctive rooftop extension, while preserving the fine Art Deco legacy of the original building, was a major challenge for the design team. It required the integration of a new steel frame within the existing loadbearing masonry, while maintaining the historic fabric below. Two new cinemas – the Electra and the Roxy, with 144 and 100 seats respectively – are linked by a foyer bar enclosed in translucent lightweight polycarbonate sheeting that at night appears as a glowing opaque box, while reflecting the quality of the sky during the day to blend into the existing skyline.

The requirement for all areas to be accessible was achieved through careful adaptation of the diverse floor levels within the existing building and the introduction of digital-technology facilities to assist partially sighted and blind visitors, as well as those with hearing difficulties.

The existing lightwell provided the space for essential modern facilities, including new projection rooms and improved public circulation. The original auditorium, the Classic, was carefully restored with 200 new seats in the stalls and 60 luxurious armchairs and sofas in the circle. For experimental work, the new 'Digital Lounge' is a multi-purpose space designed to show locally produced digital films and double as a venue for educational events. Film-makers of the future can develop their skills in digital-cinema technology in a new education suite with film-production space, editing suites and meeting rooms.

The Tyneside's detailed conservation plan, including guidance on the long-term maintenance and upkeep of the fabric, was prepared by the veteran Newcastle architect Cyril Winskell, a specialist in building conservation, supported by social historian Tom Yellowley. Patrons were heavily involved, too; focus-group research at the cinema showed that audiences regarded the building's heritage as equally important as film-going itself.

The restoration and transformation of the building revealed a great deal of the original, ornate interior, much of it influenced by Dixon Scott's travels in the Far East. Analysis of the original paintwork also revealed a palette of subdued period colours that have been faithfully replicated. Information on the original interior fittings and furnishings was obtained from period photographs and drawings. Additionally, the highly decorative glass-mosaic floors were revealed and restored, and existing light fittings refurbished.

During reconstruction, the unusual mural, *Lights and Shadows on The Wall: Improving Amusements*, executed by the eminent regional architect Peter Yates in 1976 when he redesigned the club cinema, was rediscovered. After many years hidden from view it was reinstated in the new Electra cinema, close to its original position.

The restored and extended building retains the ambience of the original, with sophisticated technology that places it at the forefront of the industry and probably makes the cinema the best of its kind in Britain: truly a mix of 1930s splendour and 21st-century technology.

Moreover, the importance of the restored 'Coffee Rooms' on the second floor as a local institution – it is also an informal, café-style restaurant – has been further underlined. Close to Newcastle's shopping area, it has a dedicated clientele. Now much expanded thanks to restoration, it is one of the post popular meeting places in the city.

PROJECT EVALUATION

The completed project will develop the demand for 'alternative' and cultural films, which is growing annually. In its first year following the reopening, ticket sales increased by 70 per cent and 350,000 people visited the cinema. Further research has demonstrated that 87 per cent of people who use the Tyneside Cinema engage with the history and heritage of the building. This might involve watching newsreels, looking at the interpretation displays, and taking part in guided and self-guided tours.

Both digital-media companies and members of the public use the Tyneside's state of-the-art film-production facilities, which aim to encourage young people in the art of film-making. These facilities offer high-speed connectivity between offices, production and cinema spaces. The Tyneside Outreach Programme brings learning opportunities in so-called moving-image media and emerging technologies to over 6,000 children, young people and adults every year. Current forecasts indicate that this will increase to around 9,000 over the next three years.

Since its reopening, the Tyneside Cinema has scooped a number of prestigious awards, including the 2009 RICS North East Renaissance Project of the Year title. Critics have been mightily impressed with the restoration. The *Guardian* was typical of many, noting that 'Newcastle is blessed with perhaps the finest independent cinema in the country.'

Client **Tyneside Cinema**
Architect **Fletcher Priest Architects**
Main Contractor **Wates Construction**
Quantity Surveyor **Gleeds**
Structural Engineer **Adams Kara Taylor**

Services Engineer **Cundall**
Project Manager **Turner & Townsend plc**
Conservation Architect **Cyril Winskell Architect**
Access Consultant **Burdus Access Management**
Acoustic Consultant **Sandy Brown and Associates**

Newcastle Library

New Bridge Street,
Newcastle upon Tyne

Construction value **£24 million**
Date of completion **March 2009**
Project type **New-build**

INTRODUCTION

Libraries nationally have been facing their biggest challenge since the growth of public book-lending in the mid-19th century, with an estimated 80 closing over the past decade. Until recently, few would have dared to predict a turnaround for this once-hallowed symbol of municipal pride. However, in some cities the first decade of the millennium saw a re-assessment of the role of the public library as a vital community resource, marking a determination by councils to reverse a tide of retrenchment. Nationally, Newcastle is leading the field with the emergence of one of the country's first 'super-libraries', acclaimed by some experts as an inspiration for others.

Procured through the Private Finance Initiative and opened in mid-2009, the city library, a highly transparent building on six levels complete with excellent café and welcoming staff, arrived with a mission to inform, educate and encourage people to visit and enjoy its range of new facilities. Its policy of open access, without ticket counters, gives the building the feel of a friendly bookshop at ground level: embracing reading areas and soft seating alongside low book shelves.

The previous city library, designed by Sir Basil Spence in the 1960s on the same site, was at best imposing rather than welcoming. The main entrance was off the drab backwater of the pedestrian Princess Square, a legacy of the era's over-enthusiasm for Modernism-turned-Brutalist. Its interior was relatively closed and cellular, with staff separated behind counters or in offices.

CLIENT'S BRIEF

From the outset, it was important to make the library a key city-centre attraction, with prominent signposting from Grey's Monument and the City's principle shopping street to the new building a few hundred metres eastwards, reinforced by directions to the neighbouring Laing Art Gallery and a square rejuvenated in 2002 by the artist Thomas Heatherwick.

The Commission for Architecture and the Built Environment (CABE) supported the city council and advised on the brief for the new library, later commenting on the final designs. This led to a brief from the city council, which not only called for a building that would 'delight and inspire' – a guiding principle used by the team throughout the design process – it also required the building to be a model for 21st-century library facilities, a civic landmark and a meeting place. Equally importantly – in line with a new, inclusive community ethos – it had to accommodate a range of supporting facilities including a café, crèche, public-meeting and exhibition spaces.

'User-friendliness' became an overarching mantra: IT services were to be spread around the building, including self-issuing terminals – easy-to-use and much less intimidating than some feared – with a 24-hour return system. This released staff from more mundane duties to help users and borrowers enjoy the library and its facilities. Additionally, design proposals – for exterior and interior, including furniture, and stock arrangement – were developed through extensive consultation with staff and users.

'An inspiration for the other 148 library authorities in England ... a building that speaks of style, learning, confidence and a warm welcome.'

Roy Clare – Chief Executive of the Museums, Libraries and Archives Council

exploded axonometric illustrating the principal building elements
by Ryder Architecture

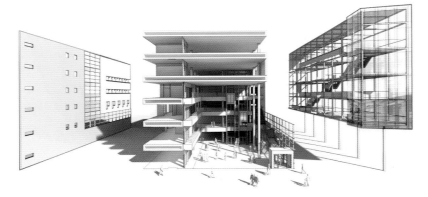

DESIGN PROCESS

A new definition soon entered the project's design lexicon: 'bookshelf for the city'. It was to become a neat way of describing both the library internally and the building itself – with a glazed steel-frame grid, reminiscent of shelving, forming its eastern elevation. This element contains the main staircase, taking visitors on a journey through the six floors of the building. The main entrance now sits on its southeast corner, attracting people in New Bridge Street alongside as they head either in the direction of the library or the neighbouring Laing Art Gallery. Surrounding the entrance, a foyer-cum-cosy-book-sampling area and information point is surrounded by a four-storey atrium, allowing easy orientation and offering a visual 'sweep' of the wide range of services offered.

A further significant design feature involves the location of the reserve book store. This large facility, which would normally either be buried in a basement or located at ground level – thus reducing the size of the more active public areas around it – is here located on the fifth floor, accessible yet relatively discreet because it does not compete for valuable space elsewhere. The sixth floor, a key reference level for archives, also gives visitors a new viewpoint to the city centre, and beyond towards Tyneside and the coast. Interior signage is colour-coded for each area in vibrant hues, directly related to the decoration on particular levels and reflecting the new branding for the library.

Building materials were chosen to represent the civic stature of the library, its immediate physical and cultural context, and its contemporary nature. The plinth and stair cores are in polished masonry block, solidly grounding the building into the wider public realm; glazing, curtain walling and metal rain-screen cladding make the modular façades pleasing to the eye.

Outside Level One, a once-drab public space – Princess Square – has been considerably enhanced by new landscaping abutting an alternative entrance to the building, which leads directly to a spacious library café boasting an attractive terrace opening out to the square as weather permits!

The library achieves a 'Very good' rating under the BREEAM criteria, the internationally recognised standard for assessing the environmental standards of buildings. Working within the constraints of a tight city-centre site, the designers have managed to draw maximum energy-efficiency from the glazed exterior, particularly on the eastern elevations facing the Laing Art Gallery, where glazing is unprotected, allowing morning sun to heat much of the building. The west elevation, facing Princess Square, has smaller windows protected by vertical blades to prevent overheating.

Further measures to maximise efficiency include high-performance construction materials and methods; high-efficiency heating, cooling and lighting systems; rainwater recovery for flushing toilets; and solar panels to preheat hot water.

PROJECT EVALUATION

This building is all the more impressive considering that it had to be delivered within the constraints of the Private Finance Initiative; in the event, it has emerged as one of the more adventurous, and better-designed PFI projects. The budget was fixed from the start, with no opportunity for amendment; thankfully, given that the project involved complex demolition and redevelopment on a tight city-centre site, there were no cost overruns.

Overall, the design has been widely praised. Roy Clare – Chief Executive of the Museums, Libraries and Archives Council – has described the project as: 'an inspiration for the other 148 library authorities in England ... a building that speaks of style, learning, confidence and a warm welcome.'

Visitor figures soon after opening show increases of 86 per cent in enquiries, 125 per cent in book issues, 197 per cent in visits and no less than 398 per cent in new borrowers compared with the old library. Through the use of self-service technology, staff are now free to focus on welcoming people and helping them use the building.

In addition, the café is proving not only extremely popular, becoming an essential meeting point for shoppers and others, but is also proving an important means of attracting more users into the library itself.

Client **Newcastle City Council**
Developer **Kajima Partnerships Ltd**
Architect **Ryder Architecture Ltd**
Main Contractor **Tolent Construction Ltd**
Quantity Surveyor **Turner & Townsend plc**
Structural Engineer **Mott MacDonald**

Services Engineer **SES**
Project Manager **Turner & Townsend plc**
Services Consultant **White Young Green**
Fire Consultant **Jeremy Gardiner Associates**
Access Consultant **All Clear Designs**

Great North Museum

Barras Bridge,
Newcastle upon Tyne

Construction value £26 million
Date of completion May 2009
Project type New-build extension and refurbishment

INTRODUCTION

Bringing together premier collections of archaeology, geology and natural history, the Great North Museum sits in a park-like setting amidst new and mature landscaping. The £26 million part-Heritage-Lottery-funded museum is an important element in a wider vision, encapsulated in a masterplan by Farrells, to create a new cultural quarter on the northern edge of the city centre.

Occupying a prominent position beside the old Great North Road and overlooking the setting of the Civic Centre – a 'green lung', near the city's heart, which few provincial cities enjoy – the overall site now provides opportunity for public, civic and cultural activities.

Subtle alterations to the Grade II* listed building reveal to best advantage the original layout and, with new openings and outside views, open up the museum, improving circulation and providing a fully accessible attraction.

A new extension complements and contrasts with the existing Hancock Museum in form and use, and provides facilities appropriate to a 21st-century museum. Contrast is achieved through the use of modern materials and detailing, and the bold use of accent colours.

The emerging cultural quarter around the museum also embraces the recently rebuilt Northern Stage theatre, reinforcing the University's importance as a cultural as well as economic driver for the city and the wider North East.

CLIENT'S BRIEF

Farrells was asked to address the museum's limited exhibition space, its setting in relation to the city, and its unsuitable environmental conditions, and to reinterpret the existing, varied collection. The project had to innovatively combine the Museum of Antiquities with the Natural History Society and other collections, under one roof within the shell of the existing Hancock Museum. It also had to integrate the expanding Newcastle University campus into the city in an upgraded garden setting, fully accessible to all.

The existing Grade II* building needed to be opened up and altered to make better use of light and space, and to improve circulation. An expanded exhibition space was required for displaying and interpreting the new collections. The historic fabric needed repairing, both internally and externally. Deteriorating 19th-century gallery conditions had to be transformed to 21st-century standards in order to allow good flexibility of display, interpretation and interaction with the environmentally delicate collections.

A new extension needed new entrances; additional large-scale, flexible exhibition space for temporary exhibitions and events – important revenue generators in their own right – a new library, bringing together the collections of three historical societies; a new flexible education facility and lecture room; and museum offices, delivery and building services areas, plus space for retail and catering opportunities.

Occupying a prominent position beside the old Great North Road and overlooking the setting of the Civic Centre – a 'green lung', near the city's heart

DESIGN PROCESS

Building on Farrells' extensive experience of working in Newcastle, the museum was integrated into the changing city, cultural quarter and university masterplan through the early design and funding stages. Farrells worked closely with curators, exhibition designers and heritage architects in order to satisfy all aspects of the client brief and to secure planning and listed-building consent. The process of achieving all this is summarised in Farrells' 10-point vision statement for the Great North Museum. This included a new public space for 'cultural and heritage activity', and noted that an open and expansive front to the museum would provide a space for public and cultural activities for both the University and the city.

In addition, the plan stressed the importance of a Northumbrian landscape setting, with local flora forming a large part of the museum and library content. This is used to derive modern, fresh colour schemes for the building. Rooms connecting with the landscape externally use soft greens. Bright colour accents, derived from Northumbrian flowers, are used for window mullions and in washrooms – contrasting with the greens in a playful yet natural way.

The project enabled the appropriate conservation, reuse and revival of the Grade II* listed building, while retaining the historic Hancock collections. Outside, the existing stone façade was repaired with a light touch, retaining a strong aged 'feel', while windows were reconditioned and painted dark to contrast with the sandstone. The roof was repaired/replaced using conservation techniques and materials. Inside, the stone stairwells were also repaired, cleaned and enhanced to 21st-century access standards; timber doors were repaired; and modern lighting was introduced in order to replicate the daylight quality of the original interiors.

The new extension pulls away from the existing building, creating a multi-functional galleria space and new entrances for societies, large groups and visitors to special exhibitions. It contrasts with the existing museum; new and old buildings are separated visually and physically by a double-height glazed galleria, allowing the identity and form of each to read strongly. In addition, the new building contextually derives its form and size from the volume of the existing central gallery; strong horizontal lines and vertical rhythms transfer from the existing structure across to the new building.

A new temporary-exhibition gallery incorporates a dedicated place for display, performance and 'celebration', providing a secure, environmentally controlled space in which internationally significant collections may be displayed. This space can be closed off from the main galleries.

The museum also brings together the Society of Antiquaries and the Natural History Society of Northumbria in a new centre, containing office space and a public library with archive facilities accommodating their most prominent collections.

PROJECT EVALUATION

Professor Paul Younger, Deputy Vice-Chancellor of the University, believes the museum has further integrated the University into the cultural life of the city and the Northeast region. Comments from visitors suggest that they are impressed with the museum's opening up, visually and physically, to allow a new clear 'reading' of its spaces and their inter-relationship. The conserved and refreshed heritage of the building is contrasted against modern architectural and display elements, providing a new 21st-century feeling and ambience which contrasts favourably with the old Hancock Museum.

The new Great North Museum is user-friendly; large new openings, of diminishing size, sit along a central axial route through the three main galleries, the new galleria, street café and special-exhibition space, with a new 'front door' opening directly to the University. Cross-views from side spaces through the central galleries to the outside link the interior with the exterior – providing orientation and contrast. The inclusive 'feel' of the new building is further enhanced by clear zoning, with retail and hospitality areas assigned to the front spaces and within the galleria.

all photography on this spread by Sally Ann Norman
drawing supplied by the architect

Client Newcastle University
Main Contractor Kier North East
Architect Farrells
Quantity Surveyor Ridge
Structural Engineer WSP

MEP Consultant WYG
Project Manager Turner & Townsend plc
Exhibition Designer Casson Mann Designers
Conservation Architect Purves Ash LLP

◐ Education

Academics and students enrich Newcastle and Gateshead, adding value to the economy of the twin cities with leading-edge research, spending power and wider civic and cultural engagement.

When Newcastle University was created in 1963, from King's College – part of Durham University, although sited in Newcastle – in a big expansion of higher education nationally, few would have dreamt that by the millennium 55,000 full- and part-time students would be registered at two universities in the city. Part of that outcome is due to both organic growth and the creation of Northumbria University, from the former Newcastle Polytechnic, in 1992. Nationally, Newcastle has a reputation as one of the most popular university cities; a relatively high proportion of students want to remain on Tyneside after graduation, adding further to its vitality and to the wider Tyneside economy.

It is no coincidence that the two universities effectively ring the Civic Centre, thus creating a relatively new academic and cultural quarter, and they are expanding and modernising substantially courtesy of two large capital programmes.

Northumbria is expanding east, across a central motorway, with a new campus; Newcastle University is in the throes of completing a campus masterplan, produced by the architect Sir Terry Farrell, a former student at the University's school of architecture. As part of this plan, the new King's Gate student and administrative services building provides a welcoming new front door to the University, behind which stands the Northern Stage theatre and a revamped public square leading to Newcastle University's traditional red-brick Quadrangle. Significantly, the new front door provides a welcome not just for

all photography on this spread by Sally Ann Norman

students but also for the wider community heading for the theatre and the remodelled Great North Museum: Hancock nearby.

Northumbria, one of the highest ranking of the new wave of universities, has sought to judiciously acquire land for expansion with a new east campus, connected to its main campus with a new footbridge over a central motorway and a Metro rail line.

But expansion, in no small part, has been due to a fusion of civic and academic ambition in the early 1960s. As Professor John Goddard recalls, an alliance between Newcastle University's then Deputy Vice-Chancellor, Henry Daysh, and the council leader, T. Dan Smith, resulted in a consolidation of the present campus as part of Smith's vision of what he termed 'Education on Tyne'. In physical terms, this meant embracing the Royal Victoria Infirmary – with its links to Newcastle University's Medical School – and the former polytechnic, in one area.

The council bought land to secure its strategy and safeguard the University at a time when some feared the institution might move outside the city to a new greenfield site. As a result, unlike many other civic universities, Newcastle was able to expand in situ and develop a single city-centre campus on one site.

Northumbria, one of the highest ranking of the new wave of universities, has sought to judiciously acquire land for expansion with a new east campus, connected to its main campus with a new footbridge over a central motorway and a Metro rail line.

For its part, Newcastle University is investing in both an emerging 'Science City' business park, a venture called Science Central and a multi-use development on the site of a former brewery with the aim of creating businesses and private sector jobs. To foster business links, and postgraduate (and graduate) enterprise, the University's business school has appointed four entrepreneurs as 'professors of practice'.

Elsewhere, the student population of the twin cities has been further underpinned by the ambitions of colleges of further education in Newcastle and Gateshead. The latter has recently invested £60 million on new campuses, including a new central Baltic Campus behind the contemporary art centre of the same name.

All photography on this spread by Sally Ann Norman

Newcastle University, King's Gate Building

Barras Bridge,
Newcastle upon Tyne.

Construction value **£34 million**
Date of completion **October 2009**
Project type **New-build**

INTRODUCTION

The main approach to Newcastle University was given a striking new frontage with the completion of this functional, blue-glass-clad building. Overlooking the city's imposing Civic Centre on Barras Bridge, and opposite the parkland of St Thomas' Green, it houses what the University calls its 'threshold' services for visitors and students. Comprising mostly open-plan accommodation, arranged over five storeys, and combining many of the University's administrative departments, it houses approximately 400 staff – including the Vice-Chancellor and Registrar – previously located in a number of disparate buildings across the campus.

The site, a former car park, lies in front of the rebuilt Northern Stage theatre; indeed, a widened route, King's Walk, beside the new building leads to an enlarged public square between the Students' Union building, a lawn in front, and the theatre itself. In turn, the route directs visitors across a service road to the red brick, Tudor-Jacobean buildings of the University's late 19th-century quadrangle.

However, the sharply contrasting style of King's Gate – the result of an architectural competition featuring several national practices – does not jar with the older buildings; rather, it complements the adjoining theatre and effectively completes the Barras Bridge streetscape with a simple form fashioned from high-quality glazing, louvres and natural sandstone cladding. It gives the University campus a front door and a point of arrival arguably for the first time.

CLIENT'S BRIEF

The need for a major gateway for the university, and a civic frontage to Barras Bridge, was laid down in a series of 'critical success factors' for the new building. These stipulated that as well as providing a high-quality, welcoming and accessible environment – it was to be a 'public face' for the University, after all – the building had to provide flexible spaces for informal meetings and interaction between staff and students, especially on the ground floor. Three principles were laid down in a university masterplan: integration between university and city, a rationalisation of administrative facilities, and high-quality public spaces internally and externally. Moreover, the building itself, incorporating largely open-plan working with minimal cellular spaces, had to achieve a 'Very good' energy efficiency, and environmental rating under the internationally recognised BREEAM standards while, at the same time, respecting adjacent buildings.

Equally importantly, the building had to symbolise the aspirations of an innovative and modern university capable of accommodating change. Flexibility in style and layout, and 'modernity', were stressed along with the importance of improving public spaces – the so-called 'public realm' – for the benefit of students, visitors and the public alike.

The building makes a wider civic statement: transforming the last remaining gap site on Barras Bridge, enhancing the streetscape and improving accessibility to King's Walk while literally bringing the University closer to the city.

all photography on this spread by Sally Ann Norman

Client **Newcastle University**
Architect **FaulknerBrowns Architects**
Main Contractor **BAM Construction**
Quantity Surveyor **Summers-Inman**
Structural Engineer **Cundall**

Services Engineer **Cundall**
Project Manager **Summers-Inman**
Landscape Architect **Colour: Urban Design Limited**

photography by Martine Hamilton Knight

Northumbria University, City Campus East

Northumbria University City Campus East,
Newcastle upon Tyne

Construction value **£47 million**
Date of completion **August 2007**
Project type **New-build**

INTRODUCTION

As one of a relatively new wave of former-polytechnics-turned-universities in England – and, consistently, one of the most successful – Northumbria has become a major academic, economic and cultural player in Newcastle, occupying a large city-centre site. Its new City Campus East further embeds its presence and extends its reach, while making a powerful architectural statement about regeneration and the importance of higher education in the city. In turn, this provided an opportunity to take a considerable step towards achieving its central vision: to become one of the world's leading teaching-based universities.

At the heart of the project was the primary need to provide the best possible class-based facilities for the 9,000 students and staff who make up the University's School of Law, Newcastle Business School and the School of Design. In addition, the project also symbolised a transformation of the eastern edge of the city centre, across the Central Motorway East, which would have a significant impact on the University and the city with an adventurous extension of its campus across a new bridge.

Advancing educational standards, stimulating urban renewal and embracing innovative designs were all part of the process that allowed the University's vision to be expressed in a bold architectural form.

CLIENT'S BRIEF

Northumbria University wanted landmark buildings, adventurous in design yet practical, which would be pleasing to the eye while symbolising the ambition to become a world-class university. That meant striving for a quality of design that embraced the principles of sustainability and energy-efficiency, combined with flexibility and value for money, on an unpromising site: that of a former multiplex cinema and surrounding car parks.

After agreeing the masterplan, developed by Shepheard Epstein Hunter, the client worked closely with architects Atkins in order to translate their aspirations and functional requirements into initial designs. Atkins responded practically to the brief, by immediately removing a number of staircases from the existing building plans and simplifying its form and footprint. The final design pushed the structural spans to the extreme in order to create generous spaces, culminating in the resulting iconic buildings, linked by an eye-catching new pedestrian bridge to the west campus across the Central Motorway East – thus extending the entire campus in an eastward direction.

'This is one of the most iconic cities in Europe. It has the Angel of the North, The Sage Gateshead and the Gateshead Millennium Bridge and I'd put this new campus in that league. This is a really world class facility, with world class design.'

Andrew Dixon, former Chief Executive of the NewcastleGateshead Initiative

 all photography on this spread by Sally Ann Norman

Client Newcastle College
Architect RMJM
Main Contractor Sir Robert McAlpine Ltd
Quantity Surveyor Todd Milburn Partnership
Structural Engineer RMJM
Services Engineer RMJM
Project Manager Turner & Townsend plc

Acoustic Consultant Sandy Brown Associates LLP
Access Consultant ADAPT
Catering Consultant The Dynamic Catering Design Partnership
Sport and Exercise Consultant Technogym UK Ltd
Hair and Beauty Consultant EXRM Solutions Ltd

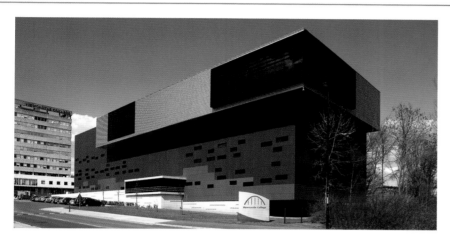

DESIGN PROCESS

The academy is clearly distinguished by its three constituent forms: a monolithic 'black box' with an abstract, pierced façade; a 'silver box' with giant windows, allowing people outside to catch a glimpse of the inner workings of the school; and a concrete plinth, on which the whole building sits.

The black façade is characterised by an array of slot windows, which draw attention to the building and generate curiosity. The building 'skin' here is a carefully developed and economical fibre-cement cladding system, with the window locations systematically considered in relation to daylight, heat gain and the spaces that they serve.

The silver box at the top of the building, open to the public, commands panoramic views over the Tyne Valley. The 'buzz' of activity within the academy is revealed to the outside world by the design and placing of windows which showcase the real working environments to the campus and the city beyond. The effect is prominent and powerful, and is a new and distinct addition to the cityscape and skyline.

Elevated on a plinth, all these elements sit together in the southeast corner of the campus – generating the maximum possible visual impact. The concrete plinth provides a level approach for pedestrians, a separate loading area for vehicles and discreet

access for mechanical and electrical plant accommodation.

The Lifestyle Academy has one clear public entrance for all, which leads to the heart of the building. From this point, students and the public are distributed separately by a clear circulation strategy. The hub of the building incorporates a service spine housing toilets, vertical circulation and service risers. The main accommodation is then wrapped around this in order to maximise natural light and ventilation from the external envelope. The surrounding landscape and public realm has been designed to link the academy back to the rest of the campus.

The majority of the Lifestyle Academy has a concrete frame and exposed BubbleDeck® concrete slabs. The use of this system significantly reduces mass, and the environmental benefits include the reduction of CO_2 and a saving of up to 50 per cent in the levels of both water and aggregate used during construction. The concrete slabs were factory finished, a process which offered greater quality control and significantly reduced the on-site construction period. The top floor of the building is constructed in a steel frame, which provides the support needed for the lightweight metal roof. A significant portion of the metal structure is reclaimed steelwork, sourced from existing buildings.

PROJECT EVALUATION

The location of the Lifestyle Academy on the Rye Hill Campus was a concern from the outset of the project. However, through close working between the client and design team this perceived weakness was turned into the outstanding strength of the building design.

A key decision taken during the design process involved the pros and cons of placing 'public activity' (restaurant, spa, gym and salons) on the top floor in a high-profile 'silver box', showcasing the activities taking place within and allowing visitors stunning views across the city. Traditionally activities such as these are located on the ground floor, in order to attract interest from passers-by. It was agreed, however, that because there has been little public 'footfall' in this part of the city – it is, after all, some way from shopping and cultural attractions – there was potential in turning the Lifestyle Academy into a 'destination', capitalising on it becoming a recognisable landmark in its own right. The architect's design solution – a 'high-impact silver box' – is now an established part of the cityscape.

Rye Hill House,
Newcastle College

**Newcastle College Rye Hill Campus
Scotswood Road, Newcastle upon Tyne**

Construction value **£5.2 million**
Date of completion **Spring 2007**
Project type **Refurbishment / renovation and new-build**

EDUCATION

INTRODUCTION

Upgrading this Grade II listed Victorian villa, which dates from 1840, represents the fourth major project by these architects at Newcastle College's Rye Hill campus.

RMJM has restored and extended the original property, located at the north end of the campus, to house student-support and administration facilities. In the process, an architectural form, developed through the previous projects undertaken by the practice for the college, has been maintained, adopting what the architects describe as 'a consistency of design approach'. The project received listed building consent, allowing necessary enabling works: principally, the demolition of adjacent, derelict, non-listed houses.

CLIENT'S BRIEF

The principal requirement for the project was to create a new gateway to the Rye Hill Campus, and to accommodate student services and the central administration departments of the college – creating an important service area where students can go to get advice on enrolment, fees, finance and accommodation.

The 3,300 m2 Rye Hill House project incorporates a striking Victorian residence, which was abutted by two further, unlisted, derelict terraced houses and had been unoccupied for several years at the time of the proposals. Early feasibility considerations included the retention and refurbishment of all the existing buildings, including their façades, with new building behind. The preferred outcome was to demolish the adjoining, derelict terraced houses and incorporate a major new development to the side and rear of the refurbished Victorian villa.

The development has been applauded as a stimulating regeneration project, receiving a commendation from the Lord Mayor's Design Awards.

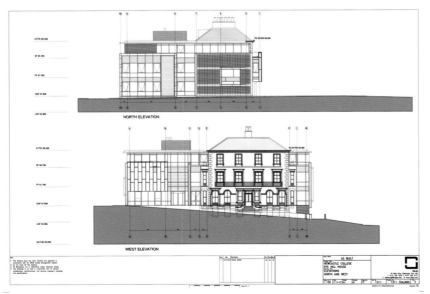

 all photography on this spread by Sally Ann Norman
drawing supplied by the architect

Client **Newcastle College**
Architect **RMJM**
Main contractor **Sir Robert McAlpine Ltd**
Quantity surveyor **Todd Milburn Partnership**
Structural engineer **RMJM**

Services engineer **RMJM**
Project Manager **Turner & Townsend plc**
Enabling Works **Contractor Thompsons**

DESIGN PROCESS

The design strategy adopted by the architects involved maintaining the listed building as cellular, private offices and meeting rooms, providing flexible and adaptable open-plan offices in the new portion and separating the two elements with triple-height atria. This allowed the historic building 'room to breathe' without compromising a confident, modern design. The atrium spaces have vibrant café facilities; as such, they have achieved an exciting yet relaxed environment.

The west-entrance atrium forms a striking entrance hall to the entire development and is top lit, stretching up to the height of the listed building eaves. The east atrium acts as a circulation route at ground level and a lightwell above, in order to maintain the operation of the rear rooms in the listed building. The glazed roof is set one floor below the eaves of the listed building, and the rear brick façade of the latter is fully exposed to the atrium. Underfloor heating and mechanical ventilation are provided in order to maintain environmental conditions in both the atria and the adjacent spaces.

The renovation to the existing building included strengthening existing floors in order to accommodate higher loads, the introduction of a new part-timber trussed roof, new tanking to the existing basement, and chimney breast removal and support. A concrete raft foundation was used for both upper and lower ground levels, and concrete retaining walls were erected around the north end of the site with temporary sheet piling used to form the retention.

PROJECT EVALUATION

This 'new for old' project has added a new, exciting dimension to this ambitious college, which lies adjacent to the Summerhill Square conservation area – comprising magnificent, well-maintained houses built between 1820 and 1840, surrounding a large garden-cum-park and close to the city centre. The project incorporates the Grade II listed property, Rye Hill House. Reaction from local people has been positive, largely owing to the extensive consultation carried out prior to commencement

On completion, the development has been applauded as a stimulating regeneration project, receiving a commendation from the Lord Mayor's Design Awards.

Cardinal Hume Catholic School

Old Durham Road,
Gateshead

Construction value **£24 million**
Date of completion **August 2007**
Project type **New-build**

INTRODUCTION

In common with many other large towns and cities in the UK, Gateshead has seen a transformation in its primary and secondary schools over the past 15 years and proudly boasts that there has been a large scale programme of rebuild/refurbishment in our schools. The new £24 million Cardinal Hume Catholic School was opened in September 2007.

The building, in the suburb of Wrekenton, was designed to replace the old and outdated St Edmund Campion School – a 1,200-place secondary school for 11–18 year olds – in order to meet modern-day teaching and learning requirements on a new site close to the old school site.

CLIENT'S BRIEF

Extensive early briefing sessions were held with the school, in the course of which staff, governors and pupils were interviewed over a number of days to establish their vision for a new school. During the construction period, these were fine-tuned through further consultation in order to ensure that the teaching and non-teaching staff members were fully aware of design developments.

From the outset, there was a consensus that the new environment created should not feel like a 'standard school' and that the architecture and quality of its internal and external environment should have a more mature and collegiate 'feel'. This was achieved with a cost-per-square-metre ratio that the Department for Education and Skills (subsequently the Department for Education) believed to be very economical. For over two years, the project manager held a Monday-morning briefing with the school's Head and senior leadership team to appraise them of progress and consider refinements to the brief. This resulted in a first-class working relationship between the project manager, the architect and the client.

In terms of IT-technology provision, the school is rated within the top three educational establishments in Britain. In addition, a 'wireless cloud' from the school provides the local community with lifelong learning opportunities.

all photography on this spread by Sally Ann Norman

style houses alongside a multi-storey 'wall' of flats with small windows on the north side (overlooking a major road) and balconies looking south. The overall development now needs substantial improvement in order to safeguard its future.

Before the First World War, it is estimated that around half the population of Newcastle and Gateshead lived in flats – a far higher proportion than in other English industrial cities. While some have fallen into disrepair, many remain structurally sound and still provide excellent accommodation.

The task facing the local housing market renewal Pathfinder project, called 'Bridging NewcastleGateshead', is no less challenging. In seven years, it has already refurbished over 6,000 houses, demolished at least 2,370, built approaching 300 new homes and acquired 14 hectares of land for redevelopment.

Part of the Pathfinder challenge is addressing the housing structure of inner Newcastle and Gateshead. For almost 30 years, up to 1914, large numbers of terraces were built – some by developers, and others by industries for their workers. Many

of these terraces incorporated 'Tyneside flats', which embraced an imaginative two-storey design – quite unlike, say, Glasgow tenements or maisonettes elsewhere – with one house above the other, each with its own front and back door. Before the First World War, it is estimated that around half the population of Newcastle and Gateshead lived in flats – a far higher proportion than in other English industrial cities. While some have fallen into disrepair, many remain structurally sound and still provide excellent accommodation.

In the 2010–11 financial year, the Pathfinder will be spending almost £30 million in the twin cities – from Walker Riverside in the east of Newcastle to Scotswood in the west and Felling in the east of Gateshead. Scotswood, overlooking the Tyne, represents a particular challenge; demolition has left large, green open spaces for redevelopment on a prime, south-facing site. In a joint venture between the city council and a private developer, up to 1,800 new family homes are planned with the aim of creating a 'suburban' feel. In the east end of the city, similar plans are further advanced.

In short, while renewing and replacing an aged housing stock has presented challenges in Newcastle and Gateshead, the scale of the problem in the twin cities is considerably less than in other northern conurbations, notably Manchester-Salford and Liverpool-Bootle; indeed, on some estimates, only four per cent of the housing stock is empty – much less than the national average.

Perhaps inevitably, during the late 1990s and early in the millennium, Newcastle and Gateshead, like other large cities around Britain, fell victim to the speculative craze of building new, city-centre apartment blocks, with good design sometimes an afterthought. Buy-to-let investors acquired a disproportionate number of flats, many of which now remain empty.

Some developments, however, stand out as above average: new apartments in Trinity Gardens, overlooking a new public square, blend well into a mixed-use development. Additionally, the relatively recent redevelopment of the bright-red brick Turnbull Building in Hanover Square, central Newcastle, shows how sympathetic conversion into prestigious apartments can add considerable value to an old property – in this case, a late 19th-century printing works-turned-warehouse. Similarly, the conversion of the former Wills tobacco factory, on Newcastle's Coast Road, into apartments has enhanced one of the finest Art Deco buildings in the city; in many ways, the style – albeit by a different architect – is similar to the recently refurbished Moor Court flats, overlooking the Town Moor.

all photography on this spread by Sally Ann Norman

153

The Staiths, South Bank

Team Street, Dunston, Gateshead

Construction value **£80 million**
Date of completion **Ongoing – Phase 1 completed 2003**
Project type **New-build, with emphasis on landscaping and the public realm**

INTRODUCTION

Rarely does a new housing project catch the public imagination. This one does, largely through the input of designers Wayne and Gerardine Hemingway, working with Wimpey, and an innovative architect. The result, the Staiths, South Bank – so named after an adjoining Grade II listed coal-loading jetty (or 'staith') – is a residential development mercifully breaking with standardised, speculative building convention. It dares to be different, with a variety of styles and materials – render, brickwork, timber – grouped around public spaces to create that 'sense of place' so lacking in many other developments. Situated on the south bank of the Tyne, occupying a third of the 1990 Gateshead Garden Festival area, the site has been the subject of 43 development proposals – all of which foundered.

Bordered to the north by the river and its staiths, this 'brownfield' site – a former gasworks – has its attractions: it lies beside a Site of Special Scientific Interest, while riverside cycle routes link it with Gateshead Quays and Newcastle Quayside.

Wimpey appointed IDPartnership Northern to develop design proposals for the site in conjunction with Hemingway Design in 2001. By this time, the site had been remediated for residential use, and detailed studies had been undertaken to determine ground conditions, and ecological and other constraints.

CLIENT'S BRIEF

The outline plan was to develop the site for 700–750 units in a mix of low-density two/three-storey houses and flats, together with higher-density apartment blocks.

The detailed brief developed through a series of intensive team meetings in which ideas from IDP and Hemingway Design were explored and fine-tuned to inform the brief and final design.

The provision of affordable, high-quality units to first-time buyers, young families and key workers on Tyneside was fundamental. The design also needed to be contemporary – rather than the standard, traditional response – in terms of layout, architectural form and choice of facing materials. Tyneside has strong historic trading links with the Baltic and the Low Countries, and developments in Malmö, Sweden, and Amsterdam's Borneo Dock were used as precedents.

The design team was committed to the principles of 'Home Zones' – pedestrian, car-free/restrained areas – and the site has been designed around 'walkability' and, importantly, the ability of young children to play and explore in safety. The layout is traffic-calmed throughout, and was one of the UK's first major new-build schemes with Home-Zones and play streets.

An essential design element is the attempt to reintroduce 'sub-neighbourhoods' and reinforce the importance of 'community'. Neighbourhoods of 20 to 24 houses or flats have been grouped around a communal garden area. Each unit has its own private space, and the residents also have shared use of the courtyard garden in the centre.

In response to an Arts Council funded survey in 2003, most residents felt that 'they had bought into a development that was individual, flexible, stylish, tranquil and spacious, with a strong community feel'.

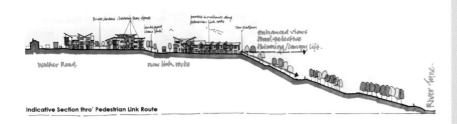

Indicative Section thro' Pedestrian Link Route

DESIGN PROCESS

The city council was determined to involve local residents as much as possible in planning the development. The architect (the Bowker Sadler Partnership) was chosen following a competitive 'place-making' event, in which the client pitched three architectural practices to work with each other over two days in design workshops along with a variety of other interests including city-council planning and highways officers, community representatives and neighbours to the development site. The clear message was that the new development should have a strong 'sense of place, with a community ethos and a neighbourhood "feel"', while being family-focused. Achieving this level of involvement at such an early stage proved its worth during later consultation events, as interested parties were familiar with the design proposals and their evolution – partly because of the contribution they had made to the process.

The aspiration was to create a place that had a distinctive character while, at the same time, reflecting the changing needs of the modern family. Local people involved in the process seemed happy that the development could be contemporary in its architectural language while, at the same time, having a clear contextual identity to avoid alienating neighbours. Because the market for new housing in this area had not been tested, it was also important that a high-quality development of some distinction could be marketed to attract interest from outside Walker. Keeping nearby residents 'on board' was seen as crucial; prior to site work commencing, the city council began a programme of environmental work to improve the local streetscape and nearby open areas, while 'face-lifting' surrounding housing stock, to show locals that they had not been forgotten.

The identity of the development evolved during the design process. It included clearly defined and varied public spaces and streets, incorporating pedestrian-prioritised 'Home Zones', to calm and restrict traffic, and a centrally located, crescent-shaped open space that connected two neighbouring communities with the new development. A strong and varied building line and roofscape, projecting bays and corner windows added an additional layer of architectural richness, along with distinctive entrance canopies and coloured wall tiles that gave identity to individual properties.

The housing blocks were laid out to maximise the use of available land and create 'active' street frontages. These would complement the public spaces and streets by creating an attractive, safe living environment with a strong identity, promoting a community spirit and, ideally, encouraging 'neighbourliness'. The inclusion of Home Zones encourages children's play, walking and cycling, and discourages the risk of over-dominance by the car.

A change in level of 5.5 m across the site allows the development to exploit views out, over and between buildings – with steps, ramps and retaining walls defining and containing spaces, as well as creating important 'defensible spaces' for individual properties.

To ease construction and deliver high energy standards, the development was constructed in timber frame with either a robust brick or a concrete-block-and-render finish, which contributes to the thermal mass of the buildings. Renewable energy was harnessed through efficient solar hot-water roof panels, taking advantage of the site's southerly aspect.

PROJECT EVALUATION

As planned, the development, with its largely traditional forms mixed with contemporary detail, has attracted both local people and those from outside the area.

The success of the Home Zones is evident as children have taken safe 'ownership' of some streets and public spaces, ensuring that cars move through the area at walking pace. However, the requirement to provide generous car parking has restricted the areas of soft landscaping, resulting in a harsher appearance to the so-called 'public realm' than had been originally envisaged.

Prospective purchasers and the new residents have been extremely positive about the development, commenting favourably on the spacious and flexible interiors, the quality of light within the dwellings, the low running costs, energy-efficiency, the 'sense of place' and the views afforded across the development.

Choice of tenure, house type and size proved successful in attracting a broad spectrum of interest. In particular, large three-storey four-bedroom houses with large roof terraces proved popular.

Hopefully completion of the second phase, fronting Walker Road, will help to realise the full potential of the development.

drawing supplied by the architect

Client **Places for People**
Architect **Bowker Sadler Partnership Limited**
Main Contractor **Mansell Construction Services Ltd**
Quantity Surveyor **Places for People**

Structural Engineer **Atkins**
Services Engineer **Atkins**
Project Manager **Places for People**
Landscape Architect **Atkins**

image courtesy of Michael Baister Photography

161

The Turnbull Building

Queens Lane,
Newcastle upon Tyne

Construction value **£6.5 million**
Date of completion **2004**
Project type **Refurbishment and conversion**

INTRODUCTION

The 'New York-style loft apartment' label became an urban cliché of the late 1990s, often stretching architectural licence and hyperbole to the limit. Not so the conversion of the Turnbull Building, whose prominent position high above the Tyne gorge overlooking Gateshead, near Robert Stephenson's High Level Bridge and close to the castle and other landmarks, made it one of Newcastle's great late 19th-century landmarks.

Northern Land Residential Developments acquired the Grade II listed building in the autumn of 1999 with the aim of creating – yes – 'New York-style apartments' close to the heart of the city. Built in 1895 as a printing works, the existing building – for the previous 40 years, an ironmongery warehouse – offered huge potential as one of the most prestigious housing conversions in a city (like so many others) with its fair share of newish, mediocre apartment blocks, built when credit was easy and investor confidence high. Not surprisingly, the city council enthusiastically supported a planning application to convert the building into stylish apartments and penthouses, with a premium price to match; indeed, one was labelled the city's first '£1m apartment' in the local media.

CLIENT'S BRIEF

The client, who was advised by several commercial and residential property agents, looked at various options for the density of the proposed development, and settled on a brief to convert the building into a series of loft apartments. These were to vary in size in order to ensure a good mix of potential spaces for sale. The 39 apartments were spread around the perimeter and vary from one-bed studios to two-bed units – with the fifth and sixth floors housing eight duplex penthouses.

From the outset, it was decreed that the immensely strong Victorian character of the building should be both retained and expressed in a conversion which would blend the glazed brickwork, exposed steel and timber beams with its contemporary design for open-plan living. In addition, it was stressed that the spectacular views across the Tyne, and west up the river valley, should be emphasised from the large, existing windows.

above: photograph by Radcliffe Photography

From the outset, the Turnbull Building proved to be a catalyst for the 'renaissance' of the area lying south of Newcastle's historic Central Railway Station.

right: photograph by Sally Ann Norman

DESIGN PROCESS

The basic masterplan was developed quickly in discussions with the council, with the agreed proposal based on several key points – for instance, recognising that the linear shape of the site would be used to create an east–west boulevard as a principal focus. This would, in turn, serve a series of open, courtyard buildings along its northern side. On the south of the boulevard, against a railway line, a 'buffer wall' of buildings would be formed to screen the interior of the site. In addition, another series of buildings would be set against the northern edge, facing the Tyne.

At the eastern end, the primary access road separated the commercial area from the rest of the site. The design of the commercial area, by others, is now under construction. The remaining land, measuring over 5 ha, was designated for residential use.

Traditional reinforced-concrete and masonry construction was used initially, but with the long southern block (constructed around 2004) timber frame was adopted. It was built off a first-floor concrete podium, which straddled the ground-floor parking – and, at over six storeys high, was one of the taller timber-frame constructions in the UK at the time. Balconies and access decks had to be built in steel, and were independent of the frame; however, in later buildings these were integrated into the timber-frame structure.

The importance of public open spaces was recognised, and several key related decisions were made during the design process, including reducing the impact of cars by placing the majority of parking within buildings. Similarly, to further enhance the importance of separating vehicles from public space, it was decided to integrate roads and cycleways to reduce pressure on roads, which were to be separated from footpaths with planting. In addition, high-quality materials and detailing for the hard landscaping could also refer to the site's industrial history, such as a railway turntable 'drawn' in brick courses in a pedestrian street.

Existing buildings

The residential site contained two buildings of architectural importance, steeped in the history of locomotive manufacturing: the Pattern Shop and the Grade II listed Boiler Shop. The design challenge here was to adapt large spaces and elements, such as windows, to the smaller-scale requirements of individual dwellings. The biggest test came with the vast internal space of the Boiler Shop, whose enormous depth made it impractical to accommodate apartments on both sides. The radical solution, fully supported by English Heritage, was to place all the accommodation on the north side, facing the river, and, by partly removing the roof covering to the south, create an enclosed garden in the remaining part of the building.

New buildings

The new buildings are predominantly three- to five-storey U- or L-shaped blocks, with a central courtyard and towers at the ends to act as gateways for each block and provide a dynamic 'avenue' running the length of the boulevard.

The client wanted a contemporary design which would, nevertheless, incorporate some familiar elements, recognisably domestic, such as brickwork and 'hole-in-wall' windows. However, a significant early decision was made to have flat rather than pitched roofs in order to free up the design.

Materials are predominantly red brick, to reflect the local context and the site's railway history. Structural steelwork was exposed over openings and balconies in order to echo this industrial past. This muted backdrop is broken up by blocks of render at entrances, coloured to indentify each block. Polished blockwork is used to give a different quality and texture to the towers along the boulevard. The river frontage is more restrained, with buff brickwork and greys used to reflect the stone and slate of the existing adjoining buildings.

PROJECT EVALUATION

This scheme is currently ongoing, with six buildings so far completed in the eastern half of the site and a further five remaining. Its success, both as a piece of urban design and as a self-contained community, will probably only be gauged when it is completed.

However, it can already been seen that the riverside elevation is both attractive and restrained, while the former Pattern Shop – now completed and occupied – has seen its exterior refurbished sensitively. Internally within the latter building, where the main windows were over a storey in height, new upper floors have been set back from the outside wall in order to create a two-storey space overlooked by internal glazed balconies – and also offering attractive views over the River Tyne.

With the site sufficiently well developed to form an initial view of the overall project, the design of each building seems to blend in well with the surrounding area. As an example, elevations along the 180 m-long southern block, beside the railway, are varied and given extra focus with, for instance, their axially situated entrance towers.

all photography on this spread by Sally Ann Norman
drawing supplied by the architect

Client Bellway Homes North East
Architect P+HS Architects
Main Contractor Bellway Homes and Tolent
Construction Limited
Quantity Surveyor Bellway Homes
Structural Engineer Entec and Patrick
Parsons Ltd

Services Engineer Bellway Homes
Project Manager Bellway Homes
Masterplanning EDAW
Timber-frame Subcontractor/Supplier
Stewart Milne Timber Systems

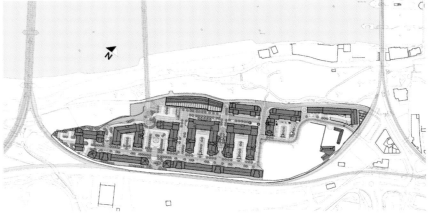

Centralofts

1–5 Waterloo Square,
Newcastle upon Tyne

Construction value £9.2 million
Date of completion July 2004
Project type Building renovation and landscape

INTRODUCTION

Alfred Wilson House was originally built in 1933 by the Co-operative Society as a drapery warehouse. In the 1970s, the Art Deco style building was converted for use as a government building as well as housing a bar, nightclub and cinema. However, it had stood vacant from 2002 and was considered for demolition until it was purchased by London & Regional Properties. The company subsequently commissioned Napper Architects to develop design proposals to bring the substantial seven-storey building back to life, allowing it to become an integral part of the rejuvenation of this previously neglected area of the city. The completed residential and commercial building, renamed 'Centralofts', is now part of the fabric of 21st-century Newcastle, and its unique architectural style has been preserved.

CLIENT'S BRIEF

Napper Architects had been commissioned by Newcastle City Council to masterplan the regeneration of this area of Newcastle, which had been identified within the Grainger Town Initiative for regeneration and remodelling. The conversion of Alfred Wilson House was to be a key part of this masterplan, along with a new dance college, a multi-storey car park and further new-build residential and office accommodation, all centred around a new landscaped piazza, Waterloo Square.

The client's brief for Alfred Wilson House called for new high-quality city-centre apartments, including penthouse suites, with dedicated basement parking. At ground level, commercial/retail accommodation was to be provided in order to ensure that activity at the street level was encouraged.

Alfred Wilson House is one of the few remaining Art Deco buildings in Newcastle, and its sensitive restoration has brought new life to a building which had previously faced demolition.

all photography on this spread by Sally Ann Norman

PROJECT EVALUATION

Alfred Wilson House is one of the few remaining Art Deco buildings in Newcastle, and its sensitive restoration has brought new life to a building which had previously faced demolition. Along with the other developments centred around Waterloo Square, its conversion has helped to rejuvenate a neglected corner of the city.

Its success has been recognised with a number of architectural design awards, whilst the apartments sold successfully at a difficult time for the residential market. Napper Architects has subsequently relocated to one of the ground-floor commercial units, fitting out the office space in the process in order to suit the firm's particular requirements.

DESIGN PROCESS

Although an initial feasibility study of the site was carried out in order to determine its viability for a new-build development, the historical context and unique architectural quality of the existing building confirmed retention of the existing fabric as the more favourable option, a view supported by the city council.

Whilst three of the existing façades were of good architectural quality and in relatively sound condition, the rear elevation, which would ultimately face onto the new Waterloo Square, had been adapted over a number of years to accommodate goods lifts, plant rooms, services risers and fire escapes. The design therefore proposed that these intrusions be removed, and a new contemporary façade erected. A lightweight façade of smooth coloured rendered panels was introduced to contrast with the more ornate brickwork of the existing elevations.

The change in ground level through the building was simply addressed by having the residential apartments accessed from the east off Waterloo Street, via a new reception hall designed with reference to the original Art Deco heritage of the building, while the commercial units were accessed from the new piazza to the west, providing the development with a dual aspect at street level. A basement level, providing dedicated parking, has been created through the formation of the new 'suspended' piazza.

Running vertically through the building is a new central service core, around which the apartments are configured with final layouts being determined by the existing window openings in the retained façades. Mezzanine levels were introduced into the apartments, which benefited from the additional space afforded by the historical storey heights and the existing tall window openings. At roof level a contemporary lightweight structure was added, which houses luxury penthouse apartments.

Some repair work was needed to the retained façades, as well as minor alterations to suit the new layout and use of the building. New specialist facing brickwork was manufactured to replicate the distinct colour, texture and proportions of the existing bricks. Contemporary iron railings were designed with reference to the distinct forms and decoration of the original ironwork. Along Waterloo Street, a contemporary cantilevered glass canopy defines the entrance to the new residential development.

Client **London & Regional Properties Ltd**
Architect **Napper Architects**
Main Contractor **Shepherd Construction Ltd**
Quantity Surveyor **Gardiner and Theobald LLP**
Structural Engineer **Shepherd Design**
Services Engineer **Shepherd Design**
Any other key consultants/sub-contractors **NG Bailey**

Hanover Mill

Quayside,
Newcastle upon Tyne

Construction value £12 million
Date of completion 2008
Project type Renovation and new-build extension

INTRODUCTION

This former bonded warehouse, an imposing eight-storey brick building on the west end of Newcastle's quayside, is an impressive reflection of the heritage of this part of the city. Whilst standing derelict, however, the building was severely damaged and gutted by a number of fires. Nonetheless, the developer, Mandale Commercial, recognised the huge potential of this Grade II listed structure and commissioned Napper Architects to develop their design proposals for a major new residential development that would give the existing building a new lease of life and represent a significant investment to the Quayside. With the addition of a new structure, stitched onto the end of the existing warehouse, the completed development provides 134 apartments – including penthouse suites, which offer stunning views along the River Tyne and its famous bridges.

CLIENT'S BRIEF

The Grade II listing of the building necessitated that the client's design brief be developed in full consultation with the planning authority and English Heritage. The primary requirement from the client was the provision of a commercially viable residential scheme with apartments of various sizes, which would allow as much as possible of the existing warehouse structure to be both retained and expressed.

Initially, the existing brick façades were made structurally stable before being carefully restored and cleaned without compromise to their aged appearance. The new-build element, located on the western half of the site (by that time vacant), was to provide further apartments but was to be designed in a contemporary style so as to complement the old with the new. As many apartments as possible were intended to have river views, and the overall layout had to successfully handle the significant level changes over the narrow, constrained site. With the original building line directly abutting the pavement along this busy urban street, the ground level was to incorporate a mix of retail units in order to provide a level of street level activity to the development.

The old warehouse no longer stands alone at the end of the riverfront as a forgotten and burnt-out ruin, but is now an integral part of the streetscape of Newcastle's vibrant new Quayside.

all photography on this spread by Sally Ann Norman

with neighbouring 19th-century, Grade II listed buildings; sympathetic landscaping, and new walkways, up the steep hill to the city centre and All Saints Church add to its appeal.

Planning – good, bad, indifferent – has naturally played a significant part in the development of Newcastle and Gateshead.

Across the city centre at Gallowgate, a new contemporary office quarter has also emerged, thankfully enhanced – unlike All Saints – by the demolition of a Brutalist 1960s office block, Wellbar House, which contained government departments. An initial plan envisaged retaining and modernising Wellbar House. When this proved impractical, a new block was designed – Wellbar Central – which, unlike its towering predecessor, largely followed the roof line of the area. Both Times Central and the recently completed Wellbar Central were the result of the enterprise and vision of the sister partnership of Sheila and Dolly Siddiqui, whose commitment to the city has survived decades.

Significantly, much of the success of this new office quarter, which also embraces Time Central – a partner to Wellbar Central – can be attributed to Newcastle City Council's Gallowgate Masterplan, which laid out the design and planning principles for the area in 1999.

Planning – good, bad, indifferent – has naturally played a significant part in the development of Newcastle and Gateshead. The Team Valley Industrial Estate in Gateshead, with functional-yet-pleasing offices alongside factories, is a good case in point. Initially a product of the 1930s, which did not reach its target employment figures until the 1960s, it had the appearance of a garden city, such as Ebenezer Howard's Welwyn or Letchworth in Hertfordshire.

Incorporating three tree-lined avenues with roundabouts interspersed with roads crossing between the main thoroughfares, it was planned by William Halford – subsequently, he became a senior official at the former Ministry of Town and Country Planning – working with a local architect, L. J. Couves. Wide open spaces and abundant landscaping characterised the layout; the estate's (still) attractive central administrative headquarters, St Georges House, Art Deco-styled and crescent-shaped beside a roundabout, provides a welcome antidote to the Brutalist blocks in Newcastle and, to a lesser extent, in Gateshead.

Newcastle, however, has its gems. Take Emerson Chambers, facing Blackett Street and Grey's Monument, the work of local architects Simpson, Lawson and Rayne. Art Nouveau and similar in style to Half Moon Chambers in the Bigg Market, its early 20th-century design, built around an iron frame, incorporates, at its eastern corner, a large copper-clad clock above a dome. The ground floor, formerly a restaurant, is now a bookshop.

Possibly the largest office block of its time, Milburn House, built into the steep incline of Dean Street leading to the Quayside, occupies a triangular, steep site. Designed by Oliver, Leeson and Wood, the building (1902–5), has some Dutch influences below the roof line. Other buildings in this attractive street – such as Cathedral Buildings (1901), opposite, by the same architects – have similar influences.

Taken together, with more Classical buildings in Collingwood Street and Richard Grainger's Grey Street, the 'sum of the parts' of Newcastle's and Gateshead's office developments add up to a generally attractive mix, blighted sadly by the blunders of the 1960s, some of which have since been rectified.

Wellbar Central

Gallowgate,
Newcastle upon Tyne

Construction value **£25 million**
Date of completion **Scheduled for autumn 2010**
Project type **New-build**

INTRODUCTION

The completion of Wellbar Central will conclude the transformation of this major city-centre location, close to St James' Park, from a Brutalist 1960s tower block, which housed government departments, to contemporary regeneration with a building design reflecting the strength of the city's varied character.

The original Wellbar House was often seen as an example of the over-zealous Modernism of the 1960s, which created buildings whose appearance quickly fell out of fashion, and its inflexible floorplates restricted the organic development of businesses within.

It was vital for the successful regeneration of Wellbar House that the redevelopment was more representative of the new form of the city: modern, yet not clashing overtly with its Classical surroundings. The building therefore needed to complement the elegant architectural principles of nearby Grainger Town, as the 19th-century core of the city has been labelled in recognition of the master builder/developer, Richard Grainger.

Wellbar Central is the second phase of the Gallowgate Masterplan, following on from the success of sister development, nearby Time Central completed in 2007, and firmly establishing Gallowgate as the commercial heart of the city.

The building stands ten storeys high and provides over 11,000 m2 of high-quality commercial office accommodation, setting a benchmark for other developments.

CLIENT'S BRIEF

Moonglade Holdings approached Lister in the summer of 2006 to undertake a thorough review of the redevelopment potential of the existing Wellbar House. At 16 storeys high, it had been empty for several years after its main occupier, the Government Office for the North East, moved to much plusher premises at the nearby development called City Gate.

However, it soon became apparent that the constraints of working with an inflexible 1960s concrete-framed building would prove too great a challenge. Consequently, it was decided that the only alternative was to demolish it and start from scratch with a new structure offering greater potential for growth and flexible use.

Both the client and Newcastle City Council were excited at the opportunities presented by this key 'gateway' site. Recognising the growing success of Gallowgate as the new business address in Newcastle, the development brief was honed towards the growing commercial-office sector and demand for high-quality accommodation – in this case, over 1,000 m2 of office space.

The city council's Urban Design Team proved a willing supporter of the redevelopment plans and, together with Lister, realised the importance of Wellbar Central interacting with its neighbour, Time Central, to create a substantial and contemporary office quarter.

The complex civil engineering of the basement excavation saw the 'arrival' of the UK's largest temporary prop, at 3 m in diameter and 30 m in length, which held back the parallel highways of Strawberry Place and St Andrews Street.

all photography on this spread by Sally Ann Norman

DESIGN PROCESS

Both the design team and the City Council were keen that the project should respect, and complement, the city's existing urban framework – including the nearby new developments of Time Central and City Gate, the medieval city walls, the magnificent St Andrew's Church opposite (the oldest church in the city, approved in 1150 by King David of Scotland when Newcastle was briefly under Scottish rule) and the gentle curve of Gallowgate.

The height of the proposed structure created a lively debate about how tall new buildings should be allowed to rise in the city; eventually, it was considered that Wellbar Central should continue the building scale along Gallowgate, with an overall height lower than the original Wellbar House tower in order to reduce its physical impact on the streetscape and the visual dominance of the building in the area.

The urban-design solution needed to improve the frontage along Gallowgate from Percy Street, removing the intrusive urban edge of the existing 1960s tower and developing a mature raising of the building scale, widening of the vista to St James Boulevard – a primary route from the new Redheugh Bridge to St James' Park, and beyond, northwards – and bringing vitality back into the street.

The main Gallowgate frontage of Wellbar Central is characterised by a sweeping façade that follows the alignment of the medieval city wall and continues the visual sweep of the nearby Time Central façade.

The four-sided nature of the Wellbar site led to each elevation being treated individually in order to provide an urban 'statement' reflective of its particular place. The aim was to integrate with the urban fabric, while creating a substantial six-storey building supported on a colonnade of tall, circular columns topped with a lightweight, glazed box. The design incorporates a series of dominant stone frames to each elevation, which encapsulate large areas of glazing modulated by an aluminium framework

Nine storeys of high-quality, flexible office accommodation extend to the perimeter of the site, maximising the space and, consequently, the commercial return. The floorplates have a central service core containing vertical circulation and staff amenities, and connecting with the entrance lobby at ground floor. Each of the office floors maximises the available daylight offering views across the city to the north and, beyond, over the Tyne Valley to the south; Level 9 presents particularly good views of the city.

Wellbar Central's external treatment continues the pattern established by the same architect at Time Central, with traditional materials such as natural stone. It also acts as a 'fulcrum' between the traditional architecture of Gallowgate and contemporary developments emerging on the site of the former Tyne Brewery, as well as a project beyond, called Science Central.

PROJECT EVALUATION

The client, Moonglade Holdings, impressed by the efficient delivery of Time Central, chose to continue with the same successful technical construction team that, once again, partnered the architects, Lister, with Tolent Construction.

Delivery problems were intensified, in comparison with Time Central, by the need for two tower cranes on this restricted site, a building that exploited available space to the full, a 10 m-deep double basement adjacent to a fully occupied office building and a shallow Metro line that clipped the edge of the site.

The complex civil engineering of the basement excavation saw the 'arrival' of the UK's largest temporary prop, at 3 m in diameter and 30 m in length, which held back the parallel highways of Strawberry Place and St Andrews Street.

Each of the subcontractors was selected for their innovative and specialist skills, and their ability to work on multi-storey projects.

At the topping-out of the building in autumn 2009, it was already clear that Wellbar Central was becoming a landmark in the city – blending well with surrounding buildings while not intruding unduly into Newcastle's valuable historic core.

all photography on this spread by Sally Ann Norman

Client **Moonglade Holdings Ltd**
Architect **Lister**
Main Contractor **Tolent Construction Limited**
Quantity Surveyor **The Millbridge Group plc**

Structural Engineer **Beattie Watkinson Ltd**
Services Engineer **Hoare Lea**
Project Manager **The Millbridge Group plc**

Time Central

32 Gallowgate,
Newcastle upon Tyne

Construction value **£15 million**
Date of completion **April 2007**
Project type **New-build**

INTRODUCTION

In 1999, Newcastle City Council approved the Gallowgate Masterplan that identified Gallowgate as the primary location for a new prestigious, commercial-office quarter within the city. Almost a decade on from the inception of the masterplan, the completion of Time Central in March 2007 announced the arrival of this new city office quarter, creating a stimulating commercial environment and providing contemporary headquarters for Muckle LLP and Brewin Dolphin Securities Limited.

The urban character of Newcastle upon Tyne was forged during the 19th century through the inspirational work of architect John Dobson and his use of the Classical language of architecture to create a formal and dignified city framework. Time Central is the first substantial intervention within the Gallowgate office quarter, and it introduces a new urban language based upon the principles adopted by Dobson that will be interpreted through the subsequent phases of the Gallowgate Masterplan.

The design of the development interacts with the immediate urban environment, and in particular seeks, with its curved primary elevation, to reinforce the medieval sweep of Gallowgate. It also responds to the citywide urban character by utilising key materials and building designs which reflect the timeless elegance of Grey Street and Grainger Town.

CLIENT'S BRIEF

The client recognised the importance of the Gallowgate quarter as a commercial hub, and their brief was very simple:

'To deliver a first class office building that will inspire the highest calibre of occupier and to leave a lasting impression on the city of Newcastle upon Tyne'.

As the initial building within the Gallowgate Masterplan, there was a sense of 'trailblazing' about Time Central. However, from the initial development team meetings and the proposal to build the first natural-stone-clad contemporary office building within the city for over 25 years the scheme gathered momentum. Both Muckle LLP and Brewin Dolphin Securities realised the potential of Time Central from an early stage, and became an integral part of this substantial landmark building.

Time Central is designed to the latest BCO (British Council for Offices) standards, and provides around 7,500 m2 of highly flexible Category A commercial office space that will accommodate the ever-changing needs of demanding occupiers.

The commercial property markets have welcomed this development in a very positive fashion. Time Central has become the primary office building within the Northeast, and one that sets a new benchmark for city-centre regeneration.

The design of the development interacts with the immediate urban environment, and in particular seeks, with its curved primary elevation, to reinforce the medieval sweep of Gallowgate.

  all photography on this spread by Sally Ann Norman

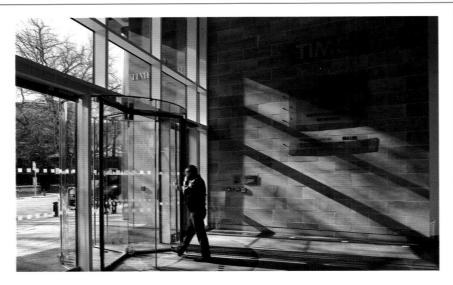

DESIGN PROCESS

Lister approached the design of Time Central in a comprehensive manner, analysing the existing urban context whilst reviewing the practical demands of a city-centre office building within the current changing commercial environment.

The building's massing is considered by the city council as wholly appropriate for this location on Gallowgate, with the curving façade responding to the alignment of the medieval city wall and a series of horizontal layers within the elevational treatment of the building contributing to the layering of the streetscape. The arrival of Time Central is announced with the bold use of architectural devices such as the vertical glazed features that highlight its primary entrances and the tall piloti that support the building mass while visually creating a delicate intervention at street level.

The building design identifies three separate horizontal masses. The recessed plinth is articulated with a perimeter of double-height slender columns and the transparent façade behind provides a vibrant, active frontage to Gallowgate. The primary mass of the building is the central four-storey band of natural stone, which is articulated by the vertical bands of glazing. A recessed lightweight glazed box, which

sits delicately above the solid building mass below, terminates this horizontal composition.

Each of the external materials was selected by the architect for quality and longevity. The Fletcher Bank sandstone cladding recreates the Classical appearance of the Tynedale sandstone of historical Grainger Town. It is combined with the stainless-steel columns and large expanses of glazing into a powerful composition, with appropriate architectural detailing creating the visual stimulus.

The double-height entrance continues the quality of building materials and detailing, with a dominant curved natural-stone feature wall leading one through the reception to the lift lobby beyond. This is combined with Lakeland slate floors and stainless-steel detailing to provide an oasis of quality and calm within the hectic commercial environment.

The decision to situate the building core within a central spine provides the key to the technical success of the office space, maximising natural daylight and views out whilst minimising the impact of the relatively 'dead' servant space. The view from the Level 7 balcony across the Tyne Valley is unrivalled elsewhere in the city, and the decision to recess the office floor has created a successful building model.

PROJECT EVALUATION

Lister and Tolent Construction developed an intensive, integrated partnership for this project, which in 108 weeks provided a building of over 11,000 m2, including a substantial basement, and fitted out around 7,500 m2 of high-quality office environment.

The primary delivery problem was one of constructing, efficiently and safely within a restricted city-centre location, to demanding programmes and to exceptional levels of quality.

The innovative building fabric comprised prefabricated natural-stone-faced concrete panels, which were delivered to site and craned into position to create the high-quality elevations evident to all users of the finished building.

Each of the subcontractors and suppliers were hand-picked, many from within the Northeast region, to work on this demanding project – and each brought their own specialist skill to the delivery team.

From the initial design concepts to the final fitting-out works, the design, development and construction teams shared a combined vision to deliver excellence at Time Central. It was the energy and professional enthusiasm of the key delivery-team members that produced a building of such quality and presence. Time Central will be a landmark with the city for many years to come.

Client **Gallowgate Properties Ltd**
Developer **Terrace Hill Group plc**
Architect **Lister**
Main Contractor **Tolent Construction Ltd**

Structural Engineer **WYG**
Services Engineer **RW Gregory LLP**
Project Manager **Terrace Hill Group plc**

Central Square 1 and 2

Forth Street,
Newcastle upon Tyne

Construction value £7 million
Date of completion April 2000
Project type Refurbishment

INTRODUCTION

Tucked behind a magnificent railway station, until recently this area was out of sight and mind to many visitors and natives alike. With elevated rail lines a physical barrier to the main city centre (access to shopping areas and the central business district provided by two 'tunnels' under the lines) it was, at best, considered workaday – with its post-office buildings, small businesses and remnants of industries past.

In truth, with intact sections of the medieval city wall and Robert Stephenson's original locomotive works nearby, this area was both rich in history and ripe for sympathetic redevelopment. The area also benefits from some fine views of the Tyne gorge and its bridges, sandwiched between the historical High Level Bridge and the more modern Metro bridge. Central Square, thus, was seen by Parabola Estates as a project 'of its time' – and, crucially, a catalyst for a much wider future regeneration of the area that is nearing coming off the drawing board with Silverlink.

The development, based around a former Royal Mail sorting office, was thus seen as providing a new vitality to a largely forgotten part of Newcastle and offering new commercial life for the railway arches beneath the station. The sorting office has been effectively rebuilt to combine the strengths of the original building with the appropriate addition of new elements. The natural materials used in this space define a calm but rich 'container', in which people's activity and the play of light provide continual animation.

CLIENT'S BRIEF

The project proposed to bring into active use a former sorting office, which had been empty since its closure in 1995. The substantial site was in a neglected area, considered to be on the 'wrong' side of the city – immediately adjacent to, but behind, the Central Station, the city's main rail and transport hub.

Parabola Estates began the Central Square project with a clear vision. The space was to be primarily for offices, but with mixed-use elements to enhance the experience of building users and visitors. Central Square was to be a landmark building and environmentally friendly, while providing an excellent working environment, with good rental value, for a range of occupiers.

At the heart of the project brief was the desire to push the boundaries in terms of good practice in environmental design. Research was undertaken with the staff of an occupier, who had committed to pre-let space, to learn what they thought constituted a 'good' office. As a framework to focus on the sustainable aspects of the design, the team adopted the Building Research Establishment Environmental Assessment Method (BREEAM) for assessing the energy-efficiency of buildings. Central Square became the first refurbished office development in the Northeast of England to achieve a BREEAM 'Excellent' rating.

above: photograph by Sally Ann Norman

A delightfully simple approach and a 'brave' project, which increased the life of an otherwise redundant building in an area badly in need of revitalisation.

Judges in a national competition in 2001 (BCO Awards)

right: photograph by Keith Paisley

CLIENT'S BRIEF

Silverlink's ambition was to create a high-quality attractive development that would meet the practical needs of both a new community and people already living in the area. The aim was to provide the best office-working environment thus far seen in Newcastle, accompanied by apartments close to all city-centre facilities yet still located in a quiet area.

Both working and living lifestyles would be supported by leisure facilities, including a hotel, neighbourhood shop, restaurants and cafés. The car-park proposal would also reinstate parking previously accommodated on the site.

Silverlink wanted to build on the rich heritage of the area with improved, landscaped pedestrian routes and better vehicle links. Chairman and owner of Silverlink, David Clouston, is also passionate about engaging with art, believing such an approach adds considerable value to developments. As such, he was determined to reinvigorate the area with a 'sense of place', underpinned by a major work of art.

Because the fringes of the site, owned by the city council, had become overgrown, dark and dangerous at night, the developers envisaged a programme of landscaping with new stairs and paths for improved public access.

However, culture, heritage and landscaping had to be balanced with making the project commercially sustainable via a design that would be affordable and generally low-maintenance. At the bidding stage, Silverlink promised to deliver, without compromise, what _space had designed and presented.

Phase 1
Client Spellcast
Architect Ryder Architecture Limited
Main Contractor Mansell
Structural Engineer Edward Bird Associates
Services Engineer Cundall

Phase 2
Client Metnor Property Group
Architect Ryder Architecture Limited
Main Contractor Metnor Construction
Quantity Surveyor Summers-Inman
Structural Engineer 3e Consulting Engineers
Services Engineer Desco Ltd

Cooper's Studio
(Hertz Building)

Westgate Road,
Newcastle upon Tyne

Construction value **£1.75 million**
Date of completion **February 2009**
Project type **Renovation**

above: photograph supplied by Ryder Architecture

INTRODUCTION

Cooper's sits within Newcastle's Central Conservation Area, and over the line of Hadrian's Wall, the remnants of which can still be found within the city's boundaries. Built in 1897 over three levels as one of the country's last city-centre livery stables, the building still has internal ramps to allow horses to walk up to first- and second-floor stalls, a central atrium auction-parade area, a first-floor ladies' viewing gallery and an open-plan top-floor area.

The building had been badly converted at various stages, lain vacant for many years and degenerated to such an extent that an application for demolition had been made. However, English Heritage established that Cooper's had national significance as a rare surviving example of this type of stable complex. It was listed Grade II, and the application for demolition withdrawn. It was subsequently acquired by the Hanro Group for redevelopment, albeit with a new approach.

In discussion with English Heritage and the City Council, the Hanro Group and Ryder Architecture developed a brief for the restoration and conversion of the building to flexible commercial floor space. The radical but sympathetic approach to the restoration and conversion works has been featured as a case study by English Heritage in their *Constructive Conservation in Practice* publication.

CLIENT'S BRIEF

In discussion with English Heritage and Newcastle City Council, The Hanro Group and Ryder developed a brief for restoration and conversion of the building for flexible commercial floor space. The brief was essentially to retain and restore key features of the existing complex, while producing an attractive building environment in order to flexibly meet the needs of business – all intended to give the building a secure long-term future. It was also important to reflect the building's history and character whilst dramatically improving natural light levels and views from the building.

This approach included finding ways of dramatically increasing natural-light penetration into the centre of the development and making access easier at first-floor level, while respecting the essential character and history of the building.

The project was developed under a design-and-build fixed-price contract, and the commercial appraisal for 'lettability' of the proposed development in a competitive market imposed a strictly defined budget.

'Ryder produced a bold scheme that acknowledged the building's most historically significant features and protected the site's archaeology. Technical problems – such as how to provide natural light in former stabling areas – have been solved and the additions are innovative, while respecting the heritage values of the building.'

English Heritage

all photographs on this spread by Sally Ann Norman

DESIGN PROCESS

Substantial elements of the original stables have been retained, including the central lightwell and horse ramps. The building consisted of three storeys of predominantly loadbearing masonry with a pitched slate roof. Some cast-iron columns serve alongside the loadbearing walls to support steel beams that carry areas of suspended floor. The second floor is timber; first floor, concrete; and entrance floor, a ground-supported concrete slab.

Natural light has been brought into the building by a radical approach with respect to the street elevation. Most of this façade comprised a series of brick panels recessed between regular brick columns, the only openings being small ventilators to the stalls behind. This pattern had been destroyed at ground level by the addition of an intrusive shopfront in the 1930s, which has now been removed and partly replaced by full-height glazing. This operation provided building material, including ventilators, for the accurate extension of the remaining brick panels to street level as originally built. Removal of original brickwork not only allows light into the development but also permits passers-by to appreciate a remarkable city-centre building for the first time.

Internally, new openings maintain the integrity of the historical subdivisions, yet also serve to interconnect spaces – visually and, at first-floor level, physically – thus linking formerly enclosed and separated stabling areas.

The original building had no usable stairs or lifts. Two new staircases, with provisions for disabled access, are positioned so as to avoid disruption to the space; one is in the former carriage lift well, the other in a natural enclosed shaft within rooms between basement and second floor in an area where floors had completely rotted away. The new passenger lift occupies the only external space associated with the building, which otherwise completely fills the site. The design team derived a great deal of satisfaction from this avoidance of any disruption to the original floorplates.

The original building was considered to be generally robust, and has withstood many years of hard use. All new structural alterations were carefully considered in order to ensure that they were kept to a minimum, and detailed so as to remain sympathetic to the historical structure.

There are no applied finishes to the office areas. Services are largely exposed, and care has been taken in the selection and location of equipment and fittings. High-efficiency lighting is suspended, providing an element of up-lighting to enhance the appearance of the structural soffits.

The re-roofing of the building permitted the addition of significant levels of thermal insulation. A mechanical-ventilation system, with heat recovery, supplies conditioned fresh air, with an air-handling unit in the east stair core incorporating a louvred intake and exhaust at roof level. All the building-services systems are zoned and controlled in order to optimise efficiency. Condensers for the heat-recovery system are located in a screened enclosure at roof level. Consequently, the internationally recognised BREEAM standards for assessing environmental standards and energy efficiency have put the new building into their 'Very good' category.

PROJECT EVALUATION

The building was completed in February 2009 and has already been highly commended by English Heritage and has achieved local and national awards.

Cooper's Studios was a commended finalist in the 2009 Lord Mayor's Design Awards in Newcastle upon Tyne in the 'Refurbishment' category. The aim of these awards is to encourage, promote and publicise the best in architecture and environmental design and to help improve the built environment. Awards are given to outstanding projects in the fields of architecture, planning, environmental, urban and landscape design.

The building is one of 20 exemplar case studies in English Heritage's *Constructive Conservation in Practice* publication. In this they state: 'Ryder produced a bold scheme that acknowledged the building's most historically significant features and protected the site's archaeology. Technical problems – such as how to provide natural light in former stabling areas – have been solved and the additions are innovative, while respecting the heritage values of the building.'

Cooper's Studios was one of the 93 buildings in the UK to win a RIBA Award in 2010 for architectural excellence, by achieving high architectural standards and making a substantial contribution to the local environment. It was also the winner (projects up to 2,000 m^2) of the British Council for Offices North of England, North Wales and Northern Ireland Award 2010.

drawing supplied by the architect

Client **The Hanro Group**
Architect **Ryder Architecture Limited**
Main Contractor **Whelan**
Quantity Surveyor **AA Projects Ltd**
Structural Engineer **Edward Bird Associates Ltd**

Services Engineer **Screen & Forster LLP**
Project Manager **AA Projects Ltd**
Fire Consultant **FiSEC**

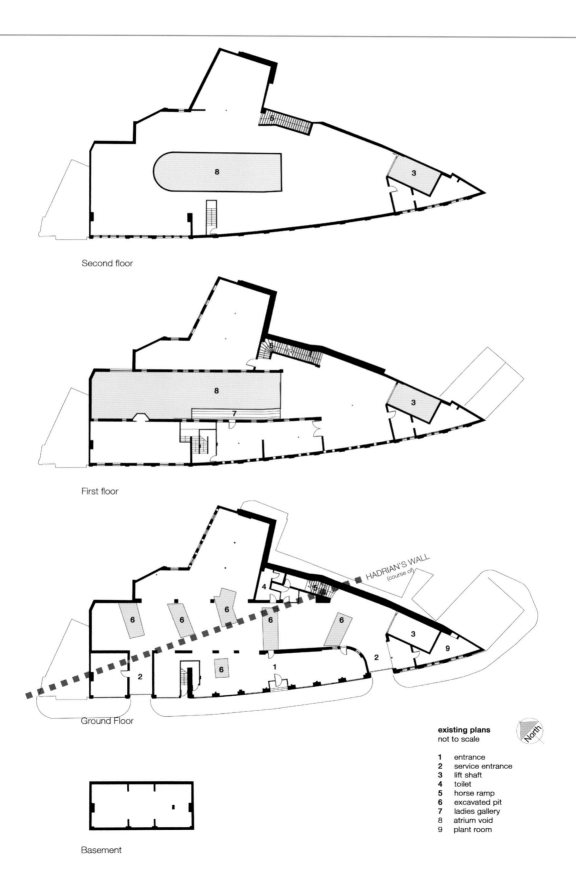

Second floor

First floor

HADRIAN'S WALL
(course of)

Ground Floor

Basement

existing plans
not to scale

North

1 entrance
2 service entrance
3 lift shaft
4 toilet
5 horse ramp
6 excavated pit
7 ladies gallery
8 atrium void
9 plant room

211

i6

6 Charlotte Square,
Newcastle upon Tyne

Construction value £1.7 million
Date of completion 2004
Project type Refurbishment and extension

INTRODUCTION

A major owner of land and property, Newcastle City Council is ideally placed to play a significant role in the creation and development of small businesses to broaden the economy of the area. In Charlotte Square, a group of buildings known as 'i6' represents the council's sixth business start-up centre – 'incubator' in commercial jargon – dedicated to the software, multi-media and IT sector.

Prior to conversion, the original buildings comprised three town houses built in 1770 by William Newton, strongly influenced by the gracious Georgian squares then emerging in London. Newton (1730–98) was probably the first architect to establish a Classical tradition in Newcastle, providing grand houses for the middle classes as they migrated from the quayside. Charlotte Square became the city's first completed formal square, a speculative development by the architect himself.

Faulkner, Beacock and Jones observe in their *Newcastle and Gateshead: Architecture and Heritage*, Newton agreed to build 'fashionable and commodious dwelling houses', and actually lived in the square for 20 years. At i6, a 1930s warehouse extension to the rear overlooks the medieval town walls, a Scheduled Ancient Monument. All the buildings were listed Grade II and lay within the Grainger Town/ Central Conservation Area. Subjected to piecemeal, unsympathetic alterations since their original construction, they had fallen vacant and were in need of considerable investment.

CLIENT'S BRIEF

In a historical area characterised by Grade II listed medieval and Georgian buildings, redevelopment clearly requires considerable skill and an appreciation of the surroundings. The brief from the city council to the architects made clear that the proposed refurbishment of 6–8 Charlotte Square for managed start-up, or 'incubator', units was no exception. Any design, which would be clearly constrained by the listed status of the existing buildings, had to be sympathetic to the integrity of the historic fabric of the area.

Importance was attached to the need for the business centre to establish a strong visual presence in the area, reflecting the nature of the modern, high-technology ventures which would be accommodated. In order to lend support and focus to other cultural industries around the square – and to help enliven the under-used public gardens, which have also been renovated – it was seen as important to retain 'Charlotte Square' as the main business address, despite a limited scope for altering the historic Georgian frontages.

The units were to be fully accessible, highly serviced and appealing to young, modern businesses, while the project was required to achieve a 'Good' energy efficiency rating under the internationally recognised BREEAM standard, notwithstanding a modest budget.

By effectively bridging the old and the modern i6 has been a success from the outset with both its client and tenants.

DESIGN PROCESS

The starting point of the design process was a group of building elements with varying floor levels and a great number of staircases. A central problem soon arose: how to join up these different levels so that any point in the building could be accessed without the use of steps.

Partial removal of some building fabric offered the opportunity to create an open atrium space to act as an efficient circulation core and communal 'hub' at the heart of the building. This atrium, as realised, contains many overlapping functions – circulation, location for the lift, refreshments and breakout/informal meeting spaces – around which all activity within the development revolves. As such, it positively promotes interaction between young fledgling businesses, all of which have an aspect or 'shop window' onto the space. The atrium, which does not compromise the Georgian exterior, also offered the opportunity to create a new, and appropriately contemporary, highly visible identity, positively advertising the presence of this new, modern business 'hub' within the city centre.

Throughout the project, the historic building fabric was carefully restored and purposefully contrasted with the clearly modern interventions. Original Georgian brick and stone features were retained alongside the 1930s warehouse elements and new contemporary insertions, in order to offer visual legibility to the continuing development of this area of the city. The design was developed in close consultation with conservation experts, English Heritage, and with the Newcastle Conservation Advisory Panel (NCAP).

The insertion of the atrium required careful structural integration with the historic building fabric. The new steel frame, which spans between the 18th-century masonry walls and the later warehouse,

provided numerous technical challenges – as did a four-storey-high structural glass assembly, which provides the building's 'window to the city around'.

The atrium also functions as an integral part of the buildings' environmental strategy. As such, i6 is a BREEAM-rated ('Very good') building. Central to this achievement is a system of natural ventilation, removing the need for air-conditioning. The glazed atrium is utilised to generate a stack effect, which draws air through individual office units via strategically placed ventilation grilles. The building fabric of the atrium space has a large amount of exposed thermal mass, principally in its new concrete walkways and historic masonry walls. These elements absorb heat during the day and radiate it back during the evening.

Although individual office units are highly serviced for IT use, ducting and cabling is carefully concealed within the historic fabric of the buildings. This has been achieved principally by creating a series of new floor levels, similar to the original ones, which contain all services in voids associated with each floor.

PROJECT EVALUATION

By effectively bridging the old and the modern – accommodating high-tech facilities in renewed and reconfigured Georgian buildings – i6 has been a success from the outset with both its client and tenants. Conservation bodies, too, recognise that in this case modernisation has not compromised a Georgian legacy. So far, the project has achieved all of its original aims: namely, that new businesses can 'grow' within the space provided by i6 before eventually expanding and moving, either into other centres or into the wider commercial world.

With the normal allowances for the ending and commencement of tenancies – pooled facilities, such as secretarial help, are available – the building has been fully occupied since completion. It even has a waiting list. It is well maintained and supported by the client, and has been commended in Newcastle City Council's Lord Mayor's Design Awards.

All photography on this spread by Sally Ann Norman
drawing supplied by the architect

Client Newcastle City Council
Architect Sadler Brown Architecture
(formerly Bill Hopper Design)
Main Contractor Turney Wylde Construction

Quantity Surveyor Gardiner and Theobald LLP
Structural Engineer WSP
Services Engineer WSP

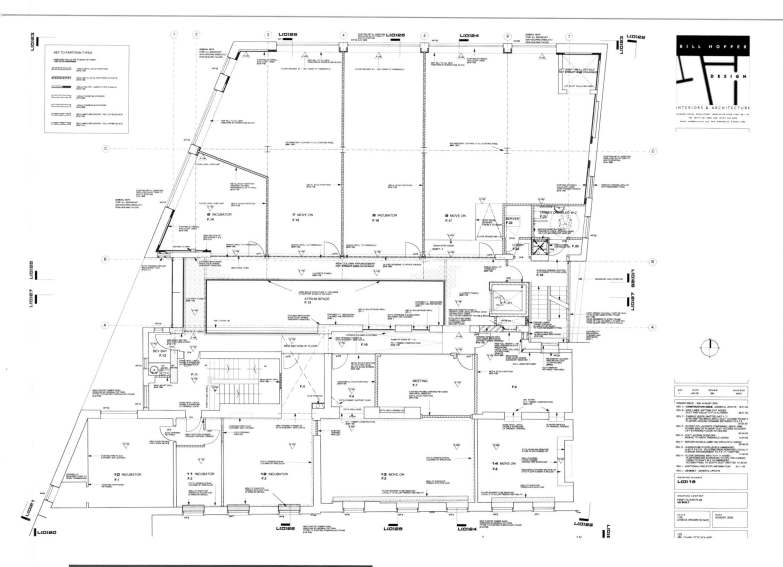

◐ Hotels

It is no accident that NewcastleGateshead has become one of the more popular short-break destinations in Britain; indeed, for four years running in the Guardian *and the* Observer Travel Awards, *it was named top city-break destination.*

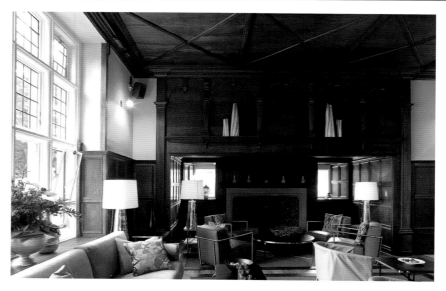

Newcastle Quayside; indeed, the hotel was the first project in the development corporation's regeneration scheme for this area. Occupying a historic site and facing the river, the rear of the hotel backs onto tall Victorian brick warehouses, some of which have been converted into flats.

Hotel supply increased by 43 per cent between 2002 and 2007 alone, with 12 new hotels and an additional 1,500 rooms.

'Stag' and 'hen' parties notwithstanding, the cultural revival on both banks of the Tyne, and further afield, has gone hand in glove with a significant increase in visitor accommodation. Hotel supply increased by 43 per cent between 2002 and 2007 alone, with 12 new hotels and an additional 1,500 rooms.

Yet until the creation of the former Tyne and Wear Development Corporation in the late 1980s, visitors would often struggle to find half-decent accommodation; the nearest modern hotel was located three miles north of Newcastle city centre at Gosforth Park.

All that was to change in 1992 with the arrival of the Copthorne Hotel, designed by Arup Associates on a fast-redeveloping

Further eastwards, the Malmaison Hotel – like Grey Street Hotel – has been created from an older structure. Sited in an old Cooperative Wholesale Society warehouse, and originally completed in 1900 – in fact, this former title is still emblazoned at the top of the building – the Malmaison is larger than a boutique hotel. In design terms, it stands head and shoulders above surrounding office blocks, some bland and anonymous. Furthermore, its location, opposite Gateshead Millennium Bridge, offers splendid views of the Tyne. Further downstream, another new hotel – The Hotel du Vin – in the former Victorian offices of the Tyne Tees Shipping Company – again highlights the potential of converting older buildings into modern accommodation.

Grey Street Hotel

2–12 Grey Street,
Newcastle upon Tyne

Construction value **£5.5 million**
Date of completion **2005**
Project type **Refurbishment and renovation**

INTRODUCTION

Perhaps it is fitting that one building, at least, should take its title from the 'architect' of the Great Reform Act, Earl Grey, whose monument in a circus at the top of Grey Street is one of Newcastle's central features.

With its gentle, rising curve and honeyed sandstone, Grey Street has won a string of awards – in any competition or survey on the 'best' streets in Britain, it invariably comes either top, or close to the top – and it was probably Grainger's finest achievement, admired by both former Prime Minister William Gladstone and architectural historian Nikolaus Pevsner, and, more recently, winning the title of 2010 Great Street of the Year in the UK's Academy of Urbanism Awards. The late Poet Laureate, John Betjeman, suggested that not even Regent Street in London 'can compare with that descending curve' of Grey Street.

The architect John Dobson, who worked with developer Richard Grainger, designed the imposing terraces that curve down to the southeast portion of Grey Street towards Nos. 2–12, which occupy the junction with Mosley Street.

No. 2 Grey Street was the last building in the thoroughfare to be completed. It stands opposite the site of Newcastle's original Theatre Royal on Mosley Street, which was built in 1788.

CLIENT'S BRIEF

Work on Grey Street Hotel, like that on many other buildings in the heart of the city, was initiated by the Grainger Town Project. Beginning in 1997, this venture sought to revive the enterprising spirit of the 19th-century master developer and builder, Richard Grainger, who created the city's Classical centre. With government money leveraging private-sector investment, the project brought an estimated 121 buildings back into use, turning round an area crying out for regeneration. Some structures – including this one – had faced an uncertain future, with demolition an option.

The building had been bought by Mr Kayu Poostchi, a local businessman and founder partner in Lazi Leisure Ltd, in 1984. The property, which had contained offices, was derelict, with both rat and pigeon infestation. Floor timbers were in poor condition and structurally unstable. The exterior of the buildings had been subjected to the ravages of time, which had affected the appearance of the 19th-century stonework and ornamental features.

Eventually, in 1999, under threat of compulsory purchase by Newcastle City Council, the practice of Ian M. Cook Architect was commissioned to submit a planning application for converting the property into a boutique hotel and leisure facility, retaining as many of its original features as possible. After detailed consultations with the city council, planning approval was granted for a 49-bedroom hotel with reception, restaurant and lounge bar at ground level and leisure facilities in the two basement floors.

above: supplied by Newcastle City Library

The late Poet Laureate, John Betjeman, suggested that not even Regent Street in London 'can compare with that descending curve' of Grey Street.

right: photography by Sally Ann Norman

DESIGN PROCESS

Building and restoration work on Nos. 2–12 Grey Street began in 2001. The works involved converting the upper floors of the former offices into bedrooms, all of which were to be provided with en-suite facilities. New structural openings were introduced between the numerous sections of the individual buildings, with timber staircases connecting the varying floor levels in order to provide a homogeneous development. Decayed wooden floors were removed, and new timber replacements provided – occasionally at revised levels, which were more suitable for a modern hotel development, without affecting the existing elevations.

The final scheme consisted of 49 bedrooms on five floor levels. Owing to the nature of the existing structure, these bedrooms varied in size. Each was different and, as a result, individually designed. New acoustic double glazing, within the existing timber frames, was provided for each bedroom. Original wall tiling in the corridor areas was retained, as were the glazed partitions. In addition, existing cornices in the bedrooms were kept and exposed where possible, with damaged examples being retained and concealed behind suspended ceilings. Lower suspended ceilings were provided in the corridors and bathrooms in order to hide new air-conditioning equipment. The impressive accommodation staircase, adjacent to the lift shaft, was retained and restored to its original condition.

The ground floor was designed to provide hotel access, reception and dining, and lounge-bar facilities for the use of both hotel guests and non-residents. An access staircase to the basement areas was provided adjacent to the building's Mosley Street entrance. A new glazed ground-floor frontage was proposed, incorporating the retention of an original timber door as requested by the City Council.

Externally, the stonework to the buildings' Grey Street and Mosley Street elevations was cleaned, and damaged stonework and ornamental features repaired where possible and replaced where necessary. Bird-repellent systems were provided to sills and cornices. The rear elevations of the buildings were built of brick, and they were similarly cleaned and repaired. Two new-build brick staircase towers were provided, together with a single-storey rear extension. The staircase tower to the Grey Street building was constructed between the ground-floor and fourth-floor levels; that to the Mosley Street building was provided between the basement levels and the fifth floor. A new-build extension was provided at the fourth- and fifth-floor levels of the Mosley Street building in order to accommodate four of the bedrooms. Limited car parking and a vehicle-delivery point were provided at the back of the property, with access from Pilgrim Street. Nearby, land suitable for car parking was leased and a 'car jockeying' service was agreed with the City Council as a condition of approval.

PROJECT EVALUATION

Given its prominent location at the junction of Grey Street and Mosley Street, the restoration and reuse of 2-12 Grey Street was regarded as a key site by the Grainger Town Project. Considerable time and effort was expended by both the Project team and its partners to start an acceptable and implementable scheme.

Although a Compulsory Purchase Order (CPO) was actually secured, the agreed conversion and restoration was as a result of negotiations and the essential architectural integrity of the buildings has been retained whilst allowing a modern hotel to function.

This group of buildings came very close to demolition and it is testament to all concerned that the buildings have not only been saved but, in their new guise as a hotel and restaurants, are proving popular and successful.

all photography on this spread by Sally Ann Norman

Client **Lazi Leisure Ltd**
Architect **Ian M. Cook Architect**
Main Contractor **Lazi Leisure Ltd**
Quantity Surveyor **Ian M. Cook**

Structural Engineer **Maughan Reynolds Partnership**
Services Engineer **SDB Engineering Ltd**
Project Manager **Ian M. Cook Architect**
Consulting Engineers **Beckett Ord**

Jesmond Dene House Hotel and Restaurant

Jesmond Dene Road,
Newcastle upon Tyne

Construction value **£8.5 million**
Date of completion **September 2005**
Project type **Refurbishment with some new-build**

INTRODUCTION

As one of the centrepieces of a park regarded by many as the finest in Newcastle – quiet woodland only minutes from the city centre – Jesmond Dene House symbolises the city's rich 19th-century manufacturing history with links to its most famous industrialist, Lord Armstrong of Cragside. Armstrong created Jesmond Dene in stages from 1853 over a period of 30 years, by which time it stretched southwards from the house to Benton Bridge. He transformed a semi-industrial and wooded valley into a garden, adding a waterfall and planting exotic trees and shrubs to create the park which exists today. As one of the city's greatest benefactors, he presented the Dene in 1883 to the city council.

The project to restore Jesmond Dene House, a fine example of an Arts and Crafts building, proved formidable. Prior to work commencing, the building fabric was in an exceedingly poor state; it had suffered from decades of insensitive alterations and extensions. However, developer and designers shared a vision of a luxurious hotel and restaurant on the site, and together commenced a two-year process of restoration, refurbishment and sensitive alteration to bring that vision to reality. Today it effectively fuses the modernity of an urban boutique hotel, or a town house, with the tranquility and relative isolation of a country-house hotel; in many ways, it is remarkable to find such a 'rural' idyll within easy walking distance of a city centre.

CLIENT'S BRIEF

The aim of Rivergreen Developments was to restore this magnificent, Grade II listed building to its former glory and to create a hotel with 32 en-suite bedrooms, a restaurant, and conference and banqueting facilities for 100 people. A further eight en-suite rooms were to be located in a new annexe on the site. In the words of the architect, some bedrooms had to be 'incorporated into the most unlikely places to make the project viable', while other key rooms had to be safeguarded to preserve the historic integrity of the building.

Not surprisingly, the designers visited other developments around the country, where similar challenges of creating hotels in listed buildings had been met, in order to assess the scale of the task. Market research was also undertaken. But on one issue they were clear: an internal, 'pastiche' make-over was seen as tasteless. Above all, this was to be a modern hotel in a fine 19th-century setting. Within the limitations imposed by the listing criteria, the buildings also clearly had to comply with the provisions of the Disability Discrimination Act, and ensure inclusivity and accessibility both for visitors and for staff.

Rudyard Kipling, Lord Baden-Powell, Chinese ministers and Japanese princes and admirals have all stayed or dined at Jesmond Dene House.

 all photography on this spread by Sally Ann Norman

DESIGN PROCESS

History

One of Newcastle's finest residential buildings, Jesmond Dene House is full of architectural bravura and historical detail – and boasts an intriguing 'cast list'. The original Georgian house, designed by John Dobson – the architect responsible for several of Newcastle's most handsome buildings – was bought in 1871 by Captain Andrew Noble, a partner in Lord Armstrong's Tyneside-based shipbuilding-and-armaments business.

As the business grew, and Armstrong took a back seat, Noble needed a grander house for entertaining. He commissioned leading Arts and Crafts architect Richard Norman Shaw – designer of Lord Armstrong's magnificent mansion near Rothbury, Northumberland, and centrepiece of his Cragside estate (now National Trust-owned) – and local architect Frank Rich to double the size of the house. They added a west wing, billiard room, Gothic porch, Great Hall and a fleet of bedrooms – all in typically grand and eclectic Arts and Crafts style, evoked by intricate panelling, plasterwork, stone carvings, exuberant chimneys and stained glass.

Knighted in 1902, Sir Andrew Noble moved in high society. Rudyard Kipling, Lord Baden-Powell, Chinese ministers and Japanese princes and admirals have all stayed or dined at Jesmond Dene House; Armstrong's industrial empire truly had a global reach, and – among other things – built much of the former Japanese battle fleet.

After Sir Andrew's widow died in 1929, the house was variously used as a college, civil-defence establishment (tunnels still exist under the building), seminary and, until relatively recently, a residential school.

The Development

In 2003, the building had been empty for ten years and, in several areas, active dry rot endangered some of the fine interior finishes. A strategy to eliminate the rot was developed using a simple monitoring system, good building management and new roof-covering to prevent water seeping into the building. Over the construction period, saturation levels reduced by 75 per cent; the dry rot was, thankfully, eradicated.

Existing modern partitions, which had subdivided the principal ground-floor rooms, were removed in order to restore former scale and grandeur. While all existing oak panelling was retained, missing or damaged panelling and other joinery features were faithfully reproduced to match the originals.

In order to re-create a logical main entry, lost during previous alterations, a modern entrance and reception extension was built of stone with oak structural columns and beams, visually linking the new with the old. And in the public areas, oak has been used for new doors, panelling and floors to provide an aesthetic link with the original materials.

A similar aesthetic theme was used for the garden-room extension to the main dining room: oak for columns, beams and floor, contrasting with the bold colours used in the restaurant. The magnificent Arts and Crafts style oak-panelled Great Hall, with its enormous carved inglenook fireplace, received only minimal repair and remains much as it was 100 years ago.

All en-suite bedrooms are bespoke, with no two identical: four have roof terraces; some sprawl amongst the eaves; some have grand stone-mullioned windows, others fine coffered timber ceilings. All have a modern sense of comfort and space. Bathrooms are large, clean and functional with big mirrors and generous baths in modern, tiled surroundings.

PROJECT EVALUATION

The hotel has been successfully delivered through close collaboration between the developer, the architect and the interior designer, which has resulted in meticulous detailing and craftsmanship. The end result is an immaculate regeneration of an abandoned, nationally important building: a successful fusion of Arts and Crafts with more modern styling.

Jesmond Dene House Hotel and Restaurant has not only added to the grandeur of the Dene itself. It has become an important element of the leisure and business infrastructures offered by Newcastle and Gateshead for both locals and the growing number of visitors to the twin cities. The hotel and restaurant employs approximately 100 full and part-time staff, from a variety of countries but with a majority of local employees.

Since completion, the hotel has won a series of local and national awards. It was named AA Hotel of the Year in 2008/2009, and has been awarded four AA red stars. The Automobile Assocation noted that that the building has been 'sympathetically converted into a stylish, contemporary, hotel'.

drawing supplied by the architect

Client **Rivergreen Developments plc**
Architect **Jane Darbyshire and David Kendall Limited**
Main Contractor **Rivergreen Developments plc**
Structural Engineer **Building Design Northern Ltd**

Services Engineer **Armstrong Rhead Partnership**
Interior Designer **Ward Robinson**
Landscape Architect **Kent Design**

courtesy of JDDK Ltd

photograph by Sally Ann Norman

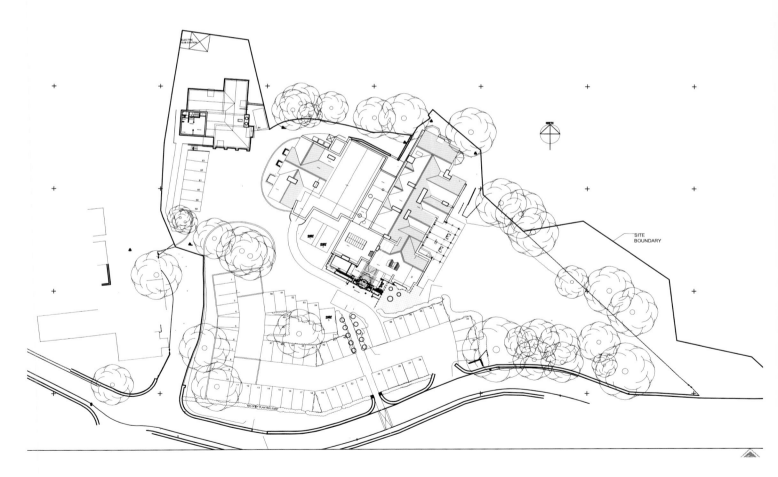

Chapter 4 ▶ Shaping the Future

The chief function of the city is to convert power into form, energy into culture, dead matter into the living symbols of art, biological reproduction into social creativity.

Lewis Mumford [1]

Cities, at their best, build confidence within their immediate boundaries and beyond into a wider conurbation. They inspire creativity, stimulate pride, reinforce a sense of belonging among inhabitants, underpin an identity – and none more so than NewcastleGateshead. Cities might be 'extraordinarily complex organisms [but they] derive from a simple formula':[2] people living closely together interact, provide services, trade, create institutions – great universities, arts and cultural centres – which, in turn, become a magnet, drawing others from further afield. Cities thus achieve a momentum of their own; at best, they become self-sustaining units, their critical masses attracting new inhabitants – the lifeblood of any economy.

Increasingly, people outside the twin cities in the wider Northeast of England identify with NewcastleGateshead. It is their city. While part of

this identity is undoubtedly underpinned by loyalty to a football club a collective mindset seems to have changed over the past few years in order to embrace a greater sense of 'belonging'. Certainly, the perception of NewcastleGateshead from beyond Tyneside has changed too – from being the place to portray the worst excesses of the 1980s meltdown of heavy industry, to the positive image of twin cities seemingly reborn (although we should not underplay the challenges of tackling generational 'worklessness', underachievement at secondary school and troubling levels of youth unemployment). It is 'cool' to be labelled a 'Geordie'.

Observing the physical variety, creative energy and social vitality of the twin cities labelled as 'NewcastleGateshead' – although, by accident or by design, the appellation 'city' is creeping into usage! – it is tempting to view a strengthening, cross-river urban partnership through the lens of the millennium and the funding that followed: the regeneration of quaysides and the artistic 'goodies' flowing partly from the largesse of Lottery funds and a (then) seemingly buoyant economy.

Furthermore, who can doubt the musing of a new masterplan for the central areas of the twin cities that 'NewcastleGateshead has the most dramatic and memorable setting of any English city, and townscape of exceptional quality: natural, historic

courtesy of Silverlink Holdings Ltd

and contemporary icons provide the setting for our daily lives.'

Well, yes. However, even a sketchy analysis of the development of the twin cities since the Emperor Hadrian set up camp almost 2,000 years ago in Newcastle – and, over the river, in Gateshead – cannot avoid the bad and the plain ugly, as well as the good and the exceptional. We should, naturally, take pride in the best: the breathtaking engineering, and the elegance, of the main bridges linking the twin cities; the stunning architecture of Georgian and Victorian Newcastle; the energy and ambition of Gateshead Council delivering the very best in cultural-led regeneration and raising the bar for the rest of Britain.

However, the test of this urban partnership is to examine relatively recent history with realism and, where necessary, with a critical eye in order to avoid the mistakes of the past; while new buildings, highlighted in the previous chapter, add considerable value to the townscape of Newcastle and Gateshead, others – let's be frank – obscure some of the city's finest areas and buildings, and are out of form and scale with their surroundings.

Planners, to be fair, have imposed tougher design standards in several areas, from near the Quayside – Trinity Gardens, for instance – and in a new Gallowgate office quarter. Similarly, a large mixed-

use development behind the central station – the Stephenson Quarter – on which preliminary work will begin in 2011 holds out the prospect of something better.

Let us not forget, however, what David Faulkner, the new leader of Newcastle City Council, has disparagingly labelled the 'concrete building spree' of the 1960s, which saw the demolition of the city's old Victorian public library to make way for an ugly relief road, ironically named 'John Dobson Street'. That spree still disfigures parts of Newcastle and Gateshead: a nondescript office block, which replaced a fine old hotel and attractive public houses opposite Dobson's splendid Newcastle Central Station; another large, unremarkable concrete slab, Pearl Assurance House, at the junction of New Bridge Street and Northumberland Street, the main shopping thoroughfare, which has sadly become a concrete and neon mish-mash in need of a makeover; and, unbelievably, a concrete office block on stilts, disfiguring Pilgrim Street a few hundred yards to the south.

More recently, the towering and uninspiring Gate leisure complex – multi-screen cinemas, restaurants, bars and all – in Newgate Street not only overshadows a stylish Art Deco (former) department store alongside. It also completely overwhelms the renovated Blackfriars area, a gem from the Middle

Ages incorporating 'the most complete medieval religious house ... in the centre of a British city'[3] as well as a mixture of architectural styles from the 13th to the 18th centuries alongside remnants of the old city wall. Similarly, a recent extension of the Eldon Square shopping complex, opposite The Gate – again out of shape and scale with its surroundings – creates an unnecessary visual barrier to the nearby Grainger Town area.

To be fair, a new strategy for the central areas of the twin cities, the NewcastleGateshead 1Plan: A vision for a great northern European city does not shy away from criticising the decisions of planners and politicians of a previous generation who inflicted a hotchpotch of concrete on their citizens in the name of progress!

One overarching mantra in this plan is 'sustainable urbanism', a label amply reinforced by a decision in both 2009 and 2010 to award Newcastle the title of Britain's 'greenest city', leapfrogging previous winners Bristol and Brighton and Hove. 'We hope this inspires others,' enthused Peter Madden of Forum for the Future, which organised this award. 'Anywhere with an industrial heritage faces genuine challenges, but Newcastle's success shows how it is possible to overcome the legacy of the past.'[4] A pity, then, that photographs in the press illustrating this award featured the classic riverscape of Newcastle and Gateshead quaysides, with the latter more prominent than the former!

The challenge now is to further reinforce a cross-river urban partnership by acting on the vision of the commendably candid 1Plan. It envisages transforming the inner areas of NewcastleGateshead, 'blighted by bad development and big roads', into more compact, accessible and sustainable twin cities (or 'city'). Boldly, the plan proclaims that some motorway-scale roads, driving through the heart of these central areas, will be turned into 'attractive streets and boulevards'.

If the centre of Newcastle has a dignity and uniformity, albeit 'broken' in places where 20th-century development has undermined its urban fabric and integrity – an intrusive and expensive-to-maintain central motorway east, for instance – Gateshead, richer in history than many imagine, has its share of 1960s blunders as well. In noting congested major roads sweeping through the space between the town centre and the vibrant riverside, signalling that 'the car is in charge', the plan observes that Gateshead is not a 'walkable town'. And the council knows it.

Armed with a new regeneration-delivery strategy, wrapped up in a masterplan – 'Fit for a City' – Gateshead Council seems determined to redress the errors of the past. Not for nothing does Sheila Johnston, the council's Director of Development and Enterprise, call it 'reinventing' central Gateshead: out will go an elevated highway (the old A1), which scythes through the central area, as well as a Brutalist 1960s shopping centre. In will come new boulevards, shopping areas, a 'cultural quarter', a park, houses and student accommodation. It is high on ambition, yet practical. But is it feasible, with public funding drying up? We should not lose heart.

Looking to the financial uncertainties of a new decade, the challenge for ambitious cities lies in developing new funding streams by pooling assets, such as land and buildings, to act as collateral for fresh ventures. The initiative, in short, will be with those councils which have taken collaboration, and joint working, onto a new, strategic level.

NewcastleGateshead should be at the forefront of this process. Who, after all, could have dreamt, in the teeth of the early 1990s recession, that by the millennium the image of these twin cities would have transformed beyond recognition? That they would have emerged as a national exemplar for culture and the arts, while becoming one of the country's more popular conference centres (plans for a convention centre, behind The Sage Gateshead, are in the making)? That the twin cities, with a string of new hotels, would top the UK's 'short break' destination league? And that – yes – once bitter municipal rivals are now the best of friends?

But how to define NewcastleGateshead: 'twin cities', or emerging 'city'? Let's put that issue to one side. We can, at least, agree with the recent 1Plan that 'This is a remarkable, stunning city [or twin-cities?], of which we can be proud.'

Notes:
1: Lewis Mumford (1895–1990), American historian noted for his study of cities and urban architecture.
2: John O. Norquist, *The Wealth of Cities*, Basic Books, Cambridge, Massachusetts, 1998.
3: Thomas Faulkner, Peter Beacock, Paul Jones, *Newcastle and Gateshead: Architecture and Heritage*, The Bluecoat Press, Liverpool, 2006.
4: Peter Madden quoted in 'It's grim down south: Newcastle pips Bristol and Brighton as Britain's greenest city', *Guardian*, 19 November 2009.

⊙ Future Vision 1

DAVID SLATER
Executive Director of Environment & Regeneration Newcastle City Council

In April 2008 David Slater joined Newcastle City Council as Executive Director of Environment & Regeneration. This includes Neighbourhood Services, Area Based Regeneration, Strategic Housing, Planning & Transportation, Regulatory Service and Public Protection, Technical Services and Resources & Performance

David was previously Executive Director Regeneration and Resources for South Tyneside Council and before that he was a civil servant in Government Office North East. He previously worked in Inland Revenue, Social Security and the Employment Department. At an early stage of his career, he led the development of Investors in People.

CHAPTER 4